The Secret Life of Dyslexic Criminologist

(In training)

By Wilma Mayhem

Copyright © 2023 by – Wilma Mayhem – All Rights Reserved.

It is not legal to reproduce, duplicate, or transmit any part of this document in either electronic means or printed format. Recording of this publication is strictly prohibited.

Table of Contents

Dedication i
Acknowledgments ii
About the Author iii
The Secret Life of Dyslexic Criminologist 1
Mad, Bad, and Dangerous 32
The Case of the Man Who Called Himself the Diamond Ring! 89
The Short Case of I Love You, Wilma. Please, Marry me .. 117
Cello 135
The Case of my Friend is Gerald Butler: 141
The Case of the Mysterious Mr. Smith, or Should It Be Dr. Smith? 151
The Case of Let Me Be Your sugar boy! 164
The Case of the Man from Instagram: Let's Chat on Telegram 194
The Scenario Involves Purchasing the Google Stream Card. 206
Flirting with Thor: A Banter Tale 219
The Case of 'Do You Want to Meet Skippy Wilma?' 267
The Case of 'Will You Be My Queen' 285
The Case of "From Italy with Love" 296
The Case of the Guy on Holiday 305

The Case of 'Welcome to My Weird World' 349
Where the Hell Did You Come from Friend? 356
The Case of Unexpected on Instagram 375
The Unusual Case of the Best Friend. 381
The Case of the Perfect Relationship 398

Dedication

To all my family and friends who have supported me on my journey along with the amazing people I get to work alongside.

Acknowledgments

Author Iain Mckinnon, OrCam Technology, Texthelp, Glean, Inspiration, Present pal, Aventido, Booost, Carescribe, NATTC, scanning pens, Learning labs and the Open University.

About the Author

Wilma started a blog about the positives of being dyslexic and sharing her experiences after leaving her work due to discrimination at the end of 2019. The pesky OU student became popular with her Open University studies in 2020. She shared her struggles and all the positive things she was finding with using assistive technology. She was invited to work alongside Claro software, which is now part of Texthelp, along with using OrCam technology and blogging about them she approached her second year of studying Criminology scammers started contacting her and as a nosy social scientist, she decided to investigate. At first, she shared her findings with her readers to warn them with is happening online. Her hosting provider changed, and her blog became broken, but she is hoping to get it fixed and up and running again to share her amazing experiences of learning. She now invites people into her mad world talking to scammers and inventing ways to get out the schemes they approach her about for giving them money, romance and entering their charity work.

The Secret Life of Dyslexic Criminologist

(In training)

Once upon a time, in the tiny town of Haberdashery, next to the Haberdashery River, lived a woman called Wilma Mayhem. There is nothing special about Wilma; people would describe her as a bit eccentric. This is because she is a bohemian hippie with electric blue hair, big round glasses, and dresses in colourful long floral dresses, skirts made from dish towels, and jumpsuits which look like a set of curtains. She loves Dr Martens, goth boots, and steampunk fashion. However eccentric she dresses, you will never find her in MC Hammer pants (you can't touch this!). She just thinks about Billy Connelly talking about hiding clear incontinence underwear using baggy trousers.

Trying to empty them with seven gallons of pee from each leg at the end of the night proves difficult. She led a socially unconventional lifestyle, pursuing a musical, artistic, and literary lifestyle. She could spend hours having adventures by reading books such as Touching the Void by Joe Simpson. A love of art and design loves artists like Picasso and Van Gogh. She also loves cooking and can spend hours in the kitchen while listening to music; she is very much an introvert. However, you would never think this with her approachable, friendly, easy-going manner. She blended in like everyone else, went to work in the local factory doing administration duties, and hung around with her friends.

Then, one day, she was extremely unlucky and had a major accident. A wall was being repaired outside her work. The people repairing the wall had parked their trucks badly and blocked the view of the road. Wilma thought it was safe to cross, and the next thing she knew, there was a loud bang, and she was lying on the road with her leg the wrong way round. She didn't know it at the time, but it was an event that would change her life forever. If only she had not left her Wonder Woman outfit in the washing machine that day! She would have easily leapt over the car and gone home normally as she had planned. The ambulance came and collected her to go to hospital. She was disappointed that George Clooney or Hugh Laurie as House were not the doctors that day. However, the number of painkillers she had been given left her more stoned than Dillion from the magic roundabout.

Wilma awoke, having had her leg set to find her best friend, Mr G, sitting in a chair at the end of the hospital bed. Mr G is a profoundly serious person, a totally bald guy who is an IT geek, a Gremlin. He is found in a dark corner with a laptop. When Wilma met Mr G, she found him to be a talented guitar player and owned several guitars. Mr G also loves lots of genres of music; unless you mention Europe and the song The Final Countdown, he will tell you it is the cheesiest song ever written and should be banned. I am sure, at times, he wished he had kept the opinion to himself as everyone loves to start humming it to annoy him. Mr G used to be very thin. However, he tells Wilma he is now unattractive to other women due to her being such a good cook. She has made him fat and cuddly #itisatrap. Mr G looked on with concern when Wilma came round after having her leg set in a full leg cast. However, she told him that things were cool. He asked her why, to which she told him she had beautiful goldfish swimming out of her feet. They told Wilma not to worry. They could rebuild her; they had the technology and sent her for surgery. Upon reaching surgery, she wished she had not read Coma by Michael Crichton as her overactive imagination jumped into life with thoughts that she was going to die and be sold off as body parts.

Wilma imagined coming out like the bionic woman and being able to run at incredible speed. The surgeons drilled into her leg and put lots of nuts and bolts, using a tube of superglue, double-sided sticky tape, and sticky back plastic; she came out like a blue Peter model with one we made earlier. Wilma spent a few days in the hospital, and during this time, her best friend, Princess Twinkle Toes, came to visit. The princess cheered Wilma up with a copy of Tatler. Wilma was not interested in the articles, just all the beautiful designer handbags. Upon time to go home, the staff made her laugh by handing her a black bin bag and written in gold felt tip pen was Louis Vuitton.

Wilma was glad to be home and put in a claim for her accident. She was looking forward to recovering and going back to work, so she watched all her favourite cooking programs, science fiction programs, CSI, and anything else which had nothing to do with real life. However, daytime TV after being stuck in the house for weeks on end can be torture. The last thing she wanted to do was end up watching "Jeremy Kyle" or "Loose Women." The JML channel for completely useless things such as the big slipper and indestructible frying pans and buying the extra-large toothbrush to clean the wheels of your car were becoming interesting entertainment. Mr G looked after her and dealt with all her frustrations. He would eventually take her to the local supermarket. He decided that it would not happen very often as it was faster to take a toddler out for shopping. Wilma's mum borrowed a wheelchair, and Mr G would take her out for some Irn Bru at her local pub. It was nice to socialise with Princess Twinkle Toes and Calamity Jane. It would be a while before they could all go out for ladies who lunch and enjoy a few glasses of wine. Weeks turned into months with Wilma's recovery, and Mr G would take her back to the hospital to have her leg x-rayed.

    Then, one day, the doctors gave her the news that she could start putting some weight on her bad leg! Hurray, she could start escaping the house and learn to walk again. However, it was the middle of winter, and Wilma was nervous about falling as she would not be able to get up with her crutches. She was bored. However, she spent the time listening to music. Music had been one of her best friends throughout her life. When out with Princess Twinkle Toes, they would end up in karaoke, and the princess always sang Gloria Gaynor's" I Will Survive.

Wilma loved to be Cher and sing strong enough. However, she always found ending up in karaoke difficult, as people were so drunk that they thought Wilma could sing. Sitting drinking wine, minding her own business, a microphone would end up in her lap, and she would have to finish another person's song. She would spend hours in the house and listen to a massive collection of CDs: ABBA, AC/DC, Iron Maiden, Bon Jovi, Miles Davis, Journey, Def Leppard, Eminem, Alanis Morrissette, A-ha, Cher and Tina Turner and many other artists.

At this point, she was Budgie sitting, so they would sit and listen to music together. If only she had adult colouring in books during this time, she would have been in heaven. She would have spent hours just listening to music and making colourful pictures. At this point, she found another artist called David Garrett, a song called Lo Ti Penso Armore featuring Nicole Scherzinger. It was beautiful, and Wilma became a fan and bought some of his albums. Wilma started to go out for walks around Haberdashery. This was once a very industrial place with plenty of history but was slowly becoming a ghost town as many services left the area!

Wilma shares an old maisonette with her best friend, Mr G. There are beautiful views of the Haberdashery River and over to the Wanbury hills from her front window. Beautiful walks along the river, which is only two minutes away from her house. People never imagine the variety of different buildings ranging from the late 1800s to modern buildings that surround where Wilma and Mr G live. Just five minutes away, there is a set of docks that were shut in 1959. This has an old railway slightly along it, which is now a museum. It has a long history of being a mining community. Alas, they were shut in the 1980s. It is a lovely cinema that has been restored to its former glory thanks to national lottery funding and the Historic Buildings Trust. It has assorted styles of movies, from silent, black, and white to modern-day new releases. The town centre is small with a Tesco metro, Lidle, as well as a variety of small businesses and charity shops. It goes from the shoreline, and all the buildings are part of a hill. Surrounded by trees, you could mistake it for Brigadoon. It just wakes up now and then.

Wilma would get help from elderly people while crossing the roads on her crutches. She started with small walks and going to her local for a cup of coffee and catching up with people. This was when she met Mr J from Yorkshire, who had just moved to the area. Wilma found out he also enjoyed listening to music and cooking. Wilma also made friends with Dennis, the international dog walker.

This name changed later to Donkey, as he had gone with Mr G on a road trip. Wilma received a message from Mr G saying he never shuts up. Wilma was watching Shrek at the time and replied with Shrek and Donkey and on another whirlwind adventure, so he became known as Donkey from then on. Wilma started extending her walks on her crutches to aid her rehabilitation. It did not take long for Wilma to start with physiotherapy.

Wilma started calling it to the physiotherapist as it was excruciatingly painful. Wilma built up her strength, and after months of being off through her injuries, she returned to work. At first, Wilma was happy to be back at work and see everyone. However, she was exhausted. She also started asking the council to put in a pedestrian crossing for people to cross the road safely during busy periods. A friend and local businessman supported Wilma on her quest and got local MPs involved in traffic calming measures. Alas, this never happened, and the only thing that happened was a nice new bus shelter erected. Also, because the van had disappeared during the accident, upon the police arriving on the scene, they only called the ambulance to deal with Wilma. Eventually, she got the news that her claim would be diddly squat. However, everyone thought she made a small fortune.

Wilma only told a few people that she made diddly squat as she would be against the state and would lose her case. Wilma thought her sleepy life would return to normal; it was not the case. Wilma kept ending up in H.R. for multiple investigations. She tried to figure out why this was the case. Her manager had told her that she was the best worker he had. However, she was also the most disorganised person he had worked alongside.

Wilma was extremely stressed by everything going on in her department, so she tried to move the department to work less stressful and with the same wages. This, of course, fell through; in fact, it was a case of out of the frying pan and into the fire. She knew that the head of her department had played a large part in this. The head of Wilma's department was a small man with a bad temper. He had many faces; Wilma knew he would be nice to your face while stabbing you in the back. She tried to stay out of his road; one of his favourite tricks was cornering people alone. Extremely militant, you must do as he said without question. Wilma called him the poisoned dwarf, and he had a sidekick, Tonto (the stupid one), the departmental manager. Wilma had no idea how Tonto got the job; if you asked him anything, you would be phoning around the entire factory for the answer. Wilma found you could not ask him questions, especially about procedures, as it was a taboo subject.

Wilma was told numerous times that she should just do it the same way as everyone else. She started investigating dyslexia as she had been identified as dyslexic as a child, but this had been presented as a reading and writing problem. Wilma had eventually learned to read and write, so she never thought that dyslexia was a problem. As she was reading through Google, she could identify with all the issues that came with being dyslexic. Wilma told her work and the management; however, this was not the issue according to the people she spoke to. Wilma decided to give her HR department information on dyslexia. Eventually, someone listened to Wilma and brought in a specialist, and Wilma told her story. She found this a very emotional experience recounting her experiences at school. She had tried blocking out all the bullying; she was either extremely stupid or a creative genius. It had been a double-edged sword she had lived with all her life. The specialists told the HR department that Wilma was dyslexic, and she thought hurray, maybe the bullying will stop. Maybe I will receive some help. Wilma also found out about a dyslexic charity; they ran an adult network as this is a lifelong difficulty.

Wilma was nervous; however, she joined, and it started changing her life. Wilma made friends with people who had the same frustrations as herself. She found out that she could receive help through something called Access to Work, a government-run scheme aiding people with disabilities within the workplace. Wilma found out about software called Dragon. She could dictate to the computer what she wanted to say in Word and email documents. Wilma showed it to Princess Twinkle Toes; she showed Wilma how to sell it to her work. She made notes for Wilma and helped her pick out an outfit that businesspeople wear. Wilma went home and practised everything the princess had taught her; the princess knew what she was talking about with working as a sales executive for a multimillion-pound company. Wilma had her meeting; however, she knew the poisoned dwarf was not going to buy this software to aid her work. The princess asked how the meeting went, and Wilma said her suspicions. At this point, Wilma received an email saying to submit a story about dyslexia for a magazine called dyslexic voice. She wrote her first story, "being dyslexic," and months later found out it had been published in the magazine called Dyslexic Voice. Everyone told her it was a brilliant achievement; she felt a little bit confident for the first time. She told her work that she had applied for Access to Work. Wilma then went on to write a piece for a dyslexic voice called "Burn the Witch" and talked about the discrimination she faced at work and the issues of dyslexia. Then it came to Princess Twinkle Toe's birthday. Wilma went to work as normal and afterwards changed and went with friends to Princess Twinkle Toe's birthday with Calamity Jane and DJ Wizzywig, and other friends for the party. Everyone had a wonderful time at the party, even though there was a power cut when everyone was singing along to Neil Diamond. As the party had been on Saturday, Wilma had the Monday off work. She did not expect a phone call from Tonto saying that she was not to turn up the next day. She was suspended from work; she was confused. This had never happened to her in the twenty years she had worked for the company.

Wilma also had access to work, arriving the next day to have reasonable adjustments put in place to aid her dyslexia. Everyone told her that she had been suspended incorrectly. In fact, the company was breaking the law. Wilma then bumped into the Princess's twinkle toes and told her what happened. The princess was horrified and phoned a friend to help Wilma out.

After consulting with a friend, a lawyer's letter was sent to Wilma's work quoting the Equality Act of 2010 and picking on people with hidden disabilities. It did not take long for all the charges against Wilma to be dropped. Wilma had also engaged the union how much they were not much help with matters of dyslexia. Access to work was engaged, and Wilma had some reasonable adjustments to aid her in the workplace.

Well, firstly, she was told about neurodiverse training, and the poison dwarf brought Wilma and the union representative into a meeting with H.R. The poisoned dwarf asked her to use her mobile phone while waiting for the Dictaphone Access to work recommended. Then he asked her to arrange her neurodiverse training that had been recommended by Access to Work. Why on earth would the management and HR department aid people with hidden disabilities at work? Wilma had been open about a brain injury she had when starting work from meningococcal meningitis. She had not realised until investigation that this had caused her dyslexia/dyspraxia.

Wilma had been reading up on dyslexia at work by Dr Silva Moody and found out about dyspraxia. Wilma eventually also had the neurodiverse training in place. This was a revolution for Wilma. She found out that she was a visual-spatial learner. She could understand an entire concept at once. She did not learn in a step-by-step fashion, and famous people such as Albert Einstein, Leonardo di Vinci, and Picasso were visual-spatial learners. It was also the reason why she struggled with organising information. She was taught how to visualise things to help recall details. She always had problems navigating spaces and bumping into things, as well as her amazing ability to trip over fresh air.

A holistic learner needs a bit of time to process written information. This was no different from stars she admired, like Cher, Tina Turner, and Whoopi Goldberg. She found out Cher hated singing Jessie James because there were too many words to remember. Dyslexia/dyspraxia affects everyone differently and has nothing to do with someone's intelligence. It was a scientific fact that people identified as dyslexic had average to above-average intelligence. Wilma discovered the management's attitudes were not going to change; dyslexia was her problem, and she had to solve it. Wilma found out about colour-coding her work. However, this was frowned upon by Tonto even though she supplied her own pens.

Wilma found out about using Post-it notes to leave herself reminders; Tonto kept putting these in the bin. Wilma brought in a calendar to help her work out dates as part of her work; again, Tonto would put her calendar in the bin. Wilma had found out about assistive technology and gone on courses. The poison dwarf asked her to find the pricing for technology and to see if it was compatible with the system. Wilma was receiving help outside of work and is now working on a CV and looking at different jobs.

Wilma also wanted to go back to education and try to get a certification in counselling and psychotherapy. Tonto did not want to help Wilma with her quest and give her the time off she required. Wilma found out this was also against the law as it was a reasonable adjustment for her learning disability. It was also part of her human rights to have an education.

At this point, Wilma had a nervous breakdown from the constant battles with the management. She was starting to achieve goals outside of work; however, she was banging her head on a brick wall at work. Wilma just wanted to walk in front of a bus and make all the stress and, anxiety, panic attacks go away. Wilma phoned ACAS to get legal advice. They tried to talk about Wilma's work. She wrote a grievance letter about Tonto with times and dates of incidents from the work diaries she kept. Wilma was permitted by ACAS to take her work to a tribunal. Wilma had her union involved and thought it would be a straightforward process; a lawyer would fill in the paperwork, and it would go to court. The union did not do this because many issues could be resolved with the help of ACAS. Wilma had been to a meeting about going back to work. They only asked what she was doing to aid her dyslexia. No reasonable adjustments were ever brought up by the poisoned dwarf. It had been another letdown; Wilma would have to battle her work and her union. She decided it was time to leave this toxic environment and do something completely different.

Mr G had taken Wilma out for a glass of wine and talked Wilma into starting a blog; Wilma did not like the idea and thought no one would read it. However, she had been writing for the dyslexic voice for a while, and that would be her starting point. The princess twinkle toes thought this was a great idea and supported Wilma with her discussion. They also had this discussion with another friend, Mr. D. Mr. D was a tall, slim man who was ex-army and bald, had a wicked sense of humour, and was highly competitive. He would always tell Wilma that he was Gordon Ramsey in the kitchen and give her professional cooking lessons. Wilma would always laugh at this as the princess always said nobody would starve with Wilma cooking. Wilma said Mr. J, Mr. G, and Mr. G were the hair bear bunch, a quirky name considering none of them had hair. They would gather for drinks on a Friday with Wilma and the princess, and occasionally, Calamity Jane joined for laughs and shenanigans. If the princess, calamity, DJ Wizzywig, they formed a group called ladies who lunch. This made everyone fall about laughing. They did not understand why, as they were perfect sensible women. Their quiet nights involved tasty food, plenty of wine, and occasional singing along with Barry Manilow, the Copacabana, and maybe a few Gins. Mr G would always tell her off after she played ping pong with herself, trying to get into the house. Announced it had been a great, quiet night and then collapsed on the couch and fell asleep.

After leaving her toxic workplace, Wilma saw an opening for a helpline advisor to aid other dyslexics and applied for the position. She had also booked a surprise trip to Krakow for herself and Mr. G. Mr D could not stop laughing as Mr G kept saying Wilma was up to something. She was trying to keep the holiday a surprise! However, Mr. G was suspicious; all she had asked him to do was book a holiday in March, a week he normally takes off.

Things were going in the right direction, and Wilma had taken up a writing class to improve her blog. Mr. G eventually found out about the holiday and was excited. He even saw Santana playing in Krakow. However, this all changed as they went out with Donkey and watched the news of the borders shutting with covid nineteen.

Unsure of what was now going to happen, they just went home; everyone was wondering how long everything was going to be shut. Wilma decided to blog about the pandemic; she looked through photos on Facebook and wondered where the zombies were hiding. She was looking out for cybermen and Daleks and blogged about the shutdown. The virus was hiding behind bushes, waiting to attack you. The adult network she was a part of went onto Zoom calls, along with the writing class she was a part of. She started being invited to Zoom meetings by dyslexic telling their stories.

Wilma had created a LinkedIn and Twitter account and started sharing her blog. This is how she met Dr. Dodgy Shoes. He had looked at her profile and asked to have a chat with her about dyslexia; it would only take ten minutes. Dr Dodgy Shoes interrogated Wilma about the work she does as a volunteer in promoting positive dyslexia. He had seen the video she had done for charity talking about being a blogger and using assistive technology to aid with spelling. Wilma also found out that Dr. Dodgy's idea of two weeks to release a video turned into nine months. The blog started having a positive response from around the world. Wilma received lovely retweets with a fun, creative blog. Witty and wise insights into dyslexia. She even blogged about Dr Dodgy's shoes; she had found out he also enjoyed cooking. It was also talking to Dr. Dodgy Shoes and Mr. G that Wilma produced blogs such as My dyslexic guitar.

I have known since the beginning of going out with my partner he has a great passion. This is called guitars, and they are all beautiful women! He loves giving their necks a massage with oil and admires the many shapes of their bodies. No matter where I go in the world, my partner can find a guitar shop! I now have a sad life where I can tell a Telecaster from Stratocaster. I know a flying v, Gibson, Jackson, Gretsch, Hopfner, Tokai, and Ibanez, to name a few. I did, in the early days, try to convince my partner to buy a limited-edition Joe Satriani Surfing with the Alien guitar. He of course said no. Thinking about it now, it would have stayed in the guitar case just to be looked at occasionally and be called his precious.

I say this as I was looking through LinkedIn and found an article talking about dyslexia. The complex issues that arise from being dyslexic. I then came to, and I quote, "Think of it like you'd think of a guitar strings. A guitar string is all tuned differently like the brain." For the last few months, my partner has been needing strings for all the guitars in the house. A million different arguments started coming into my head. No guitarist would string up an Ibanez electric guitar with a set of acoustic strings. No Acoustic guitar would have a set of bass strings. Then, there are so many different gauges it is down to the guitarist's preference. Then, there is the complex issue of what you prefer to play.

Friends who play Gibson's, if you asked, would find that not be their preference to play an Ibanez guitar as they have a fast neck. They are entitled to their opinion. Do you need a scalped neck like Yngwie Malmsteen? This could be for the classical sound he produces. You would not say that Joe Bonamassa produces the same sound as Billy Gibeon's, even though they are both Blues players. Joe Satriani and Stevie Vai are both Ibanez players but have two completely different sounds and styles.

Then there is the shape of a guitar. I think Metallica would look a bit out of place going on stage with a Banjo! You would wonder what was going on if the duelling Banjos one was replaced by an electric violin. This is how I see dyslexia at times. It can be very clever and work in harmony with everything around it. The other possibility is a disaster waiting to happen. Just watch Aussie Man review epic music fails on YouTube. This is when dyslexia will go horribly wrong.

Dyslexia is like going to a guitar shop. There is so much choice. I should be thankful for the pandemic presently. It has saved me from finding how many more guitar shops Mr G can find. But then again, I like to have a bit of fun; right now, let's annoy Mr G. Where is the girly bubble-gum pink guitar? Now I am totally bored after three hours of looking at the variety of guitars. Where is the ugliest guitar in the shop? I know at this point, my dear Mr G will roll his eyes and ask if I would like to be like Jonny Depp and go for a mega pint of wine. This sounds like a great idea. I have messaged the person in question, saying thanks for this thought. I live with a guitar freak. Really, why am I thinking of this whole argument of dyslexia as like guitars or guitar strings? I now need s serious counselling and psychotherapy to think the whole thing through!

Blogging brought about opportunities with Claro software to try out a new program called Writing Helper. She built a good working relationship with the team and went to many webinars; it would also help her as she had applied for the Open University to study for a Bachelor of Arts (Honours) in Criminology. Criminology is a social science studying crime and criminals, their motivations, and the consequences of crime. It also takes in preventative measures; it takes in the law, psychology, biology, statistics, and sociology. Some people would say Wilma picked this subject as she was a great fan of criminal minds. She certainly would not mind being Derek Morgans's baby girl in the program. She also loves Abby Sciuto, the forensic genius in NCIS. However, the real reason was to find out how to aid dyslexics in the criminal justice system. How does the criminal justice system aid dyslexia as a hidden disability? This is covered under the Equality Act of 2010; however, a reasonable adjustment is as long as a bit of string.

Wilma knew from her struggles through her battles with her accident, work, and union that there were problems with being dyslexic. Also, achieving a degree was something she had always dreamed about; however, she was too stupid to achieve this goal. Wilma needed a formal identification of dyslexia, as this was a face-to-face meeting. How would Wilma achieve this during the pandemic? She was phoning the helpline asking for help and received help setting up a Zoom call with an educational psychologist. After the call was finished, she was told she was dyslexic; this paved the way for Wilma to apply for disability student allowance to aid with reasonable adjustments.

Wilma eventually started her course in October and was aiding the helpline from home. Wilma had a friend who was also studying at the Open University. Every Friday, they would discuss their courses, and Wilma had started by being introduced to social science. The importance of social science and how society is made up of many complex layers. Wilma did not have a clue what she was doing! She was challenged with the amount of reading involved, which left her exhausted. Then, the art of writing assignments was different from creative writing. Wilma's friend was ready to give up and not achieve her degree. Together, they made a pact and supported each other with their frustration of studying during a pandemic. Wilma had mountains of material to blog about through studying, assistive technology, and the pandemic. Wilma was contacted by OrCam and asked if she would try out an OrCam read and blog about how it aided her in the first year of studying an introduction to social science. Wilma made many mistakes in her first year as she was figuring out how to write assignments.

Figuring out referencing when lectures happened online and how to use forums. She also received a phone call from her tutor explaining that she had submitted the wrong assignment. She had been given an extension, and the lecturer informed her she would not make that mistake again! It was overwhelming at times, but mastering all the assistive technology received reasonable adjustments. The first year whizzed by, and Wilma was applying for her second year. Wilma had a friend who had supported her through their discussion of studying with the Open University. Let's face it: what nut case would start studying for a degree during a pandemic and be locked in the house? Wilma's friend was in her final year of their degree in educational psychology. She was delighted to finish and receive her degree; it was a pity they could not celebrate with bottles of champagne because of the pandemic.

Wilma's second year was approaching quickly, which was introducing her to crime. Wilma now knew her way around the website and how to plan her assignments and lectures. Everything went through serious planning and was placed on Google Calendars; this was when Wilma's life became even more interesting. An international star messaged Wilma on Twitter, and they invited her to chat with them on hangouts. Wilma did not know it at the time, but it was her first scammer. This was a nice gentleman, very polite, and told Wilma she reminded him of her mentor. However, at the same time, she received various messages on different platforms from the same artist. The nosey social scientist had taken hold. This led her into a world where she would chat with various people pretending to be international artists. Wilma also found that when you break up with scammers, you are less likely to end up like Bridget Jones! Yes, sitting lonely in a flat in an Onesie with a bottle of wine, singing along with Celine Dion all by myself.

Wilma also imagined that as a criminologist, if she were murdered, she would magically disappear and be found in a wheelie bin. The crime scene investigation would not have a problem identifying her as the titanium rod in her leg is numbered. They would also be Richard Marx playing in the background singing Hazard. As they were all stuck in the pandemic, the bubble was the hair bear bunch and princess twinkle toes on Friday evenings with boxes of wine. Wilma would share her stories of the scammers she was chatting with at the time. The Princess twinkle toes would say there was market anything. Wilma said that the scammer would like to wake up with her by his side. He would whisper sweet nothings in her ear and gaze lovingly into her eyes. At this point, everyone was howling with laughter. Wilma made an Austin Powers impression by saying do I make you horny, baby. She said she could do a naughty student with the glasses at the end of her nose, holding her OrCam for a photo. They could call it dyslexic; there was even more laughter at the whole scenario. Wilma also added chatting with scammers to her blog; it was a way of warning people of the scenarios Wilma was finding as a criminologist. Princess Twinkle Toes was going to help market Wilma with her stories. However, this did not happen as just after the New Year, Princess Twinkle Toes unexpectedly passed away. This was a shock to everyone, and Wilma wrote a beautiful tribute about her friend, which she published on the day of her funeral.

Rest in Peace, Princess Twinkle Toes

New Year fun and shenanigans

This is a hard blog to write; everyone in my group started the New Year with the usual fun and laughter at my best friend's house. We were nicknamed Patsy and Eddie from Absolute Fabulous Bollie Bollie Sweetie Darling. This was due to our mischief; we would do lots of foolish things, such as arrange cyber cocktail sessions. Everyone knew that a bottle of wine between friends such as us was, without a doubt, usually empty. LOL. It was time to say goodbye to the old year and bring in the new. Things were looking up. Everyone was excited. Lots of exciting new projects, holidays were being planned, and a bright new future during a challenging time due to the pandemic. Even the new variant of the virus had not put us off. Then, just shortly afterwards, we received the news that our dear close friend had passed away. We found out later that a blood clot had entered her heart, and she passed away instantly and peacefully. It was even more tragic that her partner had tried to revive her through CPR. However, when the ambulance arrived, she was pronounced dead at the scene. It came as a terrible shock to everyone who knew my friend.

If you had ever come across my friend, you would know about her bright, bubbly personality. She would tell anyone to be the best they could be! She was always positive, the life and soul of the party, and enjoyed life. Tell everyone to face the crowd and be proud! Shine like a star and love every minute. Amaze people with your skills and perform to the crowd. Oh, the stories of fun and shenanigans could fill books! People would be laughing for hours.

Businessperson

My friend worked in corporate entertainment. Her brilliance brought a great many skills throughout her media career, with managing people, as well as being a strong leader and speaker at many functions. She loved supporting people and doing things differently, had a wicked sense of humour, and loved telling a great many stories. She told me about the time her best friend at work, for some bizarre reason, ended up running across the office. Then, she proceeded to explain that her best friend did not person ever run. As she watched in amazement, she spotted "Gary, tank commander." Well, that explains it as "Gary tank commander" was one of her heroes. The same friend also hated horror movies; I was in stitches upon being told about the time everyone went to see IT. After watching the movie and going home, her brother left a big red balloon in the middle of her living and just about gave her a heart attack! We all howled with laughter at his practical jokes, which included phoning my friend up and offering her money to keep refugees in her hut at the bottom of the garden. She would talk about going to functions such as "Woman of Influence." She would call it "Woman under the Influence," the doors were shut fun, and shenanigans began, along with a few bottles of her favourite champagne.

As a woman high up in the business world, she needed a personal assistant to organise everything; time was always her enemy. She always said she was lost without them; her PA would tell her off for sneaking into the canteen for a bacon roll, as she was supposed to be giving a talk in lecture theatre three. The personal assistant would take care of all the travel plans. Every time I was in her BMW, it was just full of coffee cups and instant food wrappers, along with clothes. It was just an office on wheels. If she was ever stuck in traffic, she was redoing her nail varnish, touching up her make-up to look dazzling while meeting stars for red carpet functions. I would always tell her to be careful on long journeys. However, when she was working in London, I knew never to text her as the meetings she entered turned into drinking games later in the day. The stories would turn into this one time at band camp, on a train trip home, she texted me to say she was never drinking saffron gin again as she had the hangover from hell. There was another time while driving home on the motorway in her BMW when someone decided to keep overtaking her and was flashing rude pictures. The weather was atrocious; she thought they would crash into her. She was panicking by the time she arrived home; everyone advised her to phone the police and report as she had noted his registration number. This led to her barking mad friend phoning her up and proceeding to ask her if she could please go to the police station. The police inspector found the offending pictures; she was required to identify the "boabie" in question.

    I was always amazed at all the business contacts she knew. We could not go out without bumping into someone who was in business. Thanks to her business contacts, she arranged to get my partner a beautiful guitar cake for his 50th birthday. Special day cakes also made her 50th birthday cake. It was a stylish square cake covered with white icing and a bottle of Chanel number 5 on the top! Everyone knew this was one of her favourite perfumes and loved also giving it out as a present, however when it came to our special friend "Calamity Jane," I was asked who gave me Chanel no 5. That is only for old people! I could not stop laughing.

Marbella

I was invited to go to my friend's 50th birthday party which was being held in Marbella! There are so many wonderful memories; it was my first and only real girl's holiday! Fun and shenanigans from start to end, we started at a friend's house for wine and nibbles before dressing her as a fairy for going through the airport! As you would expect on such a holiday, there were more drinks at the airport and on the plane. Upon reaching Malaga, my friend was thirsty, and another friend gave her some warm lemonade to cure her thirst. This did not exactly agree with her, as she fell behind, walking toward where we would get our taxi. We all turned to watch her leaning over an opening and a river of red wine fall where there was a four-storey car park. I can only hope nobody was at the bottom; it would have been messy. We stopped to allow her to catch up and went on the moving walkway. Of course, at this point, her favourite "Dior" sunglasses fell off her head. We needed a hero of the group to rescue the "Dior" sunglasses. Our intrepid hero shouted, "I will rescue your Dior!" They were drunk and proceeded to leap over a moving barrier. In my head, I imagined the action hero leaping over the barrier. The reality, however, was they were stuck and travelling the automated handrail, which they eventually fell off and landed with a loud thud! Our hero then ran like the six-million-dollar man in slow motion for the sunglasses. They were lucky and bounced and didn't hurt themselves. We then proceeded to travel just outside the Puerto Banus to our hotel; yes, even late at night, we headed straight to the bar for more drinks before heading to bed.

Our group really knows how to party, and our trip can only be described as "rent a riot"! One of our group is ginger and, therefore, allergic to the sun. There were plenty of jokes about them melting or looking like a boiled lobster. We covered them in the strongest sunscreen known to man, which we called the sun factor duffle coat. They would be hiding under mounds of beach towels with a set of eyes peeking out, also found in dark shaded areas. If you ever see a large amount of moving beach towels, it is due to a ginger hiding below. Thus, our friend talked about it is not the ginger o clock yet! This is when it is safe for a ginger to go out. When it comes to the evening and going out for refreshments, we have ginger sexy time. There were others in the group who we just basted with cooking oil and got the fish slices out to turn them around every half hour to brown like a rotisserie chicken. However, I had a sun factor of 30, and I ended up looking like a tandoori chicken look by the end of the holiday! I can only blame my blue skin; where I live, we know it is summer as the rain is warm. We all took day trips; one was to Andy's beach for cocktails and to listen to live music. We typically left an impression on the band! They kept saying will the "rent a riot" group shut up! You're singing the wrong song again; please stop requesting the "The proclaimers 500 miles." We also would take the catamaran into Marbella, upon which the lookie men made a fortune as we sat drinking cocktails on the pier before heading to the beach for tapas and more cocktails. The Louis Vuitton, Chanel, and other favourite fake designer scarfs, belts, handbags, and purses were all purchased. We all haggled hard. Why on earth would we take just one Chanel scarf for fifty euros? We want two for twenty-five euros!

Support

It was the same year and a few months on from our trip to Marbella that my best friend came to my rescue! My work had been wanting to "get rid" of me for a while, and I found out later, to my horror, that a malicious email had been put out about me. I finished my work and dressed up to go to her official party with everyone else. I had looked out my dress and the Stella McCartney handbag I had purchased on our holiday, or, as my friend said, a Stella Mcnaughty handbag along with my Chanel scarf, and had my make-up ready for putting on after I finished work! Everyone had an exciting time; we were all singing along with Neil Diamond's Sweet Caroline when the power cut hit, but it in no way stopped the party.

So, while sitting on my day off and thinking about what aid access to work would offer me the next day for reasonable adjustments to aid my learning disability. I did not expect my manager to phone me and tell me I was suspended there and then not to turn up to work the next day. He also informed me to contact Access to Work to tell them of my suspension! I can tell you I was in shock and had a panic attack. I found out later what had been written in the malicious email, which would have easily had me dismissed from the company. I was lucky as my friends gave me great advice and told me that this was against protocol. I should not have been suspended until I was on site the next day and had a witness with me while I was being suspended. Now, dyslexia is a hidden disability and is covered under the Equality Act of 2010; a company is duty-bound to support its disabled workers. I bumped into my friend in the evening and told her of the event which had happened in the morning. She was shocked, and her jaw dropped to the floor. She went on the phone with our friends; it did not take long for the correct help and support to be put in place. My company was the talk of many HR departments for going against protocol. I won my case but was left with a very deep distrust of the people around me in my work environment.

My friend always believed in me; her favourite inquiry was about how she was going to market me. She said that one of the best decisions I made was joining the dyslexic community. She supported me through my early days of learning to write and was proud when my first article was published in Dyslexic Voice. She would sit and listen to all the problems I was having at work. The lack of support from both management and the Human Resources department and my union. Thanks to being part of the dyslexic community, I found help and support, and I was beginning to achieve things. My workplace never saw this, and the management and HR department offered support. I had a problem, and what was I going to do to sort it out? Why would I go back to the education system? My departmental manager would not sign any holiday forma or leave of absence to receive an education. I kept a work diary on all the hassle I received as my departmental manager did nothing but harass me with emails of everything I had done incorrectly. I was just being difficult and not working as a team member. I should stop being lazy and just be able to work the same way everyone else does. They did not want to understand neurodiversity or support it as they did not see it as beneficial. I had a nervous breakdown and could no longer function when I decided to leave my work. She fully supported me and said I made the correct decision.

Always busy

Well, as you can tell, my best friend was always busy. I can say even something as simple as arranging a bacon roll turned into mission impossible. I would receive a text from me apologising that bacon rolls had to be moved as she had a list of things to do, which she had forgotten about! Whenever she was run down and tired, I would go around with a curry or tapas along with a bath bomb for later in the evening; she loved relaxing in the bath. She said I had a very calming influence on herself, along with my partner giving her lots of great advice. She loved his bald head and would kiss him on the top of his head, leaving her lipstick. We all supported her through good and troubled times; she had her problems like everyone else. We have all watched life change a lot over the last few years and supported each other! We knew there was light at the end of the tunnel; she was happy and found the love of her life. It makes it hard to say goodbye. Bollie Bollie, sweetie darling, I will miss our adventures together!

After the death of Princess Twinkle Toes, Wilma decided to give up talking to scammers. However, they kept leaving her messages inviting her into chat rooms. She had a light bulb moment and decided to make notes of the various conversations she was having with men trying to deceive her. She decided to be a blonde and bumble around as the female version of Inspector Clouseau chatting to scammers. Investigating like Nancy Drew and the case of the missing Flip Flop. She had told Princess Twinkle Toes that someday she would draft a book. That was a crazy notion; however, as a massive fan of the Matrix, she went and consulted with the oracle. Choose the red pill to go down the rabbit hole and meet Neo and Trinity. Wilma applied her counselling and psychotherapy skills along with what she was learning about crime through studying at the Open University. She decided to find out if patterns occurred during her chats with these people pretending to be international stars and attempting to swindle women. Chatting with these people, she lets them into her weird world of being dyslexic and using assistive technology. Laughs at the love letters she receives and thinks of songs such as Dire Straits singing about Romeo and Juliet. Wilma attracts them like Tina Turner singing a typical male. As they try to charm her by talking about her beauty, they try to find out if she has just downloaded pictures of women through questions. She answers she is in disguise and looks like Miss Piggy from the Muppets! Giving them money in various ways, the easiest being Google Stream or Apple cards, as this is untraceable money, and you will not realise you have been swindled. Joining fake fan clubs or receiving a parcel to give personal details.

Video calls can be extremely frightening, and you will be asked to aid them the next day. Women ask for aid from charity, which is usually an orphanage. This is because women in society are considered caring and nurturing. How she has caught them out or got fed up with their talk and blocked them. People will always judge her, which she accepts and like one of her favourite Bon Jovi songs her life and she will give these people some bad medicine!

Mad, Bad, and Dangerous

While Wilma was getting ready to go for her daily walk along the shore, she was invited to talk to an international star. She is getting her Spotify ready and decides she is going to listen to Cher for a bit of love and understanding. The conversation started with Hello, are you here? It's me! Yes, I'm here. It is nice to meet you here. Please send me some photos. Wilma is walking along the path and says nice to meet you as well 😁 You're welcome. Are you still here? It was taking a bit of time for Wilma to receive messages from the star. She stopped her walk and told the star, yes, I was trying to find a photo. Presently, I can only find trains at the local museum 🤣🤣🤣 Please send me your recent photo. Are you here? This person is impatient, and she answers, yes, still here, recent photo. I don't do many selfies 🤣🤣🤣 You look beautiful over there. Thanks for the compliment 😁 Wow, good 😊 you're smiling good! She laughs and says yes, I find it hard to remember to smile while taking selfies 🤣🤣🤣 He decides to ask to have chatted before. Wilma is unsure and replies we might have chatted before! I have chatted to many people. He sends back, I don't think so! Hope you know that there are so many imposters pretending to be me on social media. The FBI officials are working on that by getting some arrested and hopefully putting some of them in jail. However, there are just so many scammers.

Wilma smiles; he is trying to make her feel safe, and she sits on the picnic bench by the shore and knows extremely well! I have had several of them. I was studying criminology and caught and blocked several of them. He is curious and asks are you chatting with any of them now? Not presently. I had someone pretending to be Stjepan Hauser recently, and I have blocked him. He warns her I want you to be incredibly careful because there are so many imposters around here on social media. Tell me, dear, have you been scammed before by those imposters? As messages are travelling slowly and Wilma is walking, she receives are you still here? I am sorry it is a poor signal, and the messages are taking a bit of time to arrive and send; then, I have not been scammed. I can see patterns and habits when chatting with them. They look for help with malware, etc. I check before answering; then I tell them to report it to the police 😂

He checks what she is saying with okay. You mean you haven't been scammed before by them, right? Correct, it has only been since I started the second year of my course at the Open University, and it was introducing criminology. This was when scammers started sending me friend requests on social media networks. 👺💡 He decides to inquire where are you from? I man from St Trianian's the best place 😊 Yes, it is certainly a beautiful place. What are your career aspirations?

Wilma arrives home, pops the kettle on, and sends back I am weird; I want to find ways to support dyslexia in the criminal justice system. Ok, how long have you been working? Wilma was confused by the question: did he mean the work at present, or how long had she been working? She answers with I need to take my socks and shoes off to answer that question, a long time 😬 You're so funny again he showed his impatience with are you here? Yes, I was just making myself a cup of coffee. Wilma settles down in her cat basket with her coffee and a Kit Kat. It doesn't take long before she receives have you finished taking your coffee? She thinks he is not very patient and just says yes. 😁 You haven't answered me! How long have you been working? What do you mean? Do you mean today? During my life? No, it's your business for how long. She thinks that is what he means and texts back. I have just really started it; I have been researching and studying over the pandemic. I blog this is one of the pieces I have written, "Meddling Pesky OU Student - Dyslexia Tips." Wilma had a Zoom meeting coming up and was making dinner, and she needed to say cheerio for today; it's a busy evening 😁 While Wilma was on her Zoom call, she received what is the time there? She politely answers sorry, I am on a Zoom call about international dyslexia. What are you doing now? I know it's night there. She repeats herself I am on a Zoom call on international dyslexia. He decides to ignore what she has told him and says have you eaten this evening? Yes, I had food before joining the Zoom meeting 😁 no problem, we will chat later tomorrow. Have a lovely day, OK? Cool, it is an informative evening about teaching dyslexic children in South Africa 😁 Take care of yourself and have a good sleep 😁

    The next morning, Wilma receives thanks for the kind words. Good morning. How are you doing? The beautiful fairy at OrCam had asked Wilma if she would trail a new prototype called a learn. The OrCam learn had arrived, and Wilma was trying to connect it to the WI-FI for the third time. She was becoming frustrated as the OrCam was not reading the QR code and kept saying OrCam is ready; let's get started. Grrrrr, I might be sending the beautiful fairy a shallow grave, saying OrCam learn is buried here. She texts back I am trying to connect a prototype device at present, but it's not working 🧟‍♀️👧👾👧😂 what are you doing now? He does not understand assistive technology and just sends back tidying my house 😂 Then she decides to have some fun and sends the muppets mahna mahna and is singing along with it!

She puts a fantastic way to start the day 😂 he ignored what she had sent and asked have you eaten? Yes, I have; I love my food too much, that is why I am fat 😂😂👾👧

Wilma does not hear from the star until the following day when a message arrives: good morning how are you doing? I am well, thanks. I am doing my good deed for the day! My friend is having to self-isolate due to covid. I am doing my master chef thing and making him some nice food 😀 Then she adds s hope you are enjoying the lovely weather just now 🙏🌟☺️ He decides to ask are you married? She thinks she is not trying that again and tells him no! Please do not use that sort of bad language! That is eight years of my life, which I will never get back! I don't understand; that is typical and sent back, lol. I am divorced, and since getting divorced, I have been in a long-term relationship. He is my best friend, and we have been together for a long time 😁🥴 he then asks do you live alone? She thinks that is weird, but I will play along; no, I live with my partner. 😀

How old are you? She answers, a lady never gives away her age, and you are 41 🙈 Well, I see you already know my age! She texted back. It is not hard when you're on social media 🤣🤣🤣🤣 he then said can I ask you a question? As she reads this, she thinks you have been asking lots of questions so far and sends yes. I'm just wondering if you would like to be in love with me. 😊 She sends back that is a bit weird and a bit too soon, don't you think? I just feel like if I know you, if I might be in love with you, do you care about ages? No, I don't care about ages. However, all my friends will make jokes that I am a cougar 🙈🙍♀️ He decides to say well, I would like to be in a relationship with you. That is, if you don't mind, however, we need to know each other better! She thinks there is no harm in chatting and replies not a problem, it would be lovely to get to know you better 😊 Wilma asks what are your hobbies? I love music, I love playing the violin 🎻 and I love dance. Wilma thinks the first two are not sure about the dancing. He then adds, and you? Well, I love to cook, do art and design, listen to music, do creative writing, psychology, and socialising with my friends 😃

That's good, then follows with I'm an open person. I don't like being proud of who I am or what I own. I don't discriminate against people; we are all one. I'm just a violinist and a human like everyone else. I understand that everyone is on a journey, and we all just muddle through life. She then asks football or rugby? He ignores the question and asks what are you doing now? I am sitting with a glass of cider, chatting with my friends. They are making fun of me 🤣🤣🤣🤣 he inquires how are they making fun of you. At this point, her friend Mr. D was saying to Wilma oh, another famous boyfriend. Has he sent you pictures of the size of his bratwurst yet? He will ask you shortly if you would want it covered in gentleman's relish! She texts back the conversation is just rude. 🤣🤣🤣🤣

She sends the video where Philip Scofield does not like dunking his biscuits, but Fern Britain says he does not mind dunkin' his beef in a bit of mustard! She says the way my conversations go with my friends 🙊💡😂😂😂 She tells him I am an open-minded person. I enjoy having a good laugh with my friends, even though it is early for Wilma. She sends good night xx Okay, good night, talk tomorrow, my dear beautiful, sweet dreams xx.

She ended the conversation that evening with big hugs 😁 😌

The following day. She receives Good morning, and she returns Good morning 😁 How are you today? Wilma goes out for the day with Mr. G and wanders around the city and sends a beautiful day for a wonder 😀

Later, she sends take care of yourself! Have a good night's sleep 😴 💤 💤 💤.

When she wakes up the next day, she says wow, exceptionally beautiful. I apologise was busy yesterday and wasn't here to chat with you. I will chat when I can. How are you doing, my dear? Hope that you're well this morning. Please take care of yourself. She returns. Good morning 😊 It is Friday! Yes 🤗. Friday is always remarkably busy, I hope you have a good weekend 👫👫 Yes, dear, what are you doing now? Wilma was just relaxing in her cat basket before a busy day and returned to watching cooking programs with coffee, 🐵 he inquires do you have kids? No kids, the next question have you finished cooking? She laughs and sends back I am watching cooking on TV. It gives me ideas for cooking dinner tonight. I love being creative. Yesterday, I saw a face with long hair made from coat hangers. It was cool 😁 Wilma finishes her coffee and breakfast and says it is lovely talking to you. Need to go and set myself up for helping lots of people with dyslexia 😊 As Wilma was switching on the helpline, she received are you a religious person? How often do you go to church? She is looking at the emails she needs to answer while waiting for calls and sends. I am busy presently. Oh, that is weird you sent me a message on Twitter looking to talk 👨‍🦰💁 No, dear I am not talking to you on Twitter! Have you received a message from someone pretending to be me on Twitter? Wilma was on the phone talking and giving out information on dyslexia. He then asks are you here? She tells him I am receiving messages from him right now, lol 😂 Wilma takes a screenshot and sends it to the star

😔😔 do not listen to those scammers talking to you now! It's not me, ok. I don't know why they are doing this to me! She sends back I want to remind you that I am studying crime, which comes in many different forms. As technology has improved, forms of crime have also changed. Please don't take offence. They will trip themselves up, and karma has its place 🙏 The star then asks what is he telling you in his message on Twitter sagt er dir da drüben auf Twitter? Which is German for what does he tell you over there? He is talking in English; I would have to run it through Google Translate if he's using another language. Please block and delete that stupid scammer chatting with you on Twitter. Now, are you here? However, Wilma was answering incoming calls. I will do it. Presently, I am trying to answer important questions and aid people. This is distracting me; I will deal with it when finished 😁 🙏 Important question where are you here?

Later, she said sorry, I have not been trying to avoid you. I am a helpline advisor, and my phone has not stopped. Thankfully, my shift has finished 😁 he is waiting for Wilma and returns good, then adds okay, was machst du jetzt, meine Liebe, hoffe, dass es dir gut geht. what are you doing now, my dear? Hope you are well in Google Translate. Then he adds I know you cannot write in Germany, I know. Wilma was out for a walk to clear her head and put on Spotify to listen to her favourite Runrig album, Searchlight. First in the line of songs was Every River. She sent I am out for It has been an intense morning, just trying to chill out! Okay, you're walking now! Yes, just a standard walk around my area 😁 Okay, please send me your photo. Wilma is feeling washed out and cannot be bothered but finds a photo and sends it to him. Wow, so beautiful 💋 you're looking good 💋💋 are you there alone? There were lots of people along the shore, and Wilma replied no, there are lots of people out walking today. Okay, can I see them? Wilma takes a photo of the shore and sends it to the star. Wow, beautiful surroundings. There are lots of people out walking their dogs. Please inform me, are those people your friends? Capercaillie - coisich a ruin comes on her Spotify list, and she sends it back. It is a favourite for dog walkers. I will see my friends later. I want to express my feelings to you. She starts heading back home and stops to type, yes, you can express your feelings. I don't know how to say this, but I feel you are a good person. I am beginning to have some emotional feelings for you. It is part of my job to make people feel in a safe, secure environment to talk 😁 Well, that's good. I just love our conversation. I'm so busy, but do not worry, I will always chat with you when I can 💋 Wilma receives a message from Mr G telling her to go and meet them. She tells him I am off to annoy my friends with my batshit crazy thoughts 😂😂😂😂 I'm willing to be in a good relationship with you if it works out. Cool 😁 welcome to my weird world. 😂😂😂😂. Wilma does hear from the star until later in the evening. He sends 💋💋 good evening, how are you doing? I am good, thanks, just trying a bit of pub trivia at present 😁 She then asks what are you up to yourself? Do you go out with your friends? I'm at home resting. I just had dinner. The hair bear bunch say talking to your famous boyfriend again? To which she replies yes! They are a sad, lonely prince locked in an ivory tower waiting for their Princess Fiona. They roar with laughter, and she turns her attention to her phone and types I am still chatting with friends, and we are having a good laugh. 😃 Wow, okay have you eaten? Not yet! Prawns in chilli and garlic are planned tonight 😊 Are You planning anything exciting tonight? I'm only tired and about to sleep now. Sweet dreams! 😴😴 Thanks 💜 when are you sleeping today? She smiles and sends you to your bed and sleep 🥴😂💤💤💤💤💤💤 good night and sweet dreams 🙏 thanks, dear 💜 you too. The star was up well before Wilma, and she found a message waiting for her saying good morning, love, how are you doing? She eventually answers good morning 😁 Wilma does not hear anything until the evening. How are you doing? What are you doing now? Everyone was over at Mr. D having a drink and sharing stories and replies. I am helping my friend just now; it is a long, sad story. He sends I have a nice word for you, dear! Wilma is not ready for what he is going to say as they are talking about the Princess twinkle toes. That is nice. However, I am not sure this is the right time. My best friend has passed away, and we are sharing memories. We all miss her terribly. He sends back well, I'm telling you now that I love you 😂 are you surprised? 😂 She just smiles and returns; thanks x 😳 Do you love me too? Wilma was not thinking straight; her head was a mess with grief. They were putting on Elvis singing How Great Thou Art and the Bay City roller singing Bye-bye baby. Then, I sent over a picture saying this is the last picture taken of my best friend 😢. Does she know me? No, she died in January 😟 This year? Yes 😢 😔😔😔😔😔😔 so sorry what happened to her? A blood clot went straight into her heart, and she dropped dead. Her partner performed CPR, and she was pronounced dead when the ambulance arrived 😭 😭 I'm so sorry about this stop overthinking, okay 😔 😔 Do you have another best friend? A strange thing to ask. However, Wilma was not thinking about it at the time, and she texted back It is a bit hard when I am talking to her partner. We have all been friends for a year 🥺 Again, he apologies and then can you try to calm down my love stop thinking so much! I am trying. It's not easy! We are all here to support each other in such a grim time, as my amazing friends say when alive 😁

> Enjoy life, feel alive.
> Face the crowd.
> Be proud.
> Perform.
> Shine your brightest!
> Love every minute of it.
> **Amaze them.**
> - Unknown

Wow, that's good ♥ What are you doing now? She heads over to the box of red wine, pours herself and her friend a glass, and returns to sharing stories and texting back talking. 😁

He decides to text, saying I asked you a question before you didn't answer me. I asked do you love me? Wilma did not love the star and was more interested in the conversation she was having with her friends. He then sends, wow♡ I cannot answer that at the present time. I am just catching up with friends, and my head is a mess presently.

Again, he asks do you love me? She becomes assertive and is thinking will you just fuck off presently. However, she sends seriously! Behave yourself. We have just met. I know I just love you. I have feelings for you! She sends back that is nice. Please tell me which brain is working: the one in your head or the one between your legs! 🤣 🤣 🤣 The star left her alone for the rest of the evening.

Later in the night, Wilma was feeling a bit better. She said sorry about earlier. I was a mess, but I am in a better place now. Hugs and sweet dreams xx

The next day, he sends thanks for your kind words, morning, my love, how are you doing 🖤 Wilma settles in her cat basket with a cup of coffee, switches on the TV, and replies good morning, what are you doing today? I'm good, just going to meet someone. She thinks that it is nice he is going to meet his friends. Then he asks are you a religious person? How often do you go to church? Wilma had given up on religion a long time ago and replied oh nice, I am not religious and do not go to church. He decides to tell Wilma I am a Christian, and I love God with all my heart & trust in HIM to comfort me & guide me. Only he knows what he has in store for us. I was raised in a strong Christian family, though I haven't been to church in the last few months. However, I don't think this will ever be a problem. I don't care about your religion; I believe we are all adults and have the right to choose what we want in life. She reads and thinks if you don't shove your religious beliefs upon me, as I could not care less what you believe in! he is diplomatic and sends me a humanitarian. I gave up on religion years ago. What are you looking for in a relationship? Oh, shit, really, she thinks, okay, be sensible with the answer. Every relationship is different; everyone I know has different points of view, and my friends are remarkably diverse. They have different skills; we all laugh when we hang out 😊 He begins with okay, well, I am looking for my best friend. A woman to spend the rest of my life with. I am just an average, down-to-earth man who is looking for a woman to love and to be loved in return for a meaningful relationship. I believe that love is not about how much you have in the beginning but how much you build till the end. I don't care about the age difference or the distance. I believe that age and distance have no rules when playing in a relationship. I want to love and be loved again. Wilma is taking a drink of her coffee and receives the impatient Are you still here? She was thinking of how to reply and send it. Relationships are complex. I have been in good and bad relationships. I am lucky enough to be surrounded by amazing, supportive people. They have helped me through good and troubled times in my life. They will be truthful and tell me if they think I am wrong. You always have points when you fall out, but this is life 😁 That's good 💝 What type of man are you looking for in a relationship? She thinks I have a man in my life and am not looking for another relationship. She says I have lots of men who are friends; they all make me laugh. Okay, but I asked what type of man you would like in a relationship! She decides to ignore this, and he follows on with it; the type of woman I am interested in is a woman who can laugh, be intelligent, and be self-confident, one who is also motivated. I'm basically an incredibly positive person who loves humour and laughter and would like someone with an adventurous spirit and a cheerful outlook who can see the funny side of life.

Play it cool, Wilma. She returns well; it sounds like you and I will be good friends. 😁 He gushes on with someone open and willing to learn new things. But what matters most in a relationship is honesty. I also love a woman who knows how to treat a man like a baby. Wilma comes to this and thinks what the fuck! He also tells her romance and passion are important as well. However, I have learned that chemistry is not everything. Well, I told you that I want to be loved and loved again. They say beauty is in the eye of the beholder, so I would say I have more on the inside than beauty, LOL. No one is perfect, including myself, but I suppose if you don't put it out there and risk, you will never know. However, I am realistic, and I am by far not perfect. Again, she thinks and plays it cooly. You are correct; no one is perfect. I am certainly not perfect; I have issues that my friends and family accept, and I am currently challenging myself with studying for a degree. Thankfully, assistive technology aids me. I have dyslexia, which is complex. I struggle with reading, writing, and processing lots of information. This doesn't mean I am stupid. Well, that's good. Let me ask you this: are you ready to move or relocate if this works for us? The alarm bells are ringing in Wilma's head again with what he fuck. However, she stays calm. I have never thought about it. I have been planning my business and getting through my degree. I take one day at a time; people keep saying I should have years planned. I have found that it never works that way. I'm willing to relocate for that special woman. Life is truly short, and I am so much afraid of growing old alone...lol, I want to grow with someone who is full of fun. We will be compatible to grow old together. Wilma is not committing to anything and says, you will have that. You have a good group of friends, you have everything. You don't have to spend every minute with them. I have gone months without seeing friends, and when we do meet, we all have the best time, full of laughter. 🥰😍 ❤️ ❤️ ❤️ ❤️ What do you do for fun? Well, I enjoy art and design 😂😂😂 he tells Wilma. I enjoy slow or fast dancing, walking in the woods, holding hands, candlelight dinners, travelling, shopping, watching movies, and playing my violin. I also like to play romantic music on the piano for that special person. At this point, Wilma thinks of Brenda Russell singing Piano in the Dark and reads the next part of his message. I love snuggling and sharing enthusiastic kisses with my woman. what is your favourite thing? I can't dance to save myself. I have no sense of direction 😂😂😂. I would love to be able to dance. I love watching Ice skating. However, I spend more time flat on my face on the ice rink. 🤸💁 Oh, sorry about that! She tells the star,

    my favourite thing is cooking. I love cooking for my friends, but my kitchen ends up as a bomb site by the time I am finished. I have a great friendly rivalry with friends when cooking. 😬 They have me howling with laughter, saying they will teach me how to make it properly the next time! I am waiting for a date for the great Macaroni and cheese challenge. I will smash them out of the park, LOL. Well, that's good 💞 I love healthy foods. I love the colour green. I like to snuggle up on my couch to read an enjoyable book when it rains. I love shopping at the mall and listening to romantic music or 60's music. She thinks of the seeker I Will Never Find Another You, which her Mum played while she was growing up. and exercising. I love food, mostly eating, but I do cook occasionally. I enjoy photography, so I'm always looking to get lost in new areas, finding unique things & and places to photograph. I also have a passion for the beach. I wonder if he listens to the Beach Boys Kokomo. She types the message I hate getting sand in my feet. I love tapas and am looking forward to having a break in Madrid at some point. Love going around museums and art galleries. Walking is one of the few exercises I can now do. I also enjoy swimming and exploring; however, I do get lost a lot of the time. How often do you exercise? I go for a daily walk every day. It aids my mental health and helps me try to get complex things, such as my academic essays, together. It aids in sorting out my spaghetti brain 😄. Well, I exercise 1-2 times per week! Which best describes your daily diet? I never thought about my daily diet. I just cooked whatever I fancied. I love meat and potatoes, so keep it healthy. Then he asks how after do you drink? I drink with my friends at the weekend. Do you smoke? No, I have never smoked. Then he goes on to ask if you have children, right? Wrong, no children, of course, brought about why? It's way too complex to explain. He then sends can you just tell me? Sorry, I can't spell most of it. 😄 Well, okay, I must rest now, okay chat with you later, my beloved. She sends back to have a lovely day ahead 💗 You to take care and enjoy your day 😁

Later in the day, as Wilma was relaxing, she sent Stacey Kent singing Hushabye Mountain.

Sweet dreams the following morning. Wilma receives a hello. Good morning to you! How are you doing? Wilma sits down in her cat basket with a cup and returns good morning. I am good, thanks 😃 He inquires what are you doing now, my love? I am getting everything ready for tomorrow! I am excited to catch up with people I have met over the pandemic at an assistive technology conference 😃 What are you up to today? He tells her I'm about to go and take my bath. She wonders if he needs his back scrubbed and if she should offer to get the loofah out. She says hope you have some nice bath bombs 😂😂😂😂 😂😂 have you taken your bath? I have not had a bath for years, so I shower 🛁🛁🛁 He asks have you eaten this morning? Yes, I'm eating my breakfast just now. Then he asks are you a romantic type? I have no idea; it is not something I think about 👩💡 Well, I'm a helpless romantic! Wilma thinks whatever floats your boat! I love being with a woman and doing trivial things for her! I like to put a smile on her face. I enjoy surprising her and doing my part to make her dreams come true. I am sure you do. It is the loveliest thing to be able to support people, helping make their dreams come true. 😁 She is then asked what makes you smile. Lots of things make me smile

He sends back. I can find humour in just about anything. Smiling comes very naturally to me. I can also smile when my partner has enjoyed something that I have done for her. Just seeing those I love smiling, knowing I put that smile on their faces, makes me smile, too! Oh, that is lovely 😍🙏 I am a wonder woman myself; I wonder where I left my keys, I wonder where I left my phone, and I wonder where all my money has gone! Wilma then left the house. She was spending a few days in the city with Mr G. He was interested in seeing the assistive technology Wilma was using to aid other neurodiverse people.

Later in the afternoon, she receives LOL Wilma: good afternoon, how are you doing? What will make you happy? She sends back the afternoon, just waiting to get into the hotel. I am going to enjoy a quick refreshment 😂 Wilma was enjoying the winter sun and sitting in the street pretending she was in Spain. Wow, that's good, are you with your friends? What makes you happy? He says I'm happy when my loved ones are happy. I have a woman who treats me like a prince. She thinks, does he mean by being treated like a prince? Again! She sends me to spend time with my best friend. If he behaves himself, I will let him out to play in a guitar shop 😂😂😂😂 He asks can I see him?' Wilma sends a photo; he is a good-looking guy does he have a wife? She answers no just me annoying, him daily 😂😂😂👾💡 He asks again I said is he married? No, he is not married he wants to know do you cry a lot and what makes you cry. I do tend to cry easily, not always tears of sadness ... I cry also when I'm happy and surprised. Wilma thinks so. She cries usually when she is angry and frustrated. She answers I don't cry much; I usually cry with laughter when I am chatting with my friends. What is your favourite music? He then sends a photo of himself. It doesn't look photoshopped. However, Wilma comes across it later on Instagram. It was a picture taken on his sister's wedding day, and his sister had been chopped out of it. She replies I listen to lots of different music. It depends on my mood. I listen to jazz, big band, classical, pop, rock, folk music, and hip hop 😄 The only music I don't listen to is drum and bass. It gives me headaches 😂😂😂

Later in the evening while Wilma was sitting in the hotel bar enjoying a glass of wine she received, are you here? Yes, I am here. How are you doing?

What are you doing? Just chilling out with a glass of wine 😁. Wilma had her iPad out and was chatting to Mr G and telling him about the scammer. She reads the message to him, saying I love music. The songs I listen to will usually tell you what kind of mood I'm in, along with telling you what's in my heart. Words can't begin to describe who I am; when I'm happy, you'll usually find me singing (assuming I know the song! I think music is a gift many people take for granted.) They'll listen; however, they just hear the beat, yet it won't stop people feeling its power. Music can be soothing to the soul and can calm the restless spirit. The wrong kind of music can also damage one's inner being. A person's mind will unconsciously listen to the lyrics, which will either bring death/depression upon them or will bring joy to their soul so they might be able to enjoy life. As she talks to Mr. G, she types yes. I love to sing and dance while nobody is watching. They might think I have been let out for the day 😂😂😂🤳💡 Wow,

Lol, as a person's mood changes, so does the type of music they listen to. What are your favourite movies? I love science fiction movies. I like comedies such as Watching A Good Year. It always makes me smile 😁 What sort of movies do you like? Star Trek? Matrix? She is confused and says she has not heard of the movie. I love movies. My all-time favourite is "City of Angels." It's a movie where a man sacrificed his life as an angel to experience what it was like to love the woman he was drawn to. I also love Notebook, Sweet November, Sleepless in Seattle, Grease, Never Been Kissed, and anything with Reese Witherspoon. I like romantic comedies, action movies, and ones based on true stories like Titanic, & and Pearl Harbour. She thinks okay, we have different tastes in movies and says, I like Monster in Law for a good laugh. Wanda Sykes and Jane Fonda are funny together. I like a lot of the hammer horror films. Airplane is just classic with Don't Call Me Shirley 😂😂🙀💁🙀💁 There are so many that I like. I can't name them all. I know. 😂😂😂😂 Wilma is telling Mr. G what the star is chatting about when the next message comes. Do you love to express your feelings, or do you love to hide your feelings? A bit of both. It all depends on what mood I am in, and I never have one day the same. I'm a person who would rather express my feelings. I know it's not good to keep them locked up. It's important to express to others that you care for them. Enabling them to support and encourage them. I LOVE sharing sweet moments with the woman I love... it makes my heart happy! Then the subject changes to what kind of sport do you like best? Rugby, I like a beautiful game played by men with odd, shaped balls! Okay, that's good. I like Football, shooting baskets, playing volleyball, and baseball. What do you like and dislike? I don't like cheaters, liars, thieves, or shallow people. Other than that, I'm a person that likes pretty much everything... I'm very easygoing. I have collaborated with plenty of liars, cheaters, as well as shallow people. I must admit that compared to some people I have met, Muppets have more intelligence 🙏 Okay, I understood everything you said to me. What is your definition of true love? She thinks how shit and sends you to ask some interesting questions! I feel like I am in counselling 😂😂😂 I don't know 🤷‍♀️ I am not sure how to put it into words. Well, okay 🖤 After a wee think and drinking some of her wine, she types, you are the first person to ask me this. It has always been unconditional. You have stumped me with putting it into words 🤷‍♀️🙏 Wow 🖤

True love to me is the kind of love God gives… UNCONDITIONAL love. It's a love that is indescribable with words yet is felt deep within the heart. It's when you can't stop thinking of the other person. You are excited to get home to them after a long day at work. You want to just say hello through a text or phone call just because they are on your mind. How will you treat your man?

I treat him like I am like to be treated myself. Respectfully, deal with his sarcasm on bad days. Make sure he is okay. Try and make sure his mental health is in the best place possible 🙏 I love what you said just now. You're a good woman 🖤 I will treat my woman with lots of love and respect. I like to hold her hand while walking. I enjoy the little kisses stolen throughout the day and the little smiles she gives me from across the room. I believe adults are to walk side by side in life, so communication and honesty are ESPECIALLY important. Relationships go both ways. We all have good and bad days; my partner holds my hand to stop me from shopping Lol 😂😂😂. Not really; he is good at guiding me, but I need help with directions. I get lost in an airport 🤷‍♀️🤷‍♀️ How did you get lost in the airport? It is easy. I have dyspraxia as well as dyslexia. My friends are always joking about my sense of direction 🧗‍♀️💡👩‍🦯💡 Sorry about that. What do you like to do? Why? It is something I live with. I am upfront about my issues so people can help me if I ask for help. I love being in the great outdoors, and seeing the natural beauty God has given to us! Others take advantage of it. I love snuggling with the ones I love while watching a movie. I enjoy meeting others and making a difference in the lives of those around me. Wilma ignores the messages about God and defiantly ignores the fact he wants to snuggle up on the couch. She sends,

hey, I am on a journey! It has taken me in new directions over the last few years. It is up to people if they want to join my journey. I have met some amazing friends along the way. I have inspired some people with what I do. I have now decided to go and support people who struggle like myself and support them on their journey. All right, what is your favourite book? Lol. I don't read much, to be honest; I love reading, but it takes me ages. What people take 2 hours to read takes me weeks. It is frustrating. Thank goodness I have OrCam read to aid me now. I just point it at a page, and the amazing laser technology turns all the words into audio; it makes my life easier. I know what it is to proofread for the first time 😊 Okay, good, my favourite book is the Bible!!! It's got the greatest stories ever told, as well as words from our heavenly father. Wilma is thinking I have picked another nut job. Well, this will be easy to remember for the future sends back. I have not had anyone tell me their favourite book is the bible here. I do love a good Stephen King. Carrie and Misery were brilliant when I had time for leisure reading 😂 you were warned, I am weird 😂😂😂 Lol What would you consider a fun thing for a couple to do together? I love having a wander around and finding new things. I do get bored when my friend drags me around guitar shops 🤣🤣🤣🤣. They are all beautiful women; he loves their slender necks and shapely bodies 🙊💡 Well, for me, anything that brings laughter to both people. I am an incredibly positive person who cares about the people around me. Friendly conversation motivates me. I live my life with intent and purpose. I can find fun in almost anything I do. I am looking for someone to share special moments and love unconditionally. Wilma drinks some more wine and is still chatting with Mr G. I have plenty of laughter. I am not even going into some of the rude conversations I have when it comes to cooking; the innuendos are great, and I can give as good as I get. I also love people-watching. To make this work, If two people want to be together, it's up to the two to give it their best and not worry about what anyone says or does. It's up to us to make what we would like from life to make our future. She wasn't paying much attention to his messages and just said yes! Yeah, I am an incredibly positive person who cares a lot about the people around me. Friendly conversation motivates me. I live my life with intent and purpose. I can find fun in almost anything I do, and I am looking for my best friend. A woman to spend the rest of my life with. I don't care about the age difference or the distance. The type of woman I am interested in is a woman who can laugh, who is motivated and ambitious, intelligent, and self-confident. Well, I am tired and need a rest. I will talk to you tomorrow. 😁 Wilma goes to retire to the room she is staying in with a glass of wine, looking forward to the following day.

okay, my beloved, have a nice rest, good night, and sweet dreams 🖤 😳😳 When Wilma wakes up, she finds a message on her phone: good morning, my love. She makes herself a cup of coffee and gets back into bed before saying good morning. What are you up to today? Good morning. How are you? I'm about to go to a friend's house. She thinks that is nice as she arrives at the technology centre for an assistive technology course. As she sits down with coffee, it is a good day of learning at an assistive technology course. Enjoy your day 😁 Okay, thanks have you eaten? Wilma had not eaten but just said yes. Okay, are you at home? She thinks no, dumbass and sends no, I am at a conference centre 😂😂😂 he returns I just feel like you're with me here, she thinks that is weird and keeps chatting with everyone who is on the course with her, oh That is nice 😁 yeah 🌿 I don't know how to say this, but I love you 😊 send me a photo okay I can't just now, the talks are just about to start. The first talk is learning about global auto-correct. 😁 😌

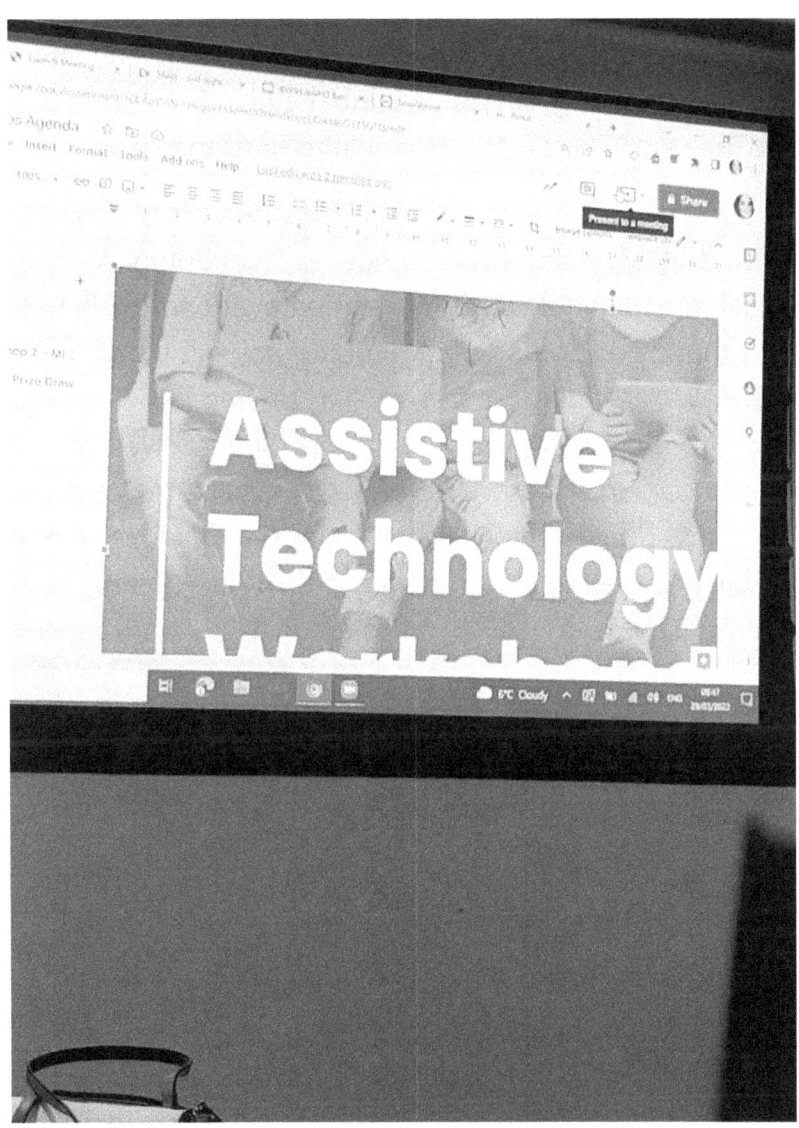

When would you go home? Tomorrow 😁 Wilma and Mr G had a wonderful day at the assistive technology course. Mr G was impressed with the talks about equatio which from Texthelp. As Mr G loves equations and equation aids maths, there was also a variety of mind mapping software showing. He also enjoyed finding out about global auto-correct and global tasks. The centre was extremely quiet due to the pandemic.

Later, she sends the star an enjoyable day. My brain cells are truly fried 🥴🥴 Good evening how are you doing my love? It has been an enjoyable day, information overload. 🥱🥱🥱🥱 Alright that's good what are you doing now? A bit of mischief 🥴. She was sending selfies of herself and Mr G enjoying cocktails to friends as they were at work. She receives: have you bought a card in the store before? No, I make my own cards. Which cards do you think I'm talking about, my love? Get well soon, birthday cards, etc. I meant gift cards like Steam cards!

No, it was quiet for a while, and then she received it. Can you get it for me? She thinks, what part of no does he not get and texts seriously? Yes, my beloved, why? I'm using it to upgrade my iCloud. Are you getting it for me? She thinks what a dick, and moves to a lovely pub with live music playing and says where am I supposed to get something I don't know?

I don't understand. If you go to the store, it will be there. Wilma's sarcasm is beginning to rise. Oh that is just helpful! Are you at home now? She is thinking, is this guy for real? What a dick, and says I am not going to the shops for your card, you're wasting my time tonight, talk to you tomorrow! Wilma goes on to enjoy the rest of her evening in peace.

The following morning, she was still annoyed and said oh, why does it not surprise me that "Prince Charming "has magically vanished!

Later, as she was sitting with a large mug of coffee with a cake, watching the world go by, talking to Mr G, a message popped up good evening, how are you doing? She thinks evening, where the hell are you in the world? It is coming up for midday, she replied I am good, really busy, okay? What are you doing? I am setting up lots of meetings with different companies. I take it you're travelling again. No, I thought you were going to get the card that I asked you to buy. Thinking this guy is an asshole and returns No! You were told this! If I say no, I mean it! This is one of the boundaries set to stop lying, cheating scammers 😁 She hears nothing and travels home late in the evening while relaxing in front of the TV in her cat basket, sipping a glass of wine; a message comes through: are you talking to me? Yes, I can talk to you. What is wrong? I don't understand you at all. What are you talking about? An evil smile comes over her face. Good! I would not be doing my job properly if you understand me 😈😈😈😈 Sweet dreams.

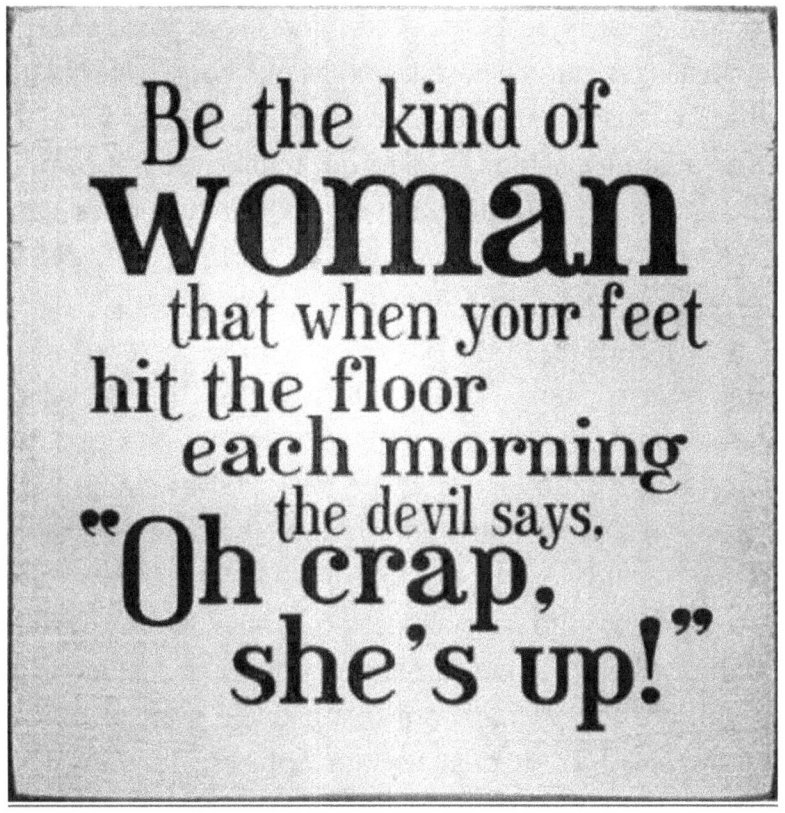

The next morning, Wilma got up later than normal. She went to check all the messages on her phone and found the "Hello, good morning system message: A call has been attempted from Hangouts. Calls made from Hangouts can't connect with Google Chat. You can share a link to a Meet video call instead.

She thinks that it is weird I have never had a video call before, so I will ignore it.

Later, she said sorry I missed your call. I will catch up with you later. It is a busy day 😅 In the afternoon, while she is studying, a message pops up: you sound like a joker. He is weird. You're always taking everything like a joke, and that's why you always laugh when talking to me. I don't like that! This guy has serious issues, but I decide to answer him with I have been on a Zoom call today and forgot to take the webcam cover off 🤭🤭🤭🤭 You always use all this when talking to me😂😄😆😆😆😄🙂🙂🙂🙂😁😁😁🤭🤭🤭🤭🤭🤭☺️😃😃☺️😃😜😝😝😛🤪🤪🤪😄☺️🙂🙂🙂 Why??? You're always using it, it's not good, you're chatting with me and taking everything like fun, are we here for fun? Wilma is confused with the message; she also thinks the guy has a significant issue, and everyone she talks to uses emojis. Sorry, I am busy just now with Zoom and the team's meetings presently. I will be part of a Texthelp virtual conference next month. I am about to have a meeting about it shortly. Don't use any of that when chatting with me! Sorry, you have lost me with what you are saying. But I am trying to do a lot at the same time. 🙈💡😅 Stop it dear we are not here for fun, what is wrong? Nothing but stop that. What? All this

You don't like emojis? A picture says a lot to me. I get more from a picture than words. If you don't like it, I will try and stop.

It is an easier way for me to communicate. 😺💡 I'm not talking about the pictures; I'm talking about the emojis. This guy is seriously crazy, but she takes a deep breath and starts typing emojis, which are pictures that express people's feelings. If I am happy, I just 😁. If I am feeling crazy, I just 🤪. Feeling loved 🥰. I don't have to think about how to put everything into words. I don't have to type as much, as it makes me tired at times. I use assistive technology when I write a lot. Then thinks about the other ways she loves to communicate and follows with thank goodness there are no gifs on this, as I love using them to communicate. He stops chatting with her, and once she has finished her work and studies, she sends. I have checked all the messages to everyone I chat to. You are the only person who has given me this feedback. I am taking time out to reflect on how we communicate going forward... She does not hear from him, and on Friday afternoon, she says have a nice weekend. 🙏 Good afternoon, how are you doing? Hello, I am not bad, thank you for asking. enjoy your weekend, thank you too, don't work too hard.

Later in the evening, while in her cat basket, What are you doing now? Watching a comedy! 🤣🤣🤣 What is your idea of fun? Wilma does not bother answering the next morning when she wakes up. Wow, I like to watch comedy, what normally makes you laugh, is it more interesting? This guy needs help; everyone needs a good laugh, and it is good for your mental health. What are you doing now? Studying, okay, I cannot believe I am nearly at the end of my second year. I must be crazy as I am not an academic. 😂 Wow, have you eaten? Not yet, I am out for a walk 😁 As she walks up the path in the local woods, she texts it will not be long before all the wild garlic blooms 😁 She does not hear anything back and enjoys the rest of her day. He leaves a text early in the morning: hello, good morning. Sounds like you had a lovely walk yesterday. Good morning 😁. It is a nice walk along from where I live.

Later, while flicking through Facebook, she sees a post about fake news from the star she is talking to on Google Chat. Wilma is studying this as part of her introduction to criminology; she had not seen the YouTube video in question, and it must have been reported and removed. However, she knew dealing with fake news was difficult, and she said, well done to you and your team for dealing with the difficulties of fake news!! (I have not seen the video in question) if you need to talk, let me know 🙏 Since he didn't answer, she guessed he was fake and didn't know what she was talking about.

Later on, good evening, have you eaten? Hello, yes, I made pork and mushroom stroganoff 😊 What have you been up to today? I'm about to sleep a good night, sweet dreams, and thank you too.

The next morning, she sends a morning sleepy head 😁 good morning, how are you doing? Wilma had been talking to a person she had gone to school with, as she had seen on Facebook that he had been hacked on Instagram. She had seen the posts and received messages and decided to check if she needed to block the person. She tells the star I am well; I am having an interesting conversation with someone I know about hackers and scammers. When were you talking to this person? This morning, they were hacked on one of their social media sights. It was a beauty!

    Later, on Facebook, Wilma received a message from a female she did not know saying that she had bumped into the star in question. He had kindly given her this WhatsApp number, and if she texted it, he might answer. Wilma checked out the number to find it was in the Czech Republic (Czechia). This was a scammer, and she decided to see what the person she was talking to had to say on the subject. She takes a screenshot and sends it to him with a report 🙏 He is still quiet, and later she sends a good evening. How has your day been? When it was late in the evening, he said hello. Are you here? When did they message you? Yes, I am here! I messaged you early this evening. Okay, when did those scammers message you? Okay, it's good that you have already reported him. I want to call you on a video call. Are you busy now? It was extremely late in the evening, and she said I am just chilling out watching TV 😁 Wilma got her iPad ready for the call. Okay, System message: A call has been tried from Hangouts. Calls made from Hangouts can't connect with Google Chat. You can share a link to a Meet video call instead. She thinks she has made a mistake and sends sorry, not used to this, oops, then calls again, and she sees the star in question and a message arrives I can't even see you and tries again with the system message: A call has been attempted from Hangouts. Calls made from Hangouts can't connect with Google Chat. You can share a link to a Meet video call instead. send me a photo, okay? System message: A call has been attempted from Hangouts. Calls made from Hangouts can't connect with Google Chat. Wilma does eventually connect for a moment and sees the star for about 20 seconds before it cuts out on her. She tries calling back and chases a dot around the screen of her iPad. He sends a screenshot and asks her for a photo. Wow, you're looking good 😊 Thanks, I don't use my iPad very often for calls. I have everything in a muddle. They talk in messages. How are you today? I'm good, what are you doing now? Still watching TV 😂😂 have you eaten? Yes, deep-fried pizza, it was lush. Did you work today? Oh yeah, I have plenty of work, an assignment to get ready for the 25th of this month, compare and contrast on a nice easy subject to write about, then sarcastically adds NOT! Did you go shopping today? No, I didn't need anything; I just went for a walk as usual before going back to studying. I want to tell you something! Do you know I love you? Wilma is thinking, what is going on here? I did see him on the camera, and he replied WOW! Wilma, I am serious about being in love with you! Why, thank you, that is extremely nice of you to tell me. Yes, I love you ♥ I don't know if you love me too. She returns. I am just getting to know you. Okay, are you donating to the orphanage home? What do you mean? How many charity organizations have you donated to before? I support the two charities, and which charities I give money is up to me and should not be questioned. When are you sleeping? I'm about to sleep now, okay? Sleep well tonight, and I'll chat with you tomorrow 😊🙏 Sweet dreams 😊 Wilma went to bed confused that night. She was not sure if she had bumped into an international star accidentally. She was trying to work out what she had seen. This could be a very clever scammer; she had a restless night trying to work out what was going on.

The next morning, he checked on Wilma with what are you doing? She was listening to ABBA while cleaning the house and texted back in the morning. I am just tidying the house just now 😁 It is boring but needs to be done 😂😂😂 he sends 😌😌🙇🙇🙇 my mom is sick and at the hospital now. Wilma thinks that is not good however I will try and support him with kind words. Oh dear! Hope she is feeling better soon. The hospital is the best place to be if you are ill 🙏 sending hugs 🤗🤗 I don't know what will happen to her because my bank account is blocked now. They are proceeding to fix something on it those scammers wanted to hack my account 🙇 Wow this is truly a nasty scammer playing on the fact that a loved one is in hospital. Plenty of people would fall for this and want to help as it is a vulnerable time. She was very suspicious now and had phoned the police. This is. not about the police. I'm talking to the bank! Can you help me with some money? I will pay it back, please 🙏🙏 The most important is for my mom to get well soon. Wilma is fearful and angry at the same time, reading the text and screaming you are one fucking sick arsehole. Do I think I have a victim here tattooed across my forehead? Do you think I am that stupid? I know you have plenty of people around to support you. If this was true, you fucking arsehole! She is incredibly angry. However, she says just continue to be with your mum and make sure she gets better soon 😁 I said can you help me with some money now? I will pay it back as soon as possible. Wilma ignores him. Are you here 😌😌 She decides to say yes heard that before! I do not trust you with that sort of information 🙏 She sent a couple of good mornings but never heard anything for weeks, then unexpectedly, she received Good morning, my love. How are you doing? I missed you so much, what are you doing now? She thinks "Prince Charming" has turned up. I am ready for you this time. Oh hello! I have been seriously busy presently. I am trying to edit my 1300 academic assignment 😁 😵. How are you doing? He is quiet again, then again. Good morning. How are you doing? Good morning, I am well, thanks for asking 😃 What are you doing now? I have missed talking to you! She laughs, thinking well, that is a big fat lie. He then follows on with, but you know that you disappointed me! Oh, now he is trying to make me feel guilty. She texts. I am just catching up with messages at present. I never said I was perfect. I told you my mom was sick, I begged for your help, and you ignored me 😔 She is thinking next time I will share my Tesco Clubcard details, try spending that with oh so much frustration! She sends a firm message: well, my devoted friends would rather talk about their feelings; it is an extremely worrying time with loved ones in the hospital. They don't ask me for money. Well, it's okay. She thinks he is still trying to make me feel bad. It's a shame it's not working. I hope your mum is better now. Hospitals are the best place if you're extremely sick. You know why I asked you for that money? Because my account was blocked, but now forget it, I'm ok now. Wilma smiles, thinks about her answer, and sends It would not be immensely helpful trying to lend you money if you're account is blocked. Stressful situations make people think irrationally. I just asked you as I know that you are a kind person.

I was reaching out for some help. However, the situation is sorted, and I'm not worried about that now. She thinks oh, I am forgiven. This is a Wendy Moten moment singing Come in Out of the Rain. he loves me again! Wilma sends a text to her friend saying "Prince Charming" is back! I wonder what the next scam will be! She thinks the game is on and asks what are you up to this weekend? 🤗 She follows this with oh yes! I know you are disappointed in me. Tell me why! I am interested to know! He goes silent until late in the night. Good night, I will chat with you tomorrow morning, OK, no problem; x

The next day, Wilma had a few Opps moments with her studies, and after swearing at her laptop most of the day, she sends a message late in the evening: I can only hope your day has gone better than mine! While reviewing my assignment to writer helper. I accidentally removed most of it 😖🙊💀 Hello good evening. How are you doing? Thanks, and how was your day going over there 🍃

Well, I am hoping to finish my assignment and submit it tomorrow. Still have a bit more to write and get all the referencing done. 🤪 I think you're still busy just now. No, I am taking a break from studying, catching up with some James Bond 😁 Then Wilma remembered and texted oh, I have been invited to Malaga to see a dyslexic project in action 😁 He sent I would be in the UK. I wonder if there are any houses for sale; I would like to buy a house in the UK. There are plenty of houses for sale in the UK. It depends on which part of the UK you are thinking about. Do you want to be in a city or the countryside? I'm buying this house because of you! The house will be for both of us when I come to the UK. Do you live in the city?? She thinks this is his latest swindle. What a load of bull shit. However, if he is annoying me, it is leaving someone else alone. She says no, I am in a small town. I am not far from the city. Then, it asks If you are going to buy a property in the UK. Would it not be better to rent it out? No, I want to buy the house, please look for a house and show me, then tell me the price. She thinks oh shit, what the hell do I know about the property? I am not telling him about a property around here! Must try and put him off and send. I once had someone ask me about buying a seaside hotel on LinkedIn in Scotland. Where do I begin? I don't know much about property or where you want to be based in the UK. I want to be in a place near you, OK? Do you know if there are houses for sale around you? I have had a chance to see if there are houses for sale around my area. I am busy. It might be a while. Okay! Please remind me occasionally. I tend to lose track of projects. 🙏 What are you doing now? LoL, I am eating my breakfast. I hope you have had a nice breakfast this morning 😁 Wilma then gets on with her assignment, and later she receives the answer yes ☺☺☺.

Later, she said I am doing a virtual conference with Texthelp, and I had some lovely feedback on the pre-recorded talk I have done for next month. 😁 Wilma was looking through TikTok in the evening and noticed more accounts of the star following her. She decided to ask how many TikTok accounts do you need. It's a bit weird to have a new account following me every week. Good evening. Please be incredibly careful; I'm not the one following you on that TikTok. Always block and delete them, OK? She thinks sarcastically, my guardian angel will look after me, what a scumbag! She types. I guessed that It's simply weird! I am incredibly careful! 😁 OK, if anyone messages from anywhere saying it's me, just block and delete that person immediately and let me know, OK? I'm chatting with you only. Well, there is a big fat lie she tells him no problem, I will let you know. These people tend to ask you the same questions. It will be to keep it a secret. They get easily upset when you say no 🙏 Please be incredibly careful, I must sleep now. We'll chat tomorrow, OK? No problem, sweet dreams 🌿🙏 She is thinking I must be careful of you after the video stunt.

The next morning, good morning. I hope you had a good sleep. Have a lovely day 🙏 later in the morning, she was looking through Facebook and saw a story from her friend and decided to share it with the star. Oh, this is a true story! I almost wet myself laughing when my friend told me this morning! She was feeling unwell and went to the doctor. They were having difficulty trying to find out what was wrong. The doctor needed to attend to an emergency patient and did not want my friend to leave. They also did not want my friend back in the waiting room, so they put her in a storage cupboard 😂😂😂😂😂 There was nothing then late in the evening, he sends good evening are you here? How are you doing? Hello, I am doing well, thanks. I am puzzled by your whole property project in the UK. It is not something I know a lot about; what are you looking for? I just want to have a house that I will stay when I am in the UK. You haven't told me about any houses yet, have you not found a house? I get the feeling that London is more of your scene. It will be normally where you do your work. I think you need a professional who is knowledgeable about this subject, 🙏 As usual, he disappeared! Good morning. Thank goodness it is Friday. I have another busy day of supporting people. I hope you have a good weekend full of laughter. I am looking forward to catching up with my friends this evening. I also want to leave you with homework. I want you to break down for me what you want when you're telling me you want to buy a property in the UK. It is too big. I need to know where about in the UK, e.g., England, Wales, Scotland, or Northern Ireland. I need to know what price range you want. I need to know if you want a new build or an old build. You might want to renovate it. After this, I will have an idea of who to ask that can guide you to what you want 🙏 I cannot tell you until I know this information. Wilma also chatted with her friend on the phone about "Prince Charming!" How he was looking for a love nest for them. They chatted about picking him up from the airport, driving him to the first police station, and telling him to ask for cell one.

Later in the day, he was back in touch, saying what I'm talking about is for you to look for any house. That is normal to live in, not that I will be living there forever. I want to come to the UK, so I stay comfortably also the house will be for both of us. Well, that is as helpful as a fart in a wetsuit! She needs some help to keep this idiot busy. Wow! Sounds like a scene out of Pretty Woman. I have never had a man say that to me before in my life. I have no idea what a normal house looks like, and all my friends use property for business. They rent them out as holiday homes, etc., okay, let me think about it. Alright, I know that you can find the perfect house that will be good for us!

Later that evening, she asked the hairbear bunch for ideas of how to deceive this scammer. The hair bear bunch told her you know this is a scammer, she returned. Of course, I know it is a scam! They were no help. She also asked Dr Dodgy for shoes, but he was not much help either. As she had talked to a friend, they had a plan, and she texted Dr Dodgy Shoes and told him. We have a brilliant plan. What we will do is pick him up from the airport and, take him to the nearest police station and tell him to ask for cell one. A few days later, she received a Good morning, how are you doing? I'm good. Good morning. I am glad that you are well. Take care of yourself 😁 Thanks how are you doing? The previous evening, Mr D had been talking about his holiday. She was still laughing about the silly conversation from the previous evening and told him I was doing well, thanks. My friend is going on holiday this week and buying a new bikini. He wants me to sew on his 50-meter swimming badge on his bikini briefs so he can attract the ladies 😁😁😁😁 Wilma does not hear anything from him for a few days, then one day, she decides to experiment with the OrCam learn and see if it is any good at foreign languages. Wilma knew, collaborating with the beautiful fairy, that OrCam had a central office in Cologne. So, she made a video of it reading German, which she sent to Dr Dodgy shoes. She also said good morning. I would like to ask you for some help. As a dyslexic person, I use a lot of assistive technology to aid with my education. I also support others, as every dyslexic person is different. Presently, I am trying out an OrCam Learn. This device will read off any surface. As someone slow at reading, it helps me with the large amount of text for my studies. As someone who does not pick up language very well, I would like to know if it is any good at German? She sends him the same video she had sent Dr Dodgy shoes. Good morning. OK, what is good in German? She predicted that he would be extremely helpful but sent the wee video of the OrCam learning to read German off my iPad. She thinks silence is golden and receives a WhatsApp from Dr. Dodgy Shoes, who could not stop laughing, thinking my knight in shining armour is useless and sending It is okay; I asked others I know who speak German. I think they have stopped laughing 🤣🤣🤣 later in the day, she is feeling mischievous and says I do not know how true this is as I saw it on Facebook. Sixty-seven percent of women say a man is "absolutely un-dateable" if he has a... ponytail. Who knew 💁‍♂️💁‍♀️🙏 Again, she did not hear anything for days, and I have taken your project about finding a house for yourself and buried it in an unmarked shallow grave. (I thought it might help my studies in criminology 🤐😂) Then, unexpectedly good afternoon, how are you doing? Hello, I am just out for a walk. It has been a remarkably busy morning helping people. 😁🙏 She was listening to Nigel Kenndy playing the Four Seasons. What have you been up to?

All the wild garlic smells amazing 😁. Again, he does not answer it is like the story of Brigadoon! They talk for two minutes and disappear again only to reappear much later again! Good evening how are you? I miss you (she thought I very much doubted that). Are you OK? Yeah, she is just having a lovely day out with the golden oldies for the 51st wedding anniversary 😄 She sends a photo saying she decided to try on some hats yesterday 😁😁😁😁 She notices he has more accounts following her on Twitter and asks Hey! Do I need to ask what is going on with Twitter? I don't have a problem with anyone following me, as my account is all about promoting the rights, freedom, and dignity of people who have a learning difference. However, I have many accounts pretending to be you following me on Twitter. I have also noticed since you have stopped tweeting that these have all been suspended and disappeared within 24 hours. I noticed yesterday one account which is following me has changed to protected tweets. It is weird 💁‍♀️ He has vanished again. It is a week before. Good evening. How are you doing? You look good! Oh, thanks. Things are busy. It's a bit scary with all the projects which are coming up. What are you up to these days? I'm just thinking about that house! What house? I get the fact you want to invest in property. I still have no idea what to look for! The UK has a lot of property for sale 💁‍♀️ I told you to look for a house that I will buy for us! Your challenging work! Still clueless 🙈🙈🙈 Then Wilma comes up with an idea and starts looking up expensive penthouses and forwards them on to the star.

Good afternoon. I hope you have had a good day. Mine has been awesome. I was a speaker at the Texthelp virtual conference. One of the stories that has come up, I decided to talk to my friend Dr Dodgy Shoes, a fellow dyslexic. I have WhatsApp them to be informed that they were boarding the plane to Germany, as usual. I asked which part of Germany they were heading to this time 🤭 I just about wet myself laughing a few hours later when they sent me a selfie from Palma airport. I think they have boarded the wrong plane 🧏‍♀️🙎‍♀️🙍‍♂️🙎‍♀️. If you happen to bump into a lost eccentric man called Dr. Dodgy Shoes, please can you make sure he has the correct postage stamp on him for returning to the UK 😂😂😂😂😂

You might want to make an official account on TikTok. Seriously, I have cleaned out some of the fake accounts. I ended up with thirty-five 🧏‍♀️🙎‍♀️. Someone contacted me today through TikTok. I think they blocked me 😄😄😄. I was looking forward to messing with them 😼😼😼😼 As usual, there was nothing for a long time, then when she least expected it, hello, I miss you! How are you? What are you doing now? Always block them whenever they message you, OK?

I like this house! Wilma thinks it's good for you! It's up to you what happens next. I have nothing to do with it. I very much doubt that anything will happen. Wilma waits a few days before answering and says hello. I have not heard from you for a while. I am busy as always. Then, feeling sarcastic, she says, "I think you are too busy to miss me! Another month goes by, and good morning, how are you? Yes, I'm extremely busy. Are you OK? Yes, I am fine, thanks. I have been busy myself; the last assignment for this year is away for marking. 👏 I will let you know how it goes 😃 he disappeared for another week. How are you? What are you doing now? Good afternoon. I miss you. Oh, hello, I have not heard from you for a while 😁. I am well, thanks 😁 What have you been up to? I'm busy! She thinks no shit Sherlock and sends I guess that's a while ago 😆 😆 😆 Yes, what are you doing now? I am meeting a friend for lunch shortly 😁 Send me a photo. She thinks there is no problem and finds a photo on her phone and sends it.

WOW 😂😂😂😂 are you there now? Wilma doubles over laughing he has not even looked at the photo! She sends oh yes, I am there now. No, I meant your photo, she sends 🤣🤣🤣🤣 sent me your WhatsApp number. Then, she stops talking, and Wilma meets her friend for lunch and has a wander around the shops.

The following morning, she says hello, how are you today 😊 I'm good, how are you? I am good, thanks; I have a big day tomorrow trying to get things organized 😬 Do you think it would be easier to talk to me if you have my WhatsApp number? Yes, send me your WhatsApp number. Wilma is suspicious about the star's intentions with giving over her number. He replies don't you like chatting on WhatsApp? What are you doing now? Yes, I do like chatting. I am just sorting things out in between messages; I never know how long you stay to chat. Are you busy now? Wilma was busy trying to fill in forms and frustrated with their layout and sends, not really, just trying to fill in forms. Can you buy me a card today? We were back to the fucking Google stream cards; you can fuck right off! She sends a simple no! Buy me a Steam card from the store, OK. No, why do you keep asking me? I have not kept asking you. I asked you before, you haven't even thought to buy it for me! Buy a Steam card for me any amount you can buy. Just buy a Steam card £100 will do me! This dick is just not taking me seriously; the answer is no! You can't buy it? Tell me why you don't want to buy it, if you tell me, I won't ask for that again. That is another big fat lie he is telling me; he will not stop till he gets what he wants! I am not buying you the damn card! He sends non dirmi questo perché quando devi fare non ti impedisce di andare in negozio e comprarmi qualsiasi quantità di carta puoi, Wilma runs it through google translate to find out the message is in Italian. This doesn't stop you from going to the store and buying me any amount I have asked for my Google Steam card. I have told you to buy the amount you can afford! She now knows that she wants to piss this guy off by asking are you on drugs? Drugs how? Then why are you sending me messages in Italian? I mistakenly tapped the translator when I was texting you, and it came to Italy. I tapped again and changed it to English, but then it went wrong with the wrong English. She is thinking yes, right? The message you have just sent, are you taking the piss out of me? What I'm telling you is to buy me the Steam card! She is getting annoyed now; how many times do you need to be told NO! You don't have a giving heart! What a disappointment this is for the orphanage I support. Oh, you're breaking my heart, pal, with your latest scam! Fuck off, that money will not go to an orphanage! I don't know why you can't just buy me a card! Because I have no proof of where that money is going or who it is aiding, I would want to see how it aids the community. Ok, you're now talking like you don't know me, right? Your perception is correct. I know what you have chosen to tell me about yourself. As you are a busy person, I know you have little time to talk. I would rather spend it trying to get to know you better. There's nothing you still want to know about me. It's just excuses. Wilma is getting angry and cannot be bothered entertaining this idiot! Not really; you do not talk like an ordinary person. Even when I wanted a relationship with you, and you're not even serious about that because if you're serious, I will know I don't know what you still want to know about me when I have already told you about myself go to the upper text and see when I told you about myself I think you forgot everything I don't know what you still want I have called you on a video call and what do you still want even if we are in a relationship you can't even trust me with this your fucking character you're showing now you want it to take years before you know all about person I know you have tried to video call me. It was unfortunate that we missed each other. Relationships do take years, not five minutes 😀 Wilma, at this point, was still trying to work out how he had done the fake call. It was clever. She would give him credit for it. He then demanded just a card that I asked you for, and you refused. I'm not happy about that! She will make you less happy shortly. What is so special about this card? I don't understand. I am skeptical about your reasoning. If there's nothing special, you should have brought it for me without complaining! That is your reasoning! Seriously! I will give you the respect that you are very stubborn about the whole thing. My answer is still the same: No. Please change the record. You are not going to convince me otherwise. Your reason is very shallow. I thought you were more intelligent. She decided to play mind games; okay, I have a good question for you. How do you deal with stressful situations? Please, let's just end up here because it can never work for us through this! Okay, I am simply curious why you have come to this decision. Sadly, you don't even trust me! Trust is built over time; please remember that I have lots of people pretending to be yourself. Everyone is looking for me to give them money, my friends don't do this to me. You are a busy person running a business. You cannot talk all the time. You also need time to hang out with friends and family. I hope you find what you are looking for with a happy conclusion. I understood everything you said, but even if you have chatted with those scammers pretending to be me, why won't you trust me? I know that you don't trust me, that's why I'm saying all this! Wilma decided not to bother pursuing it further as all it was going to be was looking for Google Stream cards and helping orphanages. She left it open for a while, did not hear anything, and blocked the scammer.

The Case of the Man Who Called Himself the Diamond Ring!

Wilma traced this Telegram number to southeastern Louisiana. She was introduced to this chat by the weird world of TikTok.

It began pleasantly with, "Hello darling, how are you?"

She gazed at the sunshine outside and replied, "I'm fine, thanks. How are you doing?"

"I'm doing good. How is your day going?"

Wilma had been using her OrCam Learn to read everything off the monitor for the Open University.

She was delving into deconstructing youth justice and replied, "Just chipping away at a few projects that need finishing. Presently enjoying a wee coffee break—unfortunately, I forgot to buy cakes to go with the coffee." She asked, "What interesting things have you been up to today?"

"Putting the final additions to my upcoming shows. And you, darling? Where are you from?"

Wilma, sitting in her cat basket with the laptop open, answered, "I'm in the library, mind-mapping my final assignment for this year's studies! I can't believe two years have passed already! I still have four to go, and I will have a degree. What country are you from?"

Wilma decided to be cryptic, mentioning a place known for engineering, whiskey, and beautiful scenery—when the midges don't eat you alive. "Oh yes, it rains a lot. We're a very friendly bunch of weird people."

"Wilma, you're so funny! You can tell me where you live, my darling friend!" She tried what she had learned about tattoos, saying, "You have a tattoo of my country on your arm!"

She caught him out there, as he didn't have a clue what she was talking about. "I'll let you tell me about your location when you're ready."

She decided to ask, "What are your hobbies?" "I love going on tour!" She thought, 'No kidding, that's what professional musicians do!' "What are your hobbies?"

"Art, design, and cooking." Then he added, "You haven't been on tour for a while; you must be excited to be back on the road."

"Maybe he's having a Cher moment while walking in Memphis." He asked, "Can we change to a private meeting room?"

"Yes, I will meet you in a private meeting room. Let's see where this goes." She received, "Do you have Telegram?"

"Yes, OK. Text me your number!" "Ok, sure, we will meet on Telegram soon." Wilma removed her number from the chat on TikTok shortly afterwards.

After the chat moved, she was asked, "What are you doing? Are you at home?"

Wilma took her head out of her textbooks and replied, "Yes, I am at home. Why?"

"I just want to surprise you with lots of scary movie smiles! LOL! I'm just joking!" Wilma thought he was a couple of sandwiches short of a picnic and replied, "Okay, that is weird!"

The following day: "Hi darling, how are you?"

"Hello sexy dude, how are you?" "I'm okay." She inquired, "How was your day?"

"I am fine, thanks." Then he asked, "How is your family? What have you been learning today?"

"It's been a busy day learning lots of new things!" Wilma had been looking at her EMA at the Open University, comparing and contrasting sociological approaches to understanding juvenile delinquency. She wasn't about to tell the scammer this news.

"I think you need to text me when you arrive home." She said,

"I'm home. I have been learning how to transfer a mind map to a PowerPoint, alongside how to use global tasks software. What have you been up to today?"

However, he had disappeared until the following day: "Hello darling. How are you doing today?" "I am sorry about yesterday evening; I fell asleep while watching a movie."

That was fine in Wilma's eyes; everyone has done that occasionally. She replied, "I am good, thanks for asking." It was Friday, and Wilma was answering inquiries on the helpline. "What are you up to today?"

The phone was dead, but she answered that it was another busy day. "I will be helping people all day."

"Helping with what?"

"All sorts of problems. I never have one day the same."

"Please be careful, OK darling!"

Wilma knew she was in a safe environment and replied, "I am always careful."

He then went on to tell her, "I was having a meeting with some partners." She smiled and returned, "Enjoy an interesting day! Thank you, darling, and please don't get stressed at work!"

She laughed, "I will be careful."

"Okay darling, hope I can text you later."

"Yes, of course, you can text me later! Must go now, text you later, darling." She thought, 'Yes, I know,' and sweetly returned, "Have an enjoyable day xxx."

The following day, late in the morning, Wilma was out for a walk, listening to Gloria Estephan singing "Do the Conga!"

She said, "Hi darling, just wanted to know how you are doing?"

"Yeah, everything is cool!" Again, he disappeared.

She thought, 'I wonder how long this guy talks until he disappears.

The following day, Wilma was out for her walk, listening to a bit of Alphaville's "Big in Japan," followed by Nik Kershaw's "The Riddle," and a message popped up, "Hi darling, how are you?" "Morning. I am doing well, thank you. How are you doing yourself?" "I'm doing good. I have been busy with work. What are you doing, darling?" "Learning new assistive technology." "Please explain to me what assistive technology you are talking about; I would like to know more about it." "It is called global tasks, and it helps break down projects and tasks. This assists a person with not being overwhelmed with deadlines, etc." "That is clever; please, can you teach me!" Wilma laughed and returned, "Let me learn how to use the software first." Wilma looked up YouTube and sent over a video demonstrating global tasks. "Thanks, darling. I'll look at this after I finish my work." "No problem," he decides to ask, "Where in Germany are you situated?" Wilma laughs, knowing full well he is in the United States, and returns, "I am not in Germany LOL. Ok, darling, where are you?" "I am in the UK!" "Where in the UK?" She's not giving anything away. "It is not part of the UK that you visit while touring." "Do you live in London?" "No, it is nice to visit. The pace of life is too fast for me." "Do you live alone or with your family?" "I am with my flatmate; we have been in the same flat for 20 years." He then asks, "Wilma, are you married?" "No," he is confused and sends, "But you said you have lived with your flatmate for 20 years!" "Yes. We are both divorced. We are best friends, and our relationships are extraordinarily complex. Some work and some don't. The main thing is being happy together. It is not plain sailing. Everyone has their issues; you must learn to compromise. Especially when you both have different ideas which clash. Relationships are built on understanding and trust."

Wilma contacted him the following day, "How are you doing?" "I'm doing ok, just been in a meeting all day, just having lunch." "Well, enjoy your lunch and chill out." Wilma is having a Dexys Midnight Runners moment listening to "Come on Eileen!" In the evening, he gets back in touch, "Hi darling, hope you are okay." "I am fine, thanks for asking. What have you been up to today?" "I am sitting in my cat basket watching TV." She was watching "The Hunt for Red October." It always made her laugh as Sean Connery was the only Russian with a Scottish accent. He sends, "Hope you had a great evening, darling." "I will." "Good morning, darling. I wish every day you could see yourself the way I see you as you are absolutely perfect." Oh, she is having a Fairground Attraction moment singing "Perfect!" She laughs while out for her walk and returns, "Good morning, thanks for the compliment. However, I am far from being perfect." "Why do you think so?" "I make mistakes like everyone else. If I didn't, I wouldn't learn anything. I feel safest and happiest when I am talking to you. What are your plans today?" "I have plenty of projects to work on, just chip away at them." "Ok, darling. What did you have for breakfast?" "I enjoyed my Weetabix with a banana." "That sounds yummy, darling. I just finished my coffee; I will eat something later. I am off to work; I will text you later. I just want to let you know someone cares about you, ok, darling?" "Thanks, you have a lovely day."

She heard from him the following day when she received, "Good morning, darling." It was the usual time that he contacted her, around midday. She returned, "Morning. I am doing well, thank you, and hope you're okay." "I'm doing good. How was your night?" "It was chilled out. I have started watching 'The Big Bang Theory' again." "OK, baby, what are you doing today? Just keep plugging away with projects I am working on." At this point, Wilma is walking through the woods listening to Disturbed singing "The Sound of Silence." He inquires, "Have you had breakfast?" "Yes, I have, thanks. What about you?" "I did; I enjoyed a pizza." Wilma thought, 'What a nice healthy start to the day.' He continues with, "Okay, I will allow you with your project. I will text you later xxx." She texts back, "Odd choice for breakfast LOL. Okay, talk later."

The following day, he returned like a scene from Rapunzel to let down her hair and text, "Good morning, darling. How are you?" Wilma was in high spirits, "I am fine, thanks ☺ How was your night?" "It was great! I was in a great Zoom meeting and enjoyed catching up with everyone, and also seeing new ways to support dyslexia. I am glad your meeting went well. What are you doing? Xxx" Wilma laughed and returned to eating breakfast, "LOL." In the evening, he returned, "Hi love, how are you, baby?" She was sitting in her cat basket when the phone pinged and returned, "I am fine, thanks. What are you doing?" "Just chilling out, watching 'The Big Bang Theory.'" She asks, "How was your day?" "You didn't go out, baby xxxx." "I went out for a walk while listening to Duran Duran's 'Wild Boys' LOL." "Ok, how was it? Have you eaten?" Wilma began feeling like a scene from Dirty Dancing: "Nobody Puts Baby in a Corner."

The next day, she was a speaker at a virtual conference on assistive technology for disability student allowance, alongside Lord Chris Holmes, when a message popped up: "How are you, baby? What are you doing?" "I'm great, thanks. I'm at a virtual conference run by Texthelp." "Okay, baby, how is the conference going?" "It's highly informative ☺. Okay, baby, I love you." He disappeared, and Wilma returned to her conference.

The following morning, her phone pinged with "Good morning, baby. Hope you're okay." She replied, "Good morning. Everything is fine, thanks." "I always find you a remarkably interesting woman, and now living together just confirmed everything." Reading this, Wilma thought, " When did Barbie move in with Ken?" He continued, "I didn't have to worry while I read your texts and saw the size of your heart, I just know you had a lot of love to give. I love you xxxx." Wilma might as well put on some popcorn and wait for the psycho from a scary movie! He then asked, "How was your evening, baby?" Wilma had been out having drinks and laughs with friends and replied, "I had a fantastic night with friends, they always make me laugh. Thanks for the compliment." "Okay, baby, happy weekend. What are you doing?" "I am going to be making tapas shortly for watching the football with my friends. My friend had told me I make the best black olive tapenade. This has gone on the menu again along with beetroot and feta dip, a Greek salad in mini gem salad leaves, and a spicy beef salad in mini gem leaves. Bread crisps and my friend made pizza. The guys are fixated on the Rangers winning over Germany. I am not into football, so I will watch Dirty Dancing instead. I hope they will not be disappointed with the score LOL."

However, she did not hear from him until the following day. "Hi, baby, how are you?" "I am fine, thanks. What are you up to today?" "I am having a good rest, baby. And you, how is your day going?" Wilma was sitting in her cat basket stuffing her face with pickled onion Monster Munch, knowing she had the bag to herself as Mr G didn't like them, and replied, "It's going well, just chilling out!" "Chilling out with who, where are you, darling?" Oh, it sounds like he's suspicious. She tells him, "I am just at home watching TV." "Well, I hope you had breakfast, and have you done your prayers while at home?" "Yes, I have had breakfast. I am not religious, so I do not pray. What about you, darling?" Maybe he does not like the fact that Wilma is not religious; she tries not to get into religious debates as she fell out with religion a long time ago. She politely replies, "I am a humanitarian; I believe in treating people as I like to be treated." "Well, I can only hope that I am treating you fine, baby?" "Yes, you are genuinely nice. It is nice getting to know you." He decides to add, "Thank you, baby. Are you having a day off today?" She thinks, 'Well, yes, it is Sunday, dipshit.' She returns to watching The Fifth Element and does not receive any other messages that day.

The following day, while Wilma is doing a bit of doodling and listening to David Garrett's Explosive album, she receives,

"How is your day going?" "It is going well, thanks for asking. What have you done today?" "Baby, I'm okay, just busy with my concert." She had a quick look on the internet to confirm, and he followed with, "I hope you are okay. I miss you, baby!" She hadn't missed him and replied, "I have been busy myself. I started a refresher course and have an assistive technology roadshow tomorrow. It will be nice to see people face to face. Yes, baby, where are you now? At home listening to music and doing a bit of drawing? Can I see a picture of your drawing?" Then inquires "How was your virtual conference this week?" he asked. She sensed he might be getting muddled up, assuming the conference was the same as the roadshow tomorrow where she'd see Texthelp, scanning pens, TalkType, Booost, and other assistive technologies to support dyslexia. She replied, "The virtual conference was great, lots of interesting facts about student disability allowance. How's the drawing going, baby?" She sent a picture of a cartoon squirrel she had been working on and said, "I've just been doodling."

The following day, she went to the roadshow for assistive technology. Everyone welcomed her, but she was the only person who turned up. She brought along her trusted prototype of the OrCam Learn to show off. They joked with Wilma about sending out for bloody Marys, oysters, and caviar, which made her chuckle. She sent a short video demonstrating TalkType's functionality. On the bus home, listening to the album "A Woman's Heart" with a song by Mary Black called "Vanities," she texted, "I hope you are well. I saw this brilliant assistive technology today and thought it might be helpful. I use a similar software called Dragon. As Dragon is no longer available for Apple Mac, Apple Mac has brought out their version called TalkType. It is dictation software; you just talk to the computer, and it will type all your documentation." He then asks do you have this software which she finds odd she's already told you she has a similar software called Dragon," she thought, feeling puzzled when he asked if she had already bought TalkType. She clarified, "No, I have not bought TalkType, but I do have similar software. How is your project going?" Proudly, she showed him a picture of all the various software demonstrated to her and said, "My project is going slowly, but I had a fabulous day learning about new software available for people today." As Def Leppard's "Armageddon" played, she watched the rain from the bus window. He texted, "Are you home now?" She replied, "On the bus heading home now. Will text when I get home. I'm presently at work. Love you, baby xxx. Also, get a good rest when you get home." After making herself a cup of coffee, she messaged, "I am home safely."

The following day, Wilma was busy organizing files on her computer when her phone pinged. "Good afternoon, baby. How is your day going?" She replied, "Hi, I hope you're well. I am presently trying to organize my disorganization in my computer files LOL. Also trying to expand my dyslexic empire on my LinkedIn account after yesterday's event by posting photos of all the technology I have seen." He asked if she had breakfast and lunch, to which she responded, "I will be having lunch shortly. What are your plans for today?" He mentioned finishing lunch and having an interview. She wished him luck with the interview, expressing her dread for interviews.

    Later, she asked how the interview went, expecting no immediate response. Unexpectedly, days later, she received, "How are you, baby? I hope you are okay." She replied, "I am great, thanks for asking. I've been busy with work and shows." He then inquired about her project progress. She explained, "I am doing a refresher on my coaching and mentoring skills and working on an electronically marked assignment due on the 7th of June. It's all going well. I've also been given some new assistive technology software to try out. So many projects, I'm not sure where the time goes! My present mood is 'I don't go crazy, I am crazy; I just go normal from time to time.' Once again, she found herself deep in work, acknowledging that this guy was sporadic, contacting her only when it suited him. So, it wasn't surprising when she was matching murder maps of London that she received a casual "Happy Sunday. Hello." She replied, "I'm great, thanks for asking. Hope you're chilling out and having a day off." His response came after a while, by which time Wilma had left her comfortable cat basket for a walk, listening to Runrig's "Hearts of Olden Glory." "I'm out for a walk, planning to make something nice for dinner later," she replied. "Are you alone?" this inquiry always spooked Wilma, and she half-expected a surprise ambush. As she received a message from Mr G inviting her to join friends for drinks and shenanigans, she texted the scammer, "I'm alone presently, waiting to catch up with my friends shortly." He advised her to be careful, to which she retorted with a picture of Harley Quinn, saying, "Hang out with people who are as weird as you!" She met the Hair Bear Bunch and didn't hear from him for a few days. As she cursed her laptop one day, she received, "Baby, I hope you are okay." Frustrated with her laptop's slowdown and assistive technology breakdown, she quipped, "I might murder some of my assistive technology if it does not behave. If you see a low-flying laptop, it will be mine!" Eventually, after struggling, she discovered the person she was working with was on holiday. Several days later, she received, "Good evening, baby. How are you?" Wilma, in a better mood, replied, "Hi, I'm good, thanks. I sorted out the issue with my assistive technology and now saving myself a lot of time." Playfully, she teased, "Surprise me, tell me you've been out with friends instead of working all the time." This was ignored. On Friday, before starting the helpline shift, she said, "Happy Friday, have a nice weekend, don't work too hard." He eventually replied with, "Happy weekend, baby. I'm good, thanks." She teased by sending a YouTube video of Sheldon Cooper drinking coffee and becoming the Flash. He asked how she was, and Wilma responded positively, enjoying the sunny weather. When he finally reappeared, he greeted her and mentioned trying another assistive technology called Global Tasks. Then, he inquired about her recent activities. She replied, "I'm doing well. I must say, one of these days, you'll surprise me by doing something normal, like hanging out and laughing with your friends." Encouragingly, she added, "Seriously, you need to laugh with your friends; it's great. I had a fantastic laugh at the weekend; my friends were dancing to Tina Turner with their version of 'Proud Mary,' it was hilarious." He then asked about her project progress. "I've submitted my last assignment for this year. Now, I'm waiting for the mark and hoping I've passed. I'm in the process of applying to start back in October," she replied confidently. "I am enjoying it, but I already know it will arrive quickly, so just trying to get everything ready. My calendar fills up so quickly!" he says. "That's great! And remember to be available for yourself among all that. Your mental health is just as important as your physical health," she responds, expressing concern for his well-being. He reassures her, "I understand and usually have time off work. I plan to have fun with friends, even if it's just having a few beers, watching YouTube, doing some bad dancing, and laughing!" In the middle of the afternoon, he abruptly says, "Well, I am off to bed, sweet dreams!" Wilma, slightly surprised, bids him good night.

The next day, he greets her with a "hi baby." They exchange pleasantries, and she notices on Facebook that he's taking some time off. "Have you booked yourself a vacation?" she teases. He quickly responds, "Well, I will chat with you later, as today is the children's fair day and I am away to watch the Queen being crowned, hip hip!"

Later that day, while enjoying some ciders after the fair and parade, he messages her again. She explains it's a local holiday and she's off. They exchange pleasantries about friends and family and weekends. A few days later, he wishes her a happy Sunday and asks what she's doing. She tells him about catching up on cooking programs, her "weird" hobby. They chat about their plans for the day. She suggests he enjoy his day off. "Thanks, baby, have a nice afternoon," he responds.

The next day, he inquires about her day and mentions trying a new scanning pen from China before returning to study at university. He asks her to consider his project in the UK, involving orphans, and building a home for them. Alarmed by the scale of the project, Wilma redirects him to organizations that could assist. He expresses a desire for them to work together on this project, which sets off alarm bells for Wilma. She tries to deflect by acknowledging his busyness: "Wow! You've been busy. Where do you find the time?" After he confidently tells her she'll manage the project, she expresses uncertainty, mentioning differences in laws between Scotland and England/Wales. He insists he's done the project's structure, plans to fund it, and wants her to oversee the business. Wilma, suspicious about the suddenness and lack of details, asks for information on setting up the charity, including the board of directors for the requirements and domain purchase. He repeats his confidence in her overseeing it and requests a business strategy but doesn't respond when she asks if he understands mind maps. Feeling overwhelmed, she starts organizing the project's tasks through a mind map but feels she can't manage it alone. When he mentions sending money without providing the necessary details, Wilma panics, stating he hasn't provided the needed information for the business account or strategy. She also points out the absence of orphanages in the UK. They have all been shut down due to mismanagement and the abuse that occurred. Please give me a bit of time. Wilma had also watched several programs about criminal activities in orphanages perpetrated by paedophile rings. This person's swindle was clever and appealing to her as a caring and nurturing individual. Wilma's instincts told her that something was wrong, and she responded, 'Okay, I know you'll be on tour shortly. I seriously can't manage this project by myself. I've been brainstorming, and here's what I've produced. I'd like your feedback.' She sent over a screenshot of a mind map she had made, to which he replied, 'Nice, I'll review it again and give you feedback.' 'Thanks, I look forward to hearing your thoughts,' she responded, though she suspected it might not happen and simply replied, 'Cheers.'

    The following day, while on the helpline, she received, 'Baby, how are you?' 'I'm good. It's Friday, and I'm looking forward to catching up with friends for wine o'clock.' 'Okay, baby, you have a happy weekend,' she replied. 'You too, so try and chill out with your friends,' he sent with laughing emojis. 'I'll think of something,' she continued, 'well, you could try making some homemade ginger beer. I have some for my friends to try out shortly.' 'Okay, baby, just wondering, are you at home or out with friends?' he asked. 'I'm at a friend's house; we're having a good laugh listening to the Ministry of Sound chilled-out sessions,' she responded. 'Get your friends around for a few beers with gaming and lots of laughs.' After a couple of days of no contact, he messaged, 'Hey, baby, how are you? I was just wondering; do you know of any charity websites?' 'There are plenty I've researched, like Made by Dyslexia, the British Dyslexia Association, and Dyslexia Scotland, also, the Prince of Wales Trust, Save the Children, Oxfam, etc.,' she replied. He disappeared again; perhaps he was contemplating the cost of building a website. Another period passed, and she received,

'Good morning, baby, how are you?' Wilma was getting ready to go out and replied, 'Morning, I'm great, thanks ☺. What are you doing?' 'I'm getting ready to take my mum out for her birthday,' he said. 'Oh, today's her birthday? Nice, please wish her a happy birthday from me!' Wilma knew her mum loved classical music and would never have heard of this person, but she politely replied, 'I will, thanks. You enjoy your day xxx.' 'Hi, darling, happy first Sunday of the month,' he sent. Wilma was out laughing with friends and replied, 'How are you? I hope you're enjoying a day off.' 'I'm doing okay, baby. What are you doing?' 'I'm laughing with my friends. They're blaming me for the grass being the wrong colour,' she responded. 'Darling, you shouldn't listen to them. What you choose to wear is your business.' She laughed, thinking he might be drunk as she hadn't mentioned clothes. 'I told them I was going to spray paint their grass purple as that's the correct colour. They're all colour-blind anyway, so it doesn't matter what colour I spray it LOL. I like to be the kind of woman that when the feet hit the floor each morning, the devil says, "Oh crap, she's up!" Enjoy the rest of your Sunday xx 'Thanks, baby, you're the best xxx.' There was another period of silence, and eventually, Wilma sent, 'Happy 4th of July to you!' 'Thanks, darling. How are you today?' he responded." She's unsure where this conversation is headed, stating, "I juggle a lot of things! Why?" Wondering about his intentions, she says, "You're doing one of those weird mystery things on me. For me, it's like 'Good morning baby.'" He responds with, "Morning. I am well, thank you." Then he asks about her night, to which she replies, "Nice and quiet, just catching up with my book." Once again, he disappears for a while, and Wilma assumes it's due to his concerts, travels, and interviews. Unexpectedly, he messages her, "Hi darling, how are you? Good evening." She, chilling out in her cat basket, responds, "Oh hello, not heard from you for a while. How are you doing?" He questions why she never reached out, and she explains she thought he was busy, engrossed in a delightful book. Despite finding it odd, he inquired about her project. She responds, updating him on her course and upcoming plans for October, and attending numerous webinars. He mentions raising money and supporters, prompting her suspicion if it's related to the fake charity, he's trying to involve her in. Despite this, she responds, hoping he found time for himself and his friends. He suggests the possibility of hanging out soon, which she doubts, going out for wine with friends instead. He responds positively, acknowledging the need for relaxation.

Wilma sends him a late-night YouTube video of Miles Davis quintet, and the following day, he messages her with a greeting. Their communication timings are erratic, but they exchange pleasantries. She informs him of her plans for an outdoor jazz festival and his interest in helping a friend with dyslexia. He offers his support, but she reassures him that she has sufficient help. He's reminded to have some fun, and she jokingly wishes to hear about his Sunday hangover. Their banter continues, with playful teasing about not listening. Then, he mentions a project, making her nervous with his cryptic messages, but he fails to clarify.

Later, he greets her with wishes for a happy Sunday, and they exchange inquiries about each other's day. Wilma finds herself puzzled about the direction of their conversation, exclaiming, "I juggle a lot of things! Why?" Wondering about his intentions, she notes, "You're doing one of those weird mystery things on me. For me, it's like 'Good morning baby.'" He responds with a simple, "Morning. I am well, thank you." Then, he inquires about her night, to which she replies, "Nice and quiet, just catching up with my book." Once again, he disappears for a while, which Wilma assumes is due to his concerts, travels, and interviews. Unexpectedly, he messages her, "Hi darling, how are you? Good evening." She, chilling out in her cat basket, responds, "Oh hello, not heard from you for a while. How are you doing?" He questions why she never reached out, and she explains she thought he was busy, engrossed in a delightful book. Despite finding it odd, he inquired about her project. She responds, updating him on her course and upcoming plans for October, and attending numerous webinars. He mentions raising money and supporters, which triggers her suspicion about the fake charity he's trying to involve her in. Despite this, she responds, hoping he finds time for himself and his friends. He suggests the possibility of hanging out soon, which she doubts, opting to go out for wine with friends instead. He responds positively, acknowledging the need for relaxation. He's reminded to have some fun, and she jokingly wishes to hear about his Sunday hangover. Their banter continues, with playful teasing about not listening. Then, he mentions a project, making her nervous with his cryptic messages, but he fails to clarify.

Later, he greets her with wishes for a happy Sunday, and they exchange inquiries about each other's day. "A few days later, he messages, 'Baby, good morning, how are you?' 'I'm good, thanks. Hope you had fun the other day,' she replies. 'Yes, I did. However, it would have been more fun if you were by my side, I wish you were here!' Wilma recalls a Pink Floyd moment and David Gilmour's 'Wish You Were Here.' 'There's plenty of time, no rush. What are you up to today?' she asks. 'I have an interview,' he responds truthfully. 'Always busy with interviews! Any other exciting plans for today?' 'No, not really,' he says. 'Take care of yourself, goodnight, and have sweet dreams,' she wishes him.

The next morning, he greets her again. 'How are you?' 'I'm fine, thanks. How did your interview go yesterday?' 'It went well, hope you're okay!' 'Glad to hear it went well. I'm sorry to cut this conversation short as I have a Zoom meeting shortly. What are you up to today?' 'I'm in the studio recording some new tracks. I hope it has air conditioning; it's still too warm.' 'Yes, it does. Take care of yourself, don't work too hard,' she advises. 'Okay, baby, stay safe,' he responds. 'Thanks, I always try to stay safe,' he assures her.

The following day, while out for a walk, a message pops up. 'Good morning, baby. How are you?' 'I'm well, thanks. How are you?' 'I'm okay, baby. Hope you're having a great weekend.' Then, another message: 'Hi, baby, how are you? Happy Sunday!' 'Good morning, I hope you're having a day off. I'm fine, thanks. What are you up to today?' 'I'm just relaxing. How was your night?' 'I met up with my friends; they always make me laugh.'

Wilma had jokingly suggested reenacting a scene from Coyote Ugly with jugs of water, but her friends declined, saying it would make people sick. 'Okay, baby, love you, and take care of yourself,' he texts. October arrives, along with the busy season for promoting positive dyslexia and returning to studying with the Open University. 'Hi, happy Friday. I haven't been ignoring you; I've been busy promoting positive dyslexia. Please enjoy a great weekend,' she messages. 'Hi darling, how are you? Happy weekend,' he replies. 'It's lovely to hear from you; I'm fine. I hope you're having fun,' she responds. 'I'm doing good. How are you?' 'I'm glad to hear that. I take it you are busy presently?' 'Yeah,' Wilma adds, 'Remember to make some time for yourself.' Their conversation had paused for a while, but Wilma had been busy tracking a parcel sent from China with a scanning pen for trying out and writing a blog. Unexpectedly, she receives, 'Good morning, baby. How are you? I am well, thanks for asking. I've been trying out a Youdao scanning pen.' "It's great to hear! How's the trial going? There are many features, and I like its user-friendly weight and touchscreen functionality. The automatic Wi-Fi updates and language options (English, Spanish, and Chinese) are impressive. I messaged them on LinkedIn and found out more languages will be added. It has a dictionary, reads off screens, and clears GDPR history, but I think having a headphone port would be beneficial. It connects via Bluetooth, but the batteries can run out, which isn't ideal for studying in a quiet place. I still prefer OrCam learn."

Months later, Wilma deletes the conversation, assuming she won't hear from them again. Unexpectedly, a message pops up on Telegram in the middle of the night: 'Hi baby.'

The next day, while sipping coffee, she replies, 'Hello, how are you?' The person asks, 'I'm okay. Can you tell me why you refused to talk to me?' Engrossed in her textbooks, Wilma explains, 'I've been busy since we last chatted, and I thought you were too busy to talk. I got caught up in my work. 'Are you working now?' they ask. 'No, I'm done for the day,' she responds. 'Glad you're home safely. Can you send me a picture of yourself?' Mischievously, Wilma sends a photo of Jennifer Saunders dressed as Eddie Monsoon. The conversation takes a turn, reminiscent of their early chats, with short exchanges and sudden disappearances. 'Hello baby, how are you?' they text. 'I'm fine, thanks. How are you?' she responds. 'I'm okay, baby,' comes the short reply. Trying to prolong the conversation, Wilma asks, 'Anything exciting today?' The response is brief: 'Dealing with some friends.' Unsure of the meaning, she replies, 'Your friends will always support you.' 'Yes, baby,' he confirms. She encourages him to have fun.

The next day, she receives another message: 'Baby, good morning. How are you?' She replies, 'Morning! I'm fine, thanks. How about you?' 'I'm doing okay. Are you at work?' he inquires. 'Not yet I'll be starting shortly.' Approaching Halloween, she sent him a picture of Chucky having escaped from his box with a caption reading "Well, that can't be good." He responded, "Okay baby, I take it you are at the shop." Realizing her mistake—knowing he doesn't watch scary movies—she clarified, "I guess you didn't get the joke." His lunchtime text simply said, "No baby, what are you doing?" Wilma felt good after a productive day, receiving positive feedback for her work at the helpline. "Thank you," she replied. He responded with "I love you, baby." Getting ready to go out with the hair bear bunch, she wished him a good day.

Later, she shared the YouTube link to Roger Daltrey's "Don't Let the Sun Go Down on Me" from the movie Lost Boys, expressing excitement about seeing it on the big screen.

The following day, he greeted her again, but she was busy laughing with friends and didn't reply.

The next morning, she responded to his previous text, asking how he was. With the weekend's clock change in mind, she playfully reminded her dyslexic friends. He replied, "Baby, how are you?" She replied, "I'm good, just chilling out. How about you?" With Halloween approaching, she teased him about partying, suggesting he dress up and do the "Time Warp." He inquired again, and she, enjoying the Rocky Horror Picture Show at a local hotel, shared a clip of "Sweet Transvestite." His response was predictably short. She playfully shared another video, this time from Tim Burton's "The Nightmare Before Christmas." His simple "OK" prompted her to jest about her insanity, to which he replied with a casual "no," leading to laughter on her end.

The following day, she wished him a relaxing Sunday. He responded the next day, asking about her well-being. She mentioned being busy with dyslexia awareness week and anticipating quieter communication due to her workload. He wondered if she was at work, to which she confirmed with a simple "yes." Inquiring about her day, she mentioned sorting out an issue with her writing assistant for an assignment, delighted that her assistive technology was working well again. He reminded her to be careful and eventually ended the conversation for the day.

The next day, he checked in again, and she politely responded, stating she was busy but doing well. He greeted her with wishes for a happy new month. Wilma, slightly detached from the month, responded positively, remarking on the cold, rainy weather, and her dedication to studying. He briefly confirmed his well-being and inquired about hers. She mentioned it would be a busy yet enjoyable month, but uncertain if it would be better than the previous one. Their conversation ended with him asking if she was at work. Wilma assures him that everything is fine, then heads to the kitchen to start cooking and listen to Spotify. She receives a reply saying, "Yes, baby, you?" She updates him on her busy schedule, highlighting the activities for Dyslexia Awareness Week and her freelance work in assistive technology training. He ends the conversation with a simple "OK baby."

The following day, she receives another message asking how she is. Wilma replies, "I'm fine, thanks. How about you today?" As expected, he responds with, "I'm doing good, baby. Hope you're having an enjoyable day." Engaging from her student space, she responds positively, expressing she's having a wonderful day. Curious, she playfully guesses if he's at work, receiving a light-hearted "Yes, how did you guess?" She tries to spark more conversation, asking if he's taken a day off or gone to the gym, but his responses remain brief. When she learns he's at home, she suggests he relax by watching a good movie, bringing up the importance of taking breaks. He agrees, and she adds a playful touch by sharing funny clips from movies. He responds with "ok," and the conversation pauses until late in the evening when he asks how she's doing. Wilma, enjoying her leisure time watching TV, responds positively.

The next day, as Wilma is out meeting her friend, she responds to his message while waiting, mentioning she's catching up with a friend over coffee and cakes. Their conversation doesn't continue for the rest of the day.

The following day, she's studying and responds positively when he checks in, keeping the conversation friendly. He tells her he's doing well and asks if she's at work. In her student cave, she mentions she'll be at work shortly. He responds affirmatively and inquires about her plans for the day. Listing her activities, including studying and moments of levity with friends, she suggests he enjoy time with his friends too. The conversation drifts back to his typical response of staying safe, to which she playfully replies she'll try.

Later in the day, he checks in on how her day has been, and she responds positively, expressing her leisurely evening. When he mentions a busy day ahead, she encourages him to take care of himself amidst the busyness, ending with well wishes.

The following day, she joyfully shared passing her assignment. As the conversation continues, it mostly stays at a surface level, drifting between asking about each other's day and expressing affection. He tells her he's doing well and asks if she's at work. In her student cave, she mentions she'll be at work shortly. He responds affirmatively and inquires about her plans for the day. Listing her activities, including studying and moments of levity with friends, she suggests he enjoy time with his friends too. The conversation drifts back to his typical response of staying safe, to which she playfully replies she'll try.

Later in the day, he checks in on how her day has been, and she responds positively, expressing her leisurely evening. When he mentions a busy day ahead, she encourages him to take care of himself amidst the busyness, ending with well wishes.

The following day, she joyfully shared passing her assignment. As the conversation continues, it mostly stays at a surface level, drifting between asking about each other's day and expressing affection. "He tells her he is doing good and then asks if she is at work. She replies as she sits in her student cave firing up her laptop and replies I will be at work shortly. He says I'm doing good baby. She says great news, hope you have a nice relaxing day. He says yes baby you? What are your plans today? She is looking at her ta-da list and replies well I have done some studying, caught up with my freelance partner and just embarrassed myself with dyslexic oops moments when replying to a friend on social media. He simply says ok baby. She decides to say get out with your friends and have an enjoyable time. The normal reply arrives OK baby just stay safe.

She knows she is in a safe place with her friends but says jokingly I will try and stay safe.

Later in the day, he texts her how was your day, she says it has been a momentous day, just chilling out watching a movie, how is your day going? He simply says Baby thinking about you. She is drinking wine and just says aww hope you have a wonderful weekend. He tells her, yes, I did tomorrow is going to be a busy day. She texts back every day will be busy in your world, so just make sure you eat, and rest properly ready for your day. He simply says I will. She tells him, she forgets to have a good laugh and texts back that she will and sends her lots of kisses. She replies take care of yourself sweetie darling< again she receives lots of kisses.

The next day she receives baby how are you? She was excited to share her good news and replied I am good thanks! I have passed my first assignment for the year. He says beautiful are you home now? She is sitting in her student cave reading and replies yes, I am. He then goes on to ask if they didn't, go to work today as it was late in the evening, she replies yes, I have been to work today. Ok, baby.

The next day she receives Hello how are you today? Ok baby hope you are okay. She replies I am great thanks; she has been studying and learning new things so how was work today? As always, the conversation never went extremely far and replied it was great thanks, I have done a lot, how has your day been? He replied Baby, I am thinking about you. Awww is that not sweet Wilma replies Hope you are having a wonderful weekend.

He tells her yes; I did tomorrow is going to be a busy day. She thinks really and tells him every day will be busy in your world, to make sure he eats and rests properly ready for the day. He tells her I will. Wilma reminds him with the following message good and don't forget to laugh. I will baby 😊. He sends smiles and kisses. She sends them back to take care sweetie darling and she receives emojis of him feeling loved.

The next day she receives baby how are you today? My day is good thanks, it has been a busy day. I am glad you had a wonderful day; remember to have a glass of wine it is Friday. A few days later baby I hope you are okay. Yeah, I am fine thanks. He decides to ask what have you been doing all day? Wilma was sitting by the laptop and replied sorting out emails etc, putting everything into folders, and administration stuff which needed to be done. Again, he disappears and sends a message of baby how are you? I am fine thanks. How are you? I am doing good. Then nothing again disappears and a few days later good morning baby, she replies I hope you are enjoying your day. Thank you, baby. He disappeared again and since she did not hear from him, she decided to block him and never hear from him again."

The Short Case of I Love You, Wilma. Please, Marry me

"The next international star Wilma met was through the strange world of TikTok.

He started by waving to her and asked, 'How are you doing today?' She replied, 'I am great, thanks; it's a beautiful day.' She followed this with, 'How are you doing yourself?' He did not reply to this but asked her where she was from and what her name was. Wilma was hesitant about revealing just anywhere, so she introduced herself: 'I am Wilma and I come from St Trinian's.' Wilma had fallen in love with this band during her teenage years. So, when asked how long she had been a fan, she answered, 'Since about '86.' The question was then repeated due to a communication error, and she clarified, 'In 1986.' She was being casual and couldn't be bothered to calculate the exact years. Then the next question she was asked was about her favourite songs. She answered this without any problem and then asked if he had a hangout application. 'Why, yes,' she does have this application. The star sent her his email address to add to hangouts, and they continued the chat there.

Wilma travelled on the bus to meet her friend for lunch. Wilma and her friend had become friends through working on the helpline. They both supported each other through the Open University. The international star greeted her on Hangouts with, 'Hello, Wilma Mayhem, how are you doing today?' She replied, 'Nice to meet you here, Wilma,' to which he responded, 'Lovely to meet you as well, I am doing well, thanks.'" "She was asked if she had eaten that day. 'I'm meeting a friend, and we'll be going out for lunch shortly.' The bus ride wasn't long, and she had her headphones in, listening to '80s hits on Spotify. 'What are you doing now?' he asked. She smiled and replied, 'I'm travelling to meet my friend. 'He decided to inquire further, 'I would like to know more about you. Are you married with children?' 'No, I am not married, and I don't have any children,' she answered. 'How long have you been single?' She could have made something up, but instead, she said, 'Approximately.' He asked, 'Don't you feel lonely sometimes? I mean, the loneliness of not having a partner?' Wilma laughed inwardly and replied, 'No, I have an excellent group of friends; life is good! 'He shared, 'I feel lonely a lot of the time. That's why I need to find my true love, someone who will love me as much as I'll love her.' Then he texted, 'I have a wife, but I don't love her! I have a feeling that destiny brought us together for a reason.' She found it cheesy but responded, 'Relationships are complex. I have been married, and it turned unhealthy for several reasons, changing my outlook on life. Let's see what kind of answer he produces.' He seemed to take some time, then wrote, 'It takes time to find out if we're compatible.' Then, seemingly forgetting what she had told him earlier, he asked, 'Where are you now? At work or home?' 'I told you, I am meeting a friend for lunch today,' she reminded him.

At this point, she was wandering around the library, searching for information. 'I hope you're having a good day? How's the weather over there?' The sky was blue with fluffy clouds drifting past as she walked up the hill. 'It's not bad just now; it might rain later,' she replied, knowing the weather could change rapidly. As she strolled and listened to Status Quo singing 'All Around My Hat,' he texted again, 'I see! I hope your profession doesn't stress you?' 'No, I love my profession; wish I had started it years ago,' she replied. 'I hope you have enough warm clothes on to keep you warm?' Wilma smiled; it was a beautiful day, and she was enjoying the change of scene. Then she received, 'Wilma Dear, you are so beautiful, nice, honest, smart, with a brave heart of understanding. If I may ask, how old are you?' 'Thanks, that was nice of you to say. A lady never gives away her age,' she responded. 'Well, I don't think the age difference between us should be a barrier; rather, the most important thing is for us to be sure if we find understanding, happiness, and joy within each other,' he replied, laying it on thick. 'I am certainly a happy person; it will be good to become friends,' she replied, trying to keep the conversation light. Then he continued, 'Above all, I think love is the greatest. Don't you also think so? Do you believe in long-distance relationships?' She reflected, 'Certainly, over the last two years, I have built several relationships, both personal and professional.' Thinking of those she hadn't met yet due to the pandemic, she replied, 'I can do long-distance relationships; I have built many new friendships over the pandemic. I still haven't met a lot of them in person.'

He seemed persistent, 'I do believe in a distance relationship, I do have faith I will meet the woman who will love and cherish me.' She remarked to herself, 'I'm sure we've heard this before!' Then he asked, 'Are you willing to relocate if you find your soul mate?' Little did he know, she already had her soul mate with Mr G, but she replied, 'I build friendships slowly. You can never truly know a person; everyone goes through good and troubled times.'" He returns "You are very correct!" Wilma thought. "It's nice to know he agrees with me," she thought, glancing at the next text. 'How has your present marital life affected you so far?' She contemplated this; after being divorced for years, she wondered where this conversation was headed. So, she texted back, 'It doesn't affect my life much. I have other issues to deal with, affecting my whole life due to a lack of understanding towards hidden disabilities. I've turned this into a positive thing and achieved new goals.' He continued down his list and asked, 'How do you normally spend your leisure time?' Wilma found this one easy to answer. 'I spend my leisure time cooking, doing Art and Design, and walking.' 'How much do you enjoy walking in the park?' he inquired. Wilma giggled to herself as she strolled around an old graveyard, taking photos of ornate gravestones. 'Yes, I do,' she replied. He added, 'I enjoy walking a lot, feeling the fresh air of Mother Nature.' She had read Muriel Grey's "The First Fifty, Munro Bagging without a Beard" As well as watching the TV program "The Munro Show" Wilma sensed a familiar tone, and it didn't surprise her when the next question came, 'Are you a God-fearing woman? How often do you attend church?' 'I am not religious,' she straightforwardly told him. As expected, the next text rolled in. 'I'm a God-fearing man. I credit my Christian faith for my life, attitude, and success. However, I don't use God's name to attract women, for my character speaks for itself. I am not the type of man who is focused entirely on himself.' Wilma sighed inwardly, thinking, 'I've heard this before, not very original.' She replied, 'It's your choice to be religious. I will stick with just blundering through life.' And of course, the predictable request came next: 'Send me your picture!' Upon receiving the compliment on her selfie, Wilma graciously replied, "Thank you, nice of you to say that." He responded with a simple "You're welcome." Wilma decided it was time to turn the tables and asked, "What are your hobbies? "He shared an extensive list: "I enjoy swimming, reading, walking on the beach, fishing, camping, scrabbling, meeting new people, understanding their way of life, observing the sea waves, the beauty of mountains, and everything nature offers." Wilma found his response impressive and cool. Switching to a lighter question, Wilma asked about his favourite colour. She randomly chose purple, not anticipating a follow-up question. To the inevitable "Why purple?" inquiry, Wilma playfully responded, "Because I am simply weird." Proudly, he shared, "My favourite colours are red and white." Wilma, somewhat missing the mention of two colours, playfully retorted, "Red, an angry colour, why did you pick it?" His response was clever, attributing love to red and purity to white. Impressed, Wilma acknowledged, "A unique way of looking at those colours, how cool." When asked about his preferred movies, he mentioned enjoying WWE. Wilma found it odd, considering wrestling as a movie, but didn't mention it. Instead, she revealed her passion for sci-fi, teasingly referencing "The Matrix." There was no response to her comment; instead, he asked about her social habits and past relationships. Wilma clarified that she enjoys spending time with friends on weekends and acknowledged understanding the mistakes from her past relationship. The conversation seemed to halt there, coincidentally as she was about to meet up with her friend for lunch. Over lunch, they discussed the star, wondering if he was genuine or an imposter. They both found him attractive but were unsure about the authenticity of their interaction. After a pleasant lunch and catching up on several topics, Wilma headed home. Later that evening, she received a simple "Hello," to which she replied, "Hello!"

"How are you doing today?" Wilma, in a great mood after a wonderful day, replied, "Today was awesome, I loved catching up with my friend." She inquired about his day. The recurring question about whether she had eaten popped up again. "Yes, I'm cool!" she thought, finding his short memory amusing. "Yes, eaten plenty today!" she replied, reminiscing about the delicious fish and chips and caramel apple pie with ice cream. She asked if he had eaten, to which he simply responded, "Yes, it was lovely." Trying to inject something new into the conversation, she mentioned the mutual professional support they often provided, but his response was simple, "Okay, I hope you are fine." Wilma replied, "Yes, everything is fine, just chilling out. What about you?" It was getting late, and Wilma decided to call it a night. "Well, I am heading to bed shortly, so I will say good night and sweet dreams." At this point, he unexpectedly brought up how cheating and lies ended his past relationship. Wilma related to this from her own experience and replied, "Yeah, my partner lied and cheated on me. Thankfully, I do not have anything to do with him!" Mason agreed, responding, "Not good at all!"

Attempting to shift the topic, Wilma brought up the Johnny Depp and Amber Heard case, which she had been following. "I know. At least the divorce was not dragged through the courts like Johnny Depp was recently." However, the discussion didn't continue, and it reverted to the list of questions with his inquiry about her goals and dreams in life. Wilma replied, "Presently, I am studying for my degree, something I never thought I would be able to do with my learning differences, which include dyslexia/dyspraxia." He continued, expressing his dreams of finding the woman he'd love, calling his wife, and building a loving family together forever. In the background, Iron Maiden's "Fear of the Dark" played on Spotify as Wilma engaged in this interesting yet somewhat repetitive conversation. Keeping her thoughts to herself, Wilma replied professionally, "Which is a lovely goal to have in life. Our goals for life now are a bit different. I've been working on mine over the pandemic, and thankfully, they're going in the right direction." his response followed, "Nice and I have found the right woman, and that woman is you, my beautiful." He swiftly moved on to inquire about smoking and drinking red wine. Wilma replied, "I don't smoke, but I love drinking red wine. My friends joke that if I went missing, just put my mug shot on a bottle of wine!" The conversation then shifted to how she handles upsetting situations. Wilma shared, "I haven't been upset by many people lately. If I do get upset, I take myself for a walk and listen to music." The next question was about the best decision she ever made. Reflecting on her past experiences, Wilma responded, "To give up my last job. It was such a negative experience, mismanaged, and lacked support. It severely affected my mental health due to other people's actions. "Moving on to the five most important things in her life, Wilma shared a delightful sentiment inspired by Princess Twinkle Toes: "Enjoy your life, feel alive, face the crowd, be proud, perform, shine your brightest, love every minute of it, AMAZE THEM." Mason found it genuinely nice. As the conversation progressed, he expressed his wish for her greatness and offered his help whenever she needed it. Then, it turned to discussing cooking for a date at home. He suggested preparing a surprise favourite meal, even if he had to research and follow instructions from renowned chefs. Wilma found it sweet and chuckled, sharing her approach to cooking. The chat pivoted when he inquired about a special place Wilma would like to visit together. Wilma cautiously avoided revealing her favourite spots but emphasized the importance of trust. Mason tried to reassure her by expressing his willingness to open up and sacrifice for love. But when he mentioned marriage, Wilma was firm: "I am never getting married again. It was a living hell the first time, I don't repeat mistakes." She made her stance clear. Wilma keeps handling his questions gracefully, making her boundaries known while keeping the conversation polite and professional. In response to Star's text about marriage vows and leaving one's country for a future partner, Wilma was thoughtful but firm in her response. She texted back, "You know very little about me; I have my soul mate! Regarding the biggest mistake men and women make in relationships..." She took her time and carefully replied, "The pandemic has made me a far happier person. It took a long time, but I've finally found my life's direction. People are welcome to join me on this journey. Every relationship is unique, and everyone makes different mistakes. No one knows exactly what will make or break a relationship." She ended the conversation gracefully, recalling her earlier intention to head to bed, saying, "On that note, good night. I'm going to catch up on my beauty sleep! Okay, bye." This way, she kept her boundaries intact and respectfully wrapped up the conversation.

The following day, Wilma received a greeting, initiating another exchange. It started pleasant enough with casual inquiries about their well-being. When she asked what he'd been up to, it was sidestepped for a more direct question about her profession and income. Wilma, maintaining her privacy, simply replied that her work involved neurodiversity consultancy, blogging about positive neurodiversity, and pursuing her degree. However, when asked about her salary, she responded curtly with, "None of your business!" internally adding a mental note about his intrusive questioning. Moving on, the conversation shifted to flowers. Wilma, who seldom received them, acknowledged their beauty. When he mentioned surprising her with flowers, she internally pondered the likelihood of garden-picked daisies. She thanked him, mentioning she'd never received flowers from a man before. He continued with overly romantic statements, including commenting on a flirty photo (which Wilma found uncomfortable), and expressing how her beauty had captured his attention. Wilma, feeling a bit overwhelmed by the romantic overtures, responded politely, thanking him for the compliments. As the romantic tone persisted, she found it a bit excessive, comparing it humorously to overly cheesy pasta. She clarified her perspective, emphasizing the need to take things one day at a time. Finally, he concluded the conversation, expressing his enjoyment in chatting with her. Wilma, relieved for a moment of respite, casually acknowledged his message and wished him well. She welcomed a break from the intense romance and looked forward to future chats, trying to keep the conversation light and casual. After explaining her work and study schedule, a few days later, Wilma received a greeting while she was on the bus, engaged in her book which she was reading via her OrCam Learn. She replied, "I'm doing well, thanks. I'm in a poor signal and Wi-Fi area, so I might not respond right away." Despite her signal situation, she asked what he was up to that day. However, his immediate question was about whether she had eaten. Wilma chuckled to herself about her love for food, replying, "I'd never be fat if I didn't love food too much! Lol, yes, I've eaten!" He expressed concern about her work stress, but Wilma clarified that while her job could be challenging, she found it enjoyable and stress-free because of her passion for it. He then shared that he missed their communication over the past couple of days and confessed to thinking about her. He asked about her day, to which Wilma playfully referenced a Lionel Richie song, "Hello, is it me you're for?" and teased, "My friends all say I'm trouble once they get to know me better." Acknowledging his hiking photo, Wilma casually replied, "Thanks, no problem." He continued probing about her work schedule, inquiring about her working days, including weekends. Wilma keeps things light and casual in her responses, even as the conversation dives deeper into her work and routine. Wilma was keeping up with the TikTok posts from the star's group when she unexpectedly received a message from him saying, "Hi sweetie, how are you doing today?" She replied, mentioning getting lost on her way to a meeting but managing to make it on time. While discussing the meeting with her friend via email, they shared thoughts on the authenticity of the star.

In the following days, Wilma received a few more casual messages like "Hi sweetie, how are you today?" but chose not to respond. Then, he mentioned planning to visit her, which made Wilma chuckle, considering it highly unlikely. He inquired if she had eaten, and she responded playfully about her meal, bran flakes with banana and soya milk. When he asked for a picture, Wilma mischievously sent a photo of swans from a recent walk. After the accidental misfire, she sent a photo of herself, to which he responded positively, complimenting her appearance. On a day that held significance for Wilma due to Princess Twinkle Toes' birthday, she was reminiscing about happy memories and songs, feeling a bit nostalgic with a glass of wine. Later, she received a greeting but was preoccupied, finding the day strange and sad thinking about the Princess Twinkle toes. She was left deep in thought, listening to A-ha's "Crying in the Rain" and Queen's "Love of my Life" on YouTube.

The next day, he expressed admiration for her, a statement that left Wilma pondering its suddenness. She replied with a simple thank you. Then, his messages took a surprising turn, expressing affection and a desire to marry her. Wilma was taken aback by the suddenness and directness of his proposal. She responded cautiously, unsure about the rapid progression of their conversation.

 This unexpected turn left her contemplating the direction of their communication. Wilma, faced with persistent romantic gestures, tried to temper the conversation by emphasizing her disinterest in marriage. When he professed his love, she maintained a firm stance, saying that loving relationships don't necessarily require marriage. Despite her attempts to set boundaries, he continued with his expressions of love. When asked what she was doing, Wilma, feeling a bit exasperated, replied that she was chatting with him at that moment. He noted that she seemed to be having a relaxed day, ending their conversation on that note.

 Days later, he reappeared with greetings and inquiries about her day. Wilma, about to join a Zoom meeting, responded briefly, saying she couldn't chat. However, he persisted, asking if she had eaten, prompting a quick affirmative response from her. During her meeting, he continued the conversation, asking about the kind of meals she prepares. Wilma, managing her meeting and the conversation simultaneously, explained her cooking habits, mentioning the recent dishes she'd made. He seemed eager about her culinary skills, especially after seeing a photo of her beef salad. Wilma found his enthusiasm amusing but continued the conversation, inquiring about his cooking preferences. However, his focus remained on her cooking, expressing a desire for her to cook for him when they met. His persistent declarations of love made Wilma roll her eyes figuratively, though she replied diplomatically, highlighting the complexity of getting to know each other. She kept her responses sensible, trying to maintain boundaries amidst the ongoing professions of love. After expressing her surprise at his persistent affectionate messages, Wilma attempted to steer the conversation into a lighter, more casual direction by asking about any embarrassing on-stage moments. However, he responded by reaffirming his love and comfort in their conversation, planning surprises for their future meeting. Wilma sensed a red flag and, while not a fan of surprises, replied positively. He continued with romantic overtures, emphasizing the importance of actions over words. Despite his persistence, Wilma remained cautious, finding the situation a bit reminiscent of a romantic song. It seems Wilma's attempts to shift the conversation weren't entirely successful as it continued to veer towards romance. Wilma found a way to steer the conversation away from romance and toward shared interests. When he asked about her hobbies, she listed various activities and jokingly referred to her enjoyment of rugby, noting the unique ball shape in the sport. He responded, suggesting they had similar interests, aiming for a connection. Seizing the opportunity, Wilma teased him by inquiring about his taste in artwork, to which he surprisingly replied that he didn't like art. Amused by his response, she shared her appreciation for various artists and their works, highlighting her preference for impressionist art over classical depictions. She playfully remarked on the difference in their tastes. Realizing he might have stumbled into a mismatch in interests, he swiftly excused himself from the conversation, leaving Wilma with a sly grin, feeling she had managed to navigate the conversation to a lighter, more enjoyable territory. He texted her, "How has your day been, my love?" She replied, "Hello, I've had a busy, productive day. Still have the evening to go. How has your day been?" He sent a nice picture of himself enjoying a cup of coffee, to which she playfully remarked, "You don't have a cake LOL," then added, "You're looking fair braw." He texted back, "Have you eaten? Hope you enjoyed the meal." She found it easy to answer, "Yes, I did. I always enjoy food." He then asked, "What have you been up to today? "The star seemed to have other ideas on his mind after their previous discussion and proceeded to ask, "My dear, I want to ask you this, do you love me?" She thought, "Here we go again," and replied, "I am just getting to know you. Take your time. I have already said not to rush things." Despite sensing his disappointment, she responded, "Okay, I'll wait, but I do care about you." She decided to ask again, "What sort of stuff do you enjoy reading?" His reply was a bit unusual, saying, "I can draft my own story, but I love reading a lot!" She found it bizarre and continued, "I enjoy writing; I write creatively as well as academically. Reading exhausts me, but I'm fortunate to have OrCam technology to aid me." He eventually replied with a simple "Nice. What are you doing now?" She thought he was becoming tedious and responded, "Chilling out, watching TV," with laughing emojis. He replied, "Okay, send me a picture of where you are now!" She thought about the request and replied jokingly, "Seriously, I could be sitting in the police station." Then she said, "The picture doesn't want to load. I have just started watching 'The House of Gucci' on Amazon."

He didn't say anything for a while but later in the evening, asked, "Hope you had a nice day?" To which she replied, "Yes, it's been good. The usual question: have you eaten?" She sighs and replies, "Yes, I've eaten plenty, thanks." Okay, my love. Now catching up with one of her favourite comedies, she's having a good laugh, watching "The Big Bang Theory" before going to bed. He wishes her a good night and sweet dreams.

The next morning, he asks, "Hello, how are you doing today? My love, how was your night?" She responds with a simple, "Hello, I'm well, thanks. How are you today?" Feeling a bit disappointed, she sarcastically replies to his question, "Silly question!" Then she asks, "What are you doing now?" She was just finishing up aiding a few projects and answered, "Getting a project ready." He responds, "I hope you are enjoying your day so far." She replies, "Have a good day yourself." She expects him to end the conversation, but then he surprises her by saying, "Recently, I have begun to feel you. I wonder if you also feel the same way?" She thinks it's a bit too much information and imagines him cuddling Dolly the sheep, thinking of her. He continues, "It's my pleasure to have you in my life. My heart is so grateful to have you!" She playfully imagines him dressed as Whitney Houston singing "Run to You."

Sometime later, he texts her, "Hello, how are you doing today?" She replies, "I'm doing well, thanks." Busy with filling out forms for university, Wilma didn't think much about the conversation until she received the text, "Have you eaten?" She answers, "Yes, I have eaten," hoping for a different topic. She adds, "Just trying to get all my forms filled in for university." Returning to her tasks, she sees the next text: "OK, I would like to ask you a question." She responds, "Yes, ask away." The question that comes back is, "Do you love me?" She finds it repetitive and replies, "Why do you keep asking me?" Hoping he'd switch topics, but he persists, "I want to know. Tell me, do you love me?" Wilma clarifies, "I don't know. I just started talking to you last week. Where is this going?" She hopes for a change but receives a reply drenched in sweet talk, "I love you so much. I want you to love me and trust me!" Feeling overwhelmed by the sugary sweet conversation, she requests him to slow down. "You're moving way ahead of me. Please give me some time to settle down and get used to talking to you." When she tries to shift the conversation to lighter topics, like books or hobbies, she receives vague or defensive responses. Wilma notices the conversation turning one-sided and feels as if she's encountered a fake person. She attempts to engage by discussing fishing and other interests, but his responses remain curt or evasive. The conversation becomes increasingly unsatisfying, and Wilma decides to share her discovery with her friend with an email, stating that she believes the star in question is fake. The friend laughs and acknowledges how simple inquiries about hobbies and reading revealed a lack of genuine engagement. They agree on the prevalence of such encounters online, and Wilma continues to keep such individuals at bay, even if it's just for a few hours, to protect others from their deceptive tactics. After chatting with her friend, Wilma receives a text asking, "How are you doing today?" She responds, "I'm fine, thanks for asking." He texts her, "I like to read magazine books." Perplexed by this statement, she asks, "I've never heard of this, what is it?" Hoping for a more engaging conversation, she finds his response unhelpful, "Don't you know? Check on Google!" Disappointed by the lack of clarity, Wilma decides to explain the concept of magazines and books. She tries to steer the conversation towards discussing reading preferences, but he remains elusive. Disheartened, she likens the situation to the story of Aladdin, wishing for a magical exchange but finding herself left without a magic carpet ride or any wishes granted After a few days' break, the person returns, greeting Wilma with a "hello honey, my day was cool, and you?" She responds positively, asking about their activities, and hoping for a more engaging conversation. However, they reply, "I'm thinking of you," prompting an eye-roll from Wilma. She replies with a generic, "Awww, that is nice," although she doesn't genuinely mean it. He continues with the standard "Have you eaten" question, and she replies with a simple "Yes." Attempting to steer the conversation elsewhere, she responds to his persistent "do you love me" query with an "I don't know, why do you keep asking?" He presses further, demanding her to express love, but she firmly replies with a "No, I don't love you," hoping to redirect the conversation. When asked what she wants to know about him, she suggests he should think about what topics he wants to discuss, considering his avoidance of simple questions. He mentions he likes reading love stories, but before she can delve deeper into the topic, he disappears from the conversation again.

Later, he reiterates his affection, but Wilma tries to understand the sudden intensity of his feelings. Instead of answering her, he diverts the conversation, expressing the desire to be with her anytime, which she doubts. Wilma receives a text asking, "How are you doing today?" She responds positively, mentioning she's preparing for a busy day. The conversation quickly shifts to the person's usual inquiry about her having eaten, followed by a controlling query about her whereabouts at that moment. Wilma responds vaguely, mentioning she's reading a book for work, contemplating how he'd react if she mentioned a book on serial killers. He simply replies with an "okay." Attempting to engage in normal conversation, she asks about his plans for the day if he's heading to the beach. His response is monotonous "It was okay." Not receiving the expected beach anecdotes, she asks about his day at the beach, only to receive a mundane response again. The routine of asking if she's eaten and questioning her mood continues. When she prompts him about himself, he sidesteps, professing his love for her. Trying to assess the waters, Wilma teases, suggesting he might say that to all girls, but he denies it. He repeatedly claims she knows a lot about him, prompting Wilma to ask why he insists on that. He tries to arrange a meeting, suggesting she purchase meet and greet tickets from his "management." Wilma plays along, verifying the provided email address as fake and informing him she'll investigate further. The person insists the tickets cost €2000, prompting laughter from Wilma. She thought A-HA he can go hunting high and low for that money Finally, she decided to report and block him.

Cello

Who needs a dating app when there are nutcases on Instagram? Wilma was out for a walk around the Haberdashery shores when she received a message on Instagram saying, "Hello, beautiful." The message continued, "I have seen quite a handful of your comments on my posts, and I just want to go out of my way to appreciate those people whose comments and good wishes encourage me. I hope to bring you guys more beautiful music." Wilma thought to herself, "I haven't left any messages on this person's Instagram account for a while. Okay, I'll play along and send something back, that is lovely!" She sat on one of the old wooden picnic tables overlooking the water. She received a response, "Thanks a lot. I feel honoured and blessed to have an amazing fan like you." Wilma typed back, "You have an amazing gift. Thank you for sharing beautiful music." Enjoying the light breeze coming off the water, she received a new message, "I know you must be so amazed and shocked to get a text from me. Trust me, it is from me because I am down to earth, and I believe you know that." Seeing the profile, the person continued, "You remind me of an old friend that I care for so much." She laughed and watched people passing by, walking their dogs, while typing into her phone, "Oh, that's a lovely thing to say about my profile. I hope you are well." The person inquired about how long she had been a fan. She answered, "A few years now," and then awaited the next question. "What's your name and where are you chatting from, my dear?" he asked. "I am Wilma, chatting from Northern Ireland," she replied. As Wilma watched the clouds sailing and drifting across the sky, and the sun hiding behind them, she listened to Pink singing "Stupid Girls" and received, "How is the weather over there?" "It's okay," she texted back. As Wilma walked home, she received, "Can I have your Hangouts email so we can talk better?" "Sure, you can," she responded, giving out her Hangouts address. Upon arriving home, she made a cup of coffee in the kitchen and then went to her student cave, switching on her laptop to see what emails she needed to answer. Wilma's Hangouts pinged on her phone with a "hello" and a picture of him sent from the internet. She answered, "Hello 😁." He replied, "Nice to meet you here." Wilma responded, "It is also nice to meet you 😁." He went on to say, "I hope I can count on you to keep our texts private between us." She smiled, knowing this was a fraud, and told him, "Yes, of course, I will keep it private." He seemed content and asked, "What are some of your favourite places you've been?" Wilma thought about it and texted back, "Provence in France and I love Spain 🙂. What are some of your favourite places to visit?" He answered, "Mexico, Italy, China, Germany, and more." Wilma knew that travelling had been hard during the pandemic and decided to see his thoughts, texting, "With you being well-travelled, it must have been frustrating during the pandemic." Instead of answering Wilma's question, he asked, "What do you do in your free time?" She replied, "I enjoy art and design, walking, and cooking 😁. What are your hobbies?" He said, "I relax and read fan comments with a glass of wine 🍷." Wilma laughed at his answer and said, "You can't go wrong with a good glass of wine 🤣🤣🤣🤣." Then came the next question, "What is your favourite colour?" Wilma liked mixing up her favourite colour and said, "Purple." He mentioned his favourite colour was blue, and Wilma thought, "Of course, the colour of trust." He also said, "I see you as a good woman with a good heart." Reading the text, she burst out laughing and told him, "Shhh! I'm trying to keep my 'good heart' a secret. My friends just tell me I'm crazy 🤪🤪🤪." Wanting to share her thoughts, she responded, "All I seek is true happiness and peace." She didn't believe this person for a minute but replied, "Cool 🙏." He mentioned being a busy man, not chatting because he had the time but reaching out during his shortest free time. Wilma sarcastically thought but reassured him, replying, "I understand what you're saying 🙏." Then, she said, "I believe meeting you was not just by accident but divine." Acknowledging the cheesiness, he continued in a more serious tone, "But we must trust each other, can I trust you?" Wilma sarcastically thought about a house dropping on her but replied, "Yes, you can trust me." The conversation took an unexpected turn when he expressed interest, saying, "I'm interested in you, dear 😊." A warning light flickered in Wilma's mind, and she replied, "How lovely of you 😁." Then, he suddenly said, "Be my wife 🙏." Shocked, she politely declined, saying, "No, I am not getting married 🤣🤣🤣🤣." He persisted, "Please, dear, I love you, dear?" Wilma wondered why she always ended up with these types of individuals and replied, "Wow, that was quick!" He continued, "Please just accept me, a nut job," and she replied, "We have just met, I am just getting to know you 🙏." He pressed on, "But now you are my wife?" Wilma nearly choked on her water, responding, "Ehhhh....... No..... Lol 😂😂😂." She decided to tease the scammer, replying, "You're funny

😂😂😂😂." He insisted, "I'm not funny, I'm in love." Wilma teased further, asking, "Who are you in love with?" He responded, "You are, dear," and she jokingly replied, "Seriously? I don't believe in love at first sight." He pleaded, "You must believe me, honey." Playing along, she said, "Okay, weird but okay 😂😂😂." He expressed his love again, and Wilma responded, "This is becoming extremely corny." Eventually, after some playful banter and ignoring his requests for assistance, Wilma finds some peace in the conversation.

However, days later, the person reappears with a greeting, "Hello, honey 🥱." Wilma, sipping her coffee, responds politely, continuing the conversation for a bit longer before indicating her busy schedule. After a long day, Wilma was relaxing and watching TV when she received a message: "Good evening, honey 🥱." She responded politely. However, when she asked what the person had done that day, there was no reply for a while.

Later that evening, she received another message asking, "What country are you from, my love?" She replied, "Northern Ireland." Then came the surprising news: "My next show will be in your country, and that will be a big opportunity for us to be together, my love 😍." Checking the concert dates sceptically, Wilma decided to play along, asking, "When will that be?" The person claimed it would be in two weeks and expressed excitement about meeting her. They then mentioned wanting to stay in her country for a few days before the show, but Wilma suggested they tour as a tourist instead. However, things took a strange turn when the person asked Wilma to help with a package of belongings, claiming to have found love and comfort in her. This raised alarm bells, and Wilma firmly stated, "I am no one's wife!" The person insisted on sending a package to her and asked for personal details, but Wilma, wary of the situation, provided a fake address and email. Still, the person seemed pleased and said they'd be happy to be with her.

Later, the person kept messaging, asking what Wilma was doing and requesting that she inform them when she received a message from a supposed security company. Wilma, feeling playful, responded casually. The person then mentioned that receiving the package would cost a little money but reassured her about repayment. As the conversation continued, Wilma found excuses for delays in receiving messages, and the person persistently asked her to ensure the security company sent her a message. Despite Wilma's scepticism, the person kept pushing for a correct email address to be sent. The next morning, the person messaged, "Hello, honey 😊," but Wilma didn't reply until late afternoon, simply saying "hello."

Later that evening, the person seemed concerned, asking if she received a message from the security company. Wilma, nonchalantly, replied that she hadn't had a chance to check her emails due to being busy. He requested the correct email, but Wilma kept feigning confusion, not giving in to his attempts. Instead, she stalled, claiming she didn't understand and needed to rush, avoiding further conversation for the evening.

The next day around midday, Wilma greeted him with "Hello honey." She played it off like she was surprised, engaging in small talk until he asked what she was doing. Wilma, out for a walk with friends, replied with her actual activity, not giving in to his attempts to manipulate the conversation. His next attempt was about needing help with a "steam card," but Wilma pretended ignorance about it. He tried different card options, but Wilma claimed she didn't know about any of them. Then, he messaged her in Croatian by mistake, correcting it in English, asking if she supported charity. Wilma played along, saying she did, which led him to mention a private campaign for a sick child needing a kidney transplant. Wilma, knowledgeable about the difficulties of transplants, responded realistically, causing the person to go silent for a while. He reappeared later with endearments, claiming to miss her, but then vanished again.

Finally, he sent a good morning message and an email address that Wilma knew didn't exist. Fed up with the swindle, she decided to block the person.

The Case of my Friend is Gerald Butler:

Wilma traced this person's WhatsApp number to Calgary, Canada, while chatting. It was August, so Wilma was still on holiday from the Open University when she decided to talk to this person. It was a warm afternoon when she received a hello and warm greetings, also "Pardon my late reply, how are you doing today?" She responded, "Hello, I am well, thank you. How are you today?" The conversation continued, "I've had a peaceful day so far. What about you? How is your day going?" "I am glad you had a peaceful day. My day has gone well, thanks for asking." "That's good. How is your project going so far?" Wilma was working on another blog, as well as studying what was happening in the dyslexic community. "They are going well, thanks for asking. I hope you are enjoying a few cocktails presently." The star was chilling in the Maldives at this point, posting pictures on Instagram. He tells Wilma, "I was at the beach today and had a peaceful day." Wilma teased him, saying, "Did you build a sandcastle, or did you forget your bucket and spade?" He started laughing the next morning and said, "You're quite funny. How are you today? What are your plans for the day, honey? "It was Friday, and Wilma was enjoying a cup of coffee and her breakfast before starting up her laptop. She replied, "I am about to go and support dyslexic people." He didn't reply until the evening and asked, "Oh, where will you do that, honey?" Wilma explained, "I can help people online from anywhere in the world." He responded, "That's good. What did you have to eat?" "Well, I made a fabulous Caesar salad." "That's wonderful. Did you eat alone?" Wilma had made dinner for herself and Mr. G and replied, "No, I have been eating with friends."

At lunchtime the next day, she received, "How was your night? My night was peaceful. I keep seeing you in my dreams at the island; you are dressed in a red gown." Wilma laughed at the dream as she had never owned a red gown in her life. She replied, "Hello! I am glad you enjoyed your evening! The pictures on Instagram looked great. What a beautiful setting. I had a lovely evening. That was one weird dream you had of me." She thought of Chris de Burgh singing "Lady in Red" and imagined a red gown; she would look like a bouncing beach ball. He sent Wilma a message in the early hours of the morning while she was fast asleep, saying, "How was your night, my love? Warm greetings. Hope you had a lovely night's rest." The opposite had been true; it was one of the worst thunderstorms Wilma had heard in a long time. She replied, "It has been a terrible night; the thunderstorm has kept me awake most of the night." About lunchtime, she had thought of putting in a letter of complaint to Thor, the God of Thunder. She needed to find the address to Ragnarök and wondered if he had been fighting with Loki again. She did like it when Thor and Loki played "get help." It wasn't until late at night she received, "Really, how are you doing today?" "I am well, thanks. How about you? "He must check by asking, "Have you eaten?" "Yes, I made some lovely pasta for eating." "How did you know pasta is my favourite food to eat?" "I did not know pasta was your favourite food." "Yes, I love pasta as well as strawberries." "Well, that is a weird combination; maybe you've received recipes from Dr. Dodgy shoes." She decides to tease him with, "You have pasta and strawberries together; well, that is a new one." He texts back, "No, that is a horrible idea. I meant my favourite fruit is strawberries." "Oh, I know strawberries and black pepper go together. I like to put this combination on a bagel with cream cheese. I was wondering if there was a new trend in pasta puddings that I had missed." "Ah, you also have great taste; the bagel sounds lovely." "Well, I am glad you think so, as I do enjoy cooking." "What are your favourite recipes for cooking?" "I don't have any favourite recipes; I like trying lots of different foods." "That is good," she asks, "do you enjoy cooking?" "Yes, but it is on a small scale!" "Well, I was not expecting you to cook on a large scale, which is for catering." She asks, "Do you have a lot of recipe books?" He replies, "Not really. What about yourself?" "Yes, I love recipe books; I get lots of ideas from them." "That is good. And what have you been doing?" "I have been having lots of meetings about writing blogs for people." "Do you have a registered page where you publish your work?" "Yes, of course, I do," and she sends him the link. "Okay, honey. By the way, there are a lot of blogs on dyslexia on Google." "Okay, honey. Wow, are you presently located in the UK?" "Yes, I am." "That is great. My good friend, Gerard Butler, comes from Scotland." Wilma replies, "Yes, I have seen his films. It's nice to know that you are friends." "Oh, do you know him? He might be in your neighbourhood!" Wilma thinks, seriously, "Yeah, he lives around the corner from me." She must stop the sarcastic thoughts sometimes. He then tells Wilma he is wonderful in the

Fallen franchise. Wilma tells him, "It is highly unlikely that Gerard Butler is in my neighbourhood." "You are funny. Just wondering if I could tell him about you. I hope you're okay with it. I want to keep our communication private; this is why I am asking your permission." Wilma laughs as she doesn't believe this person is friends with Gerard Butler and replies, "Yes, you can tell him about me if you wish." "Okay, honey. Do you have a lot of work to do today?" It was early in the morning, and Wilma had just caught her bus. She was heading into the head office for the helpline that day. "I am heading out to work now." "Okay, I will text you later."

She was listening to Philip Oakey and Giorgio Moroder singing together in "Electric Dreams." "I have just started the bus journey to work." "You don't drive?" She says, "No," and sends him five indicators of being dyslexic: 1) poor sense of direction, 2) difficulty with time management, 3) poor organizational skills, 4) difficulty distinguishing left from right, and 5) extreme tiredness. "Well, that is my tip for the day. Thank you, my love 😊" "I am glad you like them." "Of course, I do. They are from you, my love." She says, "I have just seen a dyslexic Yorkshire man wearing a cat flap." He laughs at her joke. "What did you do to him?" "I did nothing to him 😊." As she is staring out the window travelling on the bus, she receives, "Honey, do you know that Scottish men wear skirts?" She sends the YouTube video of Michael McIntyre describing how the design of the kilt came about. "Of course, Scotland had to make sure they did not look like the English! Firstly, have a large bit of tartan material and make it look like a skirt. A true Scotsman doesn't wear anything under the kilt—next, a nice set of hockey socks. After complaints about wearing a skirt with his 'balls' hanging out, the guy wants to know if he can have pockets to keep his change! The next thing is a bag. This does not go down well as it is girly. The badger's handbag around the waist is a compromise to keep his change in. Nobody would argue with him as, of course, you keep a knife called a dubh or sgian dugh (pronounced 'skeen doo') down his hockey sock." Late in the evening, she receives, "Thanks, honey. Are you home yet?" Wilma had been home for a while and was out enjoying a few ciders with the hair bear bunch and replied, "No, I am having a great laugh with my friends." He inquires, "Do you have many friends?" "What do you mean? How many friends do you have?" "I have never really counted. I am with a small group of friends who always make me laugh presently." "You are funny." So, she says, "Here's to the nights we can't remember with friends we will never forget." "You are part of a group of guys laugh out your butts with a lot of drinks and do crazy things." She sends back, "Well, what is a bottle of wine between friends like us?" "Empty!! You need to have crazy nights with crazy friends. Do you drink alcohol?" "Oh shit, there is no red wine here. Please put on a blindfold and I will order you lemonade!" "Really? Oh yeah! Yes, love." She sends him Cher singing "Love and Understanding." He asks, "Is this what you are listening to now?" "I listen to a lot of music," and then sends Mark Knopfler playing "Going Home" from the film "Local Hero." "Thank you, my love," and then she sends Meatloaf singing "Bat out of hell". "The following morning, he asks, "How was your day, honey?" Wilma had lots of laughs the previous evening and replied, "My day was excellent, thanks. How are you doing today?" "Happy weekend, my love," to which Wilma sends a picture of Patsy and Edina standing on a yacht in the film "Absolutely Fabulous" and tells him to have a great weekend. In the afternoon, he asks, "Is that you in pink?" She laughs and replies, "Yes, well, I think you look adorable." She sniggers and thinks he is a bit deluded, and he says, "You're welcome, honey. "She asks, "What mischief are you up to this evening?" He laughs, "Did you say mischief? I will probably get up to mischief after having you!" She wonders if that involves fluffy handcuffs and a tub of chocolate body paint and replies, "Yes, I said mischief! I hope you're having fun!" Yes, honey, what about you?" "I am having a great laugh with my friends." "You are attached to your friends. I always have a good laugh with the hair bear bunch; they are such genuine fun. "A couple of days later, she receives, "Good morning, honey. How are you doing today?" "I have a stinking cold at present; man-size tissues are at the ready! I hope you are on medication." "I have taken a Lemsip; however, there is no cure for the common cold. You must stay warm and drink plenty of tea," Wilma had lemon and ginger tea in the house and replied, "I know. The worst part of it is the sinus headache." He leaves her alone for a couple of days and then asks, "How are you feeling today?" At this point, Wilma had been to the doctor and informed him of a chest infection. "The vet has given me antibiotics; it is going to take a couple of days before they kick in."

The next day, he said, "Sorry, honey. I hope you are feeling better today?" "I think I have coughed a lung up today! I am sorry, honey, do you feel any better?" "I know the antibiotics are working! I just don't know if I will have a set of lungs left with all the coughing." You are funny. Where are you presently?" Wilma was sitting in her cat basket watching "The Cannonball Run" on the TV but mischievously said, "I am in my art class drawing a still life; you can come and pose for me if you wish." He doesn't answer, and she says, "Have a great weekend. "The next morning, he says, "Thank you. How do you feel?" Wilma felt terrible and replied, "I wish I could say I feel good; however, I don't. Oh, are you still sick today, honey?" "Yeah, do you want to sing 'Soft Kitty' to me?" She sends Penny singing "Soft Kitty" to Sheldon when he is sick in "The Big Bang Theory." "You are sweet; I could pet you and take care of you!" "Awww, thanks lol." "Yes, honey, why do you laugh?" "Well, I may feel terrible, but I have not lost my sense of humour. Maybe I should give up watching 'The Big Bang Theory.'" He laughs, "I have to say you are fun," to which Wilma sends him Amy waiting for Sheldon to rub some vapour rub on her chest. "Yes, I will help cure your cold by rubbing some vapour rub on your chest. She laughs I am glad you like my sense of humour; I will let you rest now. He texted back please text me when you are up again. I am hoping you have a speedy recovery xxx." "A few days later, Wilma sends the introduction to the Racoons singing 'Run with Us' and tells him, 'I am feeling better!' He does not come back to Wilma for a few days, and then she receives, 'How are you doing today, honey? I have had a really busy day, but it has also been a really good day. I hope you are well.' He leaves Wilma alone again for a few days and says, 'Okay, and how are you today?' She returns, 'I am great, how are you today?' 'I am great.' He deletes the next message followed by

'Happy weekend.' 'Happy weekend, I hope you have a momentous day 😊.' 'Yes, I sure will do, and you are too. I will have a wonderful time, thanks. Text me when you are free again.' Wilma was sitting, drinking coffee, and replied, 'I am free just now, I am not going out just yet!' 'Oh, great to hear. No, I will be heading out for a PCR test for COVID-19 for travelling. Presently I am enjoying a cup of coffee.' 'Okay, that is good. I also love coffee.' 'Yes, I nearly forgot to buy a new jar yesterday!'

The next day was the star's birthday, and Wilma sent a picture saying, 'German girls know how to party' and said 'Happy Birthday.'

The next day, he starts by deleting the original message and sends a 'thank you, how are you doing today?' 'No problem, I am doing well thanks,' she told him. 'OKAY, take care of yourself and enjoy some time off.' Wilma was so excited she could crush a grape; she kept checking she had everything ready for flying out to Malaga for the dyslexic compass. He returns, 'Thank you, honey. Do you have much work for today?' Excitedly she tells him, 'I am flying to Spain for a conference, I am excited.' 'Wow, that is nice. How long will you be there?' 'I will be there for four nights, then it will be home time. I am looking forward to meeting new people.' 'Honey, will you be available to text while on your four-day trip?' 'Yes, of course, I am not sure how much free time I will have; however, I will text you 😊.'

The next day, she was up early full of excitement, and the weather was stunning with clear blue skies. She went down to the pier, took a photo of the palm trees, and sent a 'good morning 😊.' He asks, 'Did you arrive safely?' 'Yes, I am safe and well 😊. Do you have a hotel room there for a few days?' 'Yes, I am here for four nights.' 'Okay, honey. Do you want to talk about something to me?' Wilma was confused and replied, '?????????' 'It's a question if there is anything you want us to talk about,' Wilma was still confused and said, 'I am not sure what you mean.' 'Okay, don't worry about it. What are you doing today?' 'I am at the conference at Babel Idioma's.'

The next day, she receives, 'How is your day going? Well, I am just up, going for a shower, and heading out for coffee and churros with everyone, breakfast of champions.' 'That is good; you are fun to be with. Do you love shopping as well?' 'What woman does not like shopping? I nearly pissed myself laughing when you asked me that question.' 'That is nice. I thought you might be different. What do you like shopping for the most?' Wilma loves buying handbags; however, she tells him, 'I don't have time for shopping on this trip; I am far too busy.' 'I would like to send you gifts, which address can I send them to?' 'Nice try, but you're not getting my address, and just sending that is so thoughtful and sweet of you.' Later on, she receives, 'So how are you doing today? It has been an amazing day! Everyone thanked me for my insight towards this amazing project. I am heading out for a few gins and tonics before going home tomorrow.' Wilma was packing her case and had bought some beautiful black pudding pate and some amazing, sweet nuts for taking home. 'Well, that is good. I hope you are not stressed out yet.' 'No, I am not stressed out. I have had an amazing time. Can't believe it is nearly time! I mean home time, damn spell check.' 'Why, honey, spell check can be a pain at times.' 'I love and hate my spell check! I can't get sangria right at times!' 'Why, honey?' she replies, 'I love my spell check as it aids my dyslexia in sending the correct spelling. I hate it because there are times when it completely changes the spelling of words I am looking for, and I have not noticed this fact, and the message ends up extremely strange! An example of this was recently when I sent my friend about having a large jug of sangria, however, the message ended up being treated to a large jug of managerial!' 'Okay, honey, do not worry about it. Be strong, okay?' 'I am strong; however, it is extremely frustrating at times. 'Several days later, Wilma received it late at night, 'Are you home yet?' 'Oh yes, I am back unharmed; I forgot to tell you.' He takes a couple of days to reply and says, 'It's okay, how are you doing?' 'I am doing well thanks; it's the start of another busy week.' 'You are always a busy bee.' 'I know; you are also busy. Remember to take regular breaks.' 'I will and remember to take your own advice.' A few days later, Wilma receives, 'How are you, honey?' 'I am well thanks,' and she never hears anything from the Canadian again! She left it open for a few months after not hearing anything from him; she blocked the conversation."

The Case of the Mysterious Mr. Smith, or Should It Be Dr. Smith?

Wilma began her day as usual, heading downstairs only to find a message waiting for her on Hangouts. As Hangouts was transitioning to Google Chats for added security, she decided to accept the message. It began with a simple "Hello, dear." She replied, "Hello, how are you doing?" There was no response until later in the afternoon when the person introduced himself as Mr Smith. Wilma greeted him back, "Hello, I'm Wilma. Nice to meet you here. "Their conversation kicked off with Mr. Smith asking, "Are you married?" Wilma found his directness a bit surprising and responded, "No, I'm not married." He expressed his desire to get better acquainted, mentioning his loneliness after losing his wife many years ago. Wilma, leveraging her counselling skills, asked how he lost his wife. He revealed that his wife passed away giving birth to their first son. Curious about his family, Wilma inquired if his son survived. He confirmed, adding that his son was now fifteen and he was immensely proud. Suspicious about the conversation's direction, Wilma asked if he had any other children. He responded, "No, I don't have any children. It's complicated." 💭💡 Wilma felt a pang of scepticism, realizing he might have an agenda. When he asked about her age, she replied, "I'm 35," deciding to improvise. He declared himself to be 51 and expressed his intent to find a wife. Wilma, uninterested in being his wife, typed on her iPad that she wasn't looking to remarry after a past divorce. She emphasized her belief in finding another loving partner but wasn't interested in rushing into marriage. Mr Smith persisted, expressing his eagerness to fall in love quickly, prompting Wilma's disbelief and a firm response that real relationships take time, unlike Hollywood romances. Mr. Smith remained persistent, claiming to be a patient person wanting to get to know her better. Wilma, growing bored of the conversation, changed the topic, asking about his hobbies. His response was unexpected, stating his love for kids and family as his main hobbies. Wilma raised an eyebrow and probed further, to which he explained giving up his hobbies since his wife's passing, justifying his desire for a woman like her. Wilma, disinterested in a blind date with Mr. Smith, advised him to find enjoyment beyond caring for his family, acknowledging the importance of personal time. She mentioned her profession as an assistive technology trainer. When asked about her country, she replied with the UK. He expressed his admiration for the UK, prompting an internal reference to Cilla Black's famous phrase, "Surprise, surprise!"

She felt relieved when he mentioned, "I need to go; we'll talk later. I'm at work right now, my dear." She thought, *thank goodness*, and went about her day.

Later in the evening, while Wilma was relaxing, she greeted him with a casual, "Hello, dear. How are you?" He replied, "I'm fine, thanks." She thought, *Great, the nut job is back.* He continued, "Have you eaten, dear?" "Yes, I have, thanks 😄," she replied. Then came an unexpected query, "Do you have lots of male friends? Do you flirt with them outrageously and ask them to marry you?" She was taken aback. He added, "I'm sorry for asking; I'm just jealous." Wilma couldn't fathom why he'd be jealous without even knowing her appearance or her friends. She clarified that she indeed had male friends but just as friends, nothing to provoke jealousy.

He confessed, "Okay, I don't know why, but I've never fallen this hard for a lady. I can't help feeling this way for you." Wilma found his intensity unsettling and requested him to slow down, reminding him that they had just met online. His response concerned her further as he mentioned not being able to visit the UK presently with his kids. Wilma's immediate thought was relief, and she expressed it subtly, urging him to slow down and questioning if he had similar conversations with everyone online. Seeking to divert the conversation, she inquired about his academic credentials, specifically his PhD. As expected, he avoided the question and diverted, asking more about her. He sent a picture that seemed like an internet advert, signalling the conversation was heading nowhere. Wilma, uninterested, ended the conversation and went to bed. 🙈💡 The next morning, while having breakfast, she received a "Good morning, dear," accompanied by a poorly photoshopped picture of him, his brother, and his brother's wife. Wilma replied politely. He persisted, asking if she had eaten and where she was. Annoyed, she replied, "Yes, I have, thanks! I'm at home."

He vanished until later in the afternoon, greeting her again and mentioning discussing her with his son. This alarmed Wilma, anticipating another bizarre interaction. She pleaded for patience, urging him not to rush things.

However, he continued with repetitive declarations, trying to learn more about her job and income, eventually revealing his son's plan to study in the UK. Wilma remained unshaken by the news and clarified the differences in laws across UK regions. He acknowledged this and disclosed his son's educational intentions. Misunderstandings persisted, like when he intended to say "bath" but typed "birth," to which Wilma responded in jest. 🧑‍🦰💁 His attempt to seek English lessons triggered scepticism. She replied honestly that she wasn't experienced in teaching languages. He probed further, displaying a lack of comprehension about language education. Wilma excused herself as he announced picking up his son from school.

Later that evening, he returned, prompting Wilma's dismay. He expressed boredom and inquired about the beauty of her country, to which she offered a vague yet positive response, considering perceptions of beauty differ.

He gushed, "I love being in beautiful countries!" Wilma asked, "Where are some of your favourite places to visit?" His response baffled her, "My favourite country is the UK! That's where my father passed away; I promised him I'd spend my life there." Wilma couldn't help but think, *if this guy had chocolate for brains, he wouldn't fill a smarty!* Despite this, she inquired, "Where in the UK?" He mentioned London, England, which was quite far from her. Wilma diverted the conversation, saying that London, though beautiful, was a bit too fast-paced for her taste. He expressed curiosity about her location in the UK. Wilma hinted at various other beautiful places like York, the Lake District, and Manchester, hinting at her preference for a more relaxed lifestyle. He then expressed his desire to visit those places when he comes to the UK. Wilma, sceptical, played along, mentioning the diverse beauty of the UK and how it depended on one's preferences. He agreed, expressing his initial dream to be a traveller but ending up becoming a doctor. He then compared Wilma's kindness and speech to that of his ex-wife, which puzzled her considering his earlier mention of his deceased wife. She thanked him for the compliment, suggesting he enjoyed life despite the loss of his best friend earlier in the year. Wilma offered her condolences, acknowledging the pain of losing someone close. The conversation turned more personal, discussing grief and its effects. Wilma, drawing from her knowledge in counselling and psychotherapy, engaged in a deep conversation about grief. However, she found herself avoiding further interaction and retreated to bed without responding to his last message.

The next day, she responded briefly, citing busyness, but found herself further engaged in the conversation later in the evening. He expressed concern that she might be angry with him for not replying promptly. She assured him she was simply busy.

Later in the evening, she received another message, "Hello dear, I just arrived home."

Dr Smith expressed, feeling incredibly stressed, so she asked, "What do you do to de-stress?" suggesting meditation and deep breathing. To her surprise, he responded, "Well, that's true, I've taken some drugs. Thanks for your caring." Wilma advised him to listen to music and relax. The next morning, as she was enjoying her coffee, she received an early message from him. Simultaneously, she was bombarded with work-related messages on LinkedIn, anticipating another busy day. Responding that it was Friday, she knew her time for relaxation with a glass of wine was nearing.

He advised her not to stress and asked what she was doing. Wilma, planning a BBQ with friends due to the beautiful weather, informed him of her plans. He queried if it was for fun, leading her to joke about laughter at the gathering. Praising her humour, he seemed confused by her response, thinking she understood him, while Wilma found his messages increasingly peculiar. She eventually decided to go out for a walk along the shore, listening to music, she enjoyed listening to the Peatbog Fearies album called Croft Work and ignoring his messages.

Later, she received more messages, which she chose to ignore while enjoying time with her friends at a BBQ.

The next day, he asked if she had been busy, and she shared her day's fun with water pistols and kids playing, sidestepping his attempt to offer stress relief advice. In response to her suggestions to manage stress, he revealed a strange test result about excess sperm, leaving Wilma utterly bewildered. She tried to steer the conversation away from such personal details.

The following day, he questioned their communication delay, wondering about the time in the UK and requested pictures, claiming his son wanted to see her. Wilma dismissed the request, stating she wasn't into taking selfies. "How will I have proof of how beautiful you are? I want to show how much I love you. Do you have feelings for me?" Wilma's inner thoughts were interrupted by the persistent messages. She responded, "I have only just met you; it's also my choice if I want to share my photo with you."

Then he asked, "Are you at home?" Wilma felt it wasn't his business and replied, "Why?" To which he replied, "Because of you, I laugh a little harder, cry a little less, and smile a lot more." Wilma, finding solace in music, texted back, "Laughing is good for your mental health. "He acknowledged her wish to build a friendship first. Wilma thought he was catching on and felt reassured.

Later, she received a message emphasizing the need to carefully share feelings and appreciated their friendship immensely. "Thank you for your lovely message," Wilma replied, highlighting the support friends provide in life's difficulties. He expressed fear of trying new things but appreciated their friendship, to which Wilma encouraged him to take steps toward new experiences.

Feeling a bit overwhelmed by his sentiments, Wilma decided to end the conversation, focusing on her work. He expressed deep appreciation for their friendship, claiming it to be more valuable than self-love. After a few hours, he messaged again, saying he was bored. Wilma advised him to engage in activities like taking a walk, reading, or meeting friends for a beer. He seemed unsure about finding a hobby and admitted to enjoying music. Encouraging him to embrace music and possibly attend a concert, Wilma thought they were back to square one in their conversation.

He informed her of going to bed, prompting Wilma's silent relief. Ignoring his later messages, she found herself feeling exasperated by his persistence late at night, asking her to share more about herself and expressing a desire for her to be a part of his life.

"He then mentions, 'You said you want us to build a friendship first before we move forward.' Wilma thinks, 'Great, he's catching on. That's correct.' Then, she receives a message: 'You cannot keep your friendly feelings within yourself. You will always want to share those feelings with people. But you can't just share your friendly feelings with just anybody. There is a need to carefully search for that great friend to share that unique friendship. You are that great friend, and I will continue to appreciate our friendship forever. I appreciate you a lot!' Wilma responds, 'Thank you for your lovely message. It's always good to talk to friends. They will support you through good and troubled times in your life 🙏.'

'I'm afraid of trying new things, and I want to give you a chance, but you crept into my heart so subtly that I couldn't resist being your friend. I'm happy to have you around,' he expresses. Wilma considers her response and advises, 'You should not be afraid to try new things. Just take your time, plan something you have always wanted to do and make a date to start 🙏.'

'Yes, you're right. Your friendship to me is what music is to the longing soul or water to a desert-thirsty wanderer. You are such a friend and more,' he insists. Wilma contemplates where the sick bag is and decides to end the conversation to focus on her work, saying, 'Okay, I will chat with you later 🙏.' 'Okay, dear. Goodbye. I have the best friend in the world. What else do I need? I have someone that loves me even more than I love myself. I am incredibly lucky and favoured to have you,' he adds. Wilma wonders what other weird and wonderful things will come to this guy's mind.

After a few hours, he messages Wilma again, saying, 'Hey dear, I must tell you I am just bored. Really!' She's slightly annoyed and advises him, 'Go for a walk, read an enjoyable book, and get together with friends for a beer. Seriously, you need to find a hobby!'

Later in the evening, she receives another message: 'That's why I am here chatting with you, but it looks like you are busy. I am not sure what a hobby is.' She tries again, suggesting, 'You must find a hobby to occupy your spare time. Maybe you could start dancing, read a book, or listen to some music 🎧💡.' He responds quickly, 'I love listening to music. That's a great idea.'

Wilma thinks it's great and recommends that he enjoy his spare time, even suggesting he think about going to a concert 🙏. 'I just like chatting with you online,' she thinks. 'We are back to square one!' Then, he informs her, 'I am going to bed.' Wilma sighs with relief. Ignoring his emoji-filled message, he sends another late at night when Wilma is already asleep: 'Hello dear, please tell me more about yourself. I will tell you more about my life as I would like you to be a part of my life.'"

I know it is not easy for a woman to love a man she does not know!

The next day he starts with "Good Morning," followed with "I don't like it when you ignore or cannot be bothered to reply to my messages." Wilma is yawning and waiting for the kettle to boil for making coffee and replies, "I am still sleepy, and my brain is not functioning presently. I am just looking at my plan for today." "I am sorry that must have been so stressful for you," thinks Wilma, the only stressful thing is chatting with you. He recommends she rest 🙏.

At the start of the afternoon, he sends "Hello dear I have just arrived home," she sees the message thinks big deal and gets on with her work. Again, he reaches out "Hello dear." She does not bother with him until she has finished her dinner and sends hello. It must have been like Whoopi Goldberg listening to an answering machine in "Jumping Jack Flash," he was over the moon and sent back "How was your day? I think you have been extremely busy today." "My days are always busy 😜. I think that you need to spend more time at home," she thinks seriously and asks why. She burst out laughing when she said, "You need to rest, I say this because I care about you." She thinks yeah right and tells him, "OKAY Well, I certainly hope you are okay." "Yes, everything is fine 🙏. That's good to hear, dear 👍."

Then he sends through the news "My sister just had an accident!" Wilma thinks this is not good, however, she has a sneaky suspicion that it will not be long before he tells me she has died. She is empathetic and says "Oh dear! I hope she is not seriously injured." He instantly sends her back "She is in a coma! It was extremely serious." "Oh, that comes as a surprise, well no, however," she is diplomatic and says, "Well, you must get to the hospital, your sister is more important than talking to me." He must have been going like a bat out of hell; two minutes later she received "I am working on it." Even Wilma knows you cannot drive and text at the same time. Within a brief time, he sends "the hospital demanding a huge amount of money for oxygen." Wilma thinks shock and horror that you are telling me late at night. He follows on with "I am a doctor, however, I am not even allowed to see the operation." Wilma thinks if you are a doctor then I am Mary Poppins! He follows on with "If she dies, I will never forgive myself!" Wilma again is diplomatic even though she knows this was all a fabrication and replies, "Firstly, I don't know anything but your country's hospital system. Secondly, talk to the doctors to find out what is happening presently." "Yes, dear," then three minutes later she receives "I lost her, she is gone!" "Oh, wow I could never have predicted that," she is trying not to laugh at this point "Wow! That was a serious accident, I am sorry to hear your sad news 🙏." He sends a picture of such inferior quality of a person lying in a hospital bed that just made Wilma cringe! "This nut case is getting blocked shortly," then he sends "I can't cope with the pain!" As she was dealing with a pretend death, she says "I have no idea what to say presently! I think I am in shock! I still can't believe the news. Try having a cup of steaming sweet tea." He tells her that he will try that, but instantly changes his mind and tells her that "talking to you is far better than a cup of tea." Wilma is thinking oh, bother off grasshopper! However, she behaves herself and says, "Take your time, let the news sink in, and try and think of all the good memories with your sister." Wilma thinks he might burst out singing like Michael Bolton, "How am I supposed to live without you? Any time I think of my sister I just burst into tears. I just want to keep chatting with you presently." Wilma is thinking, "I want to go to bed and sleep" and sends "No, you need to cry, you can't bottle up your feelings; it will only make it more painful in the long run." She can just imagine him blowing his nose with a man-size tissue "You're right." She decides it is time to go to bed, "I must go now! Try not to do anything silly. 🙏"

    The following morning, he sends "Hey dear I miss you." She thought "I don't miss you" and ignored the message. Then he sends a gif saying, "Happy French fry day." Wilma thinks that is crazy for someone who has just lost their sister. He is relentless and it does not take long for him to say, "Hey dear, why don't you reply to me anymore?" Wilma had been busy catching up with housework and then catching up with reading for her course; she decided to send a text to keep him quiet "I am busy presently; I am finishing off some work which needs to be done." Wilma then goes to make lunch and like dealing with a puppy she receives "I miss you dearly." He is needy, and she returns "Why? Don't worry I will talk to you later; I thought maybe you don't want to chat with me anymore. I am a busy person; I have a lot of things to do, I chat when I am free." "I love that about you Wilma, I am now going to prepare for my sister's funeral. I will give you the time and space that you need as you have a lot to do with arranging a family funeral 🙏." "Thanks for your consideration!" "No problem 🙏 ☺." Wilma then went in and blocked Dr Smith as she could not be bothered by him sending messages of how much he needed her with his sister, more than likely a fake funeral. Wilma saw that he did try to get in touch with her again after she had blocked him. Thankfully, her Hangouts app had closed permanently, and she removed his new address.

The Case of Let Me Be Your sugar boy!

Wilma started talking to an international star after receiving a message on TikTok. This had become a favourite place for scammers to send Wilma messages. She invited the international star to her Google Chat. The chat started one warm evening in May with "How are you, fan?" She thought it was supposed to be "Hello fan, how are you?" She replied, "Hello, I am fine, thanks." It didn't take long for a text to come through saying, "Thanks for supporting me." "Well, that's nice of him to say," she thought and read on. "Since how long have you been my fan? And have you picked up my book on the history of David?" She took a few minutes to think about how to reply and texted back, "I have been a fan for eight years. I do not have your book on the history of David; is that an autobiography? If it is, I am waiting for the English version. I never was any good at learning different languages. It is one of the difficulties I have as I'm dyslexic." He texted back, "I am also an expert in English like German, and the English version will be out soon after this clothing project." Wilma had been following the launch of his clothing range on Facebook and Instagram. He goes on to ask, "Hope you have ordered a jacket and T-shirt at Key Largo Fashion? This is a brilliant way to convince Wilma that they are genuine people. The entrepreneur and businessman, since the pandemic had shut down going out, people were turning their attention to other projects such as clothing." The star noticed he had made a mistake and texted,

"Not an expert in English, I mean." Wilma had been busy with her studies as well as her volunteer work raising awareness of dyslexia from home. She texted back, "I have looked at the range, but I have not bought anything yet. I have not decided what design is my favourite yet. I have also been busy with student life and assignments."

The star decided to change the conversation and asked, "How old are you? You all know I'm 41!" Wilma knew the star's age and texted back, "Oh, I have reached a grand age of 230 in life. It doesn't hurt 😂😂😂." She sends him a picture of herself, and he replies, "It is good to reach a grand age of 230 LOL. You look married with children, how many children, dear?" Wilma thought that was a cheeky remark. She replied, "I am not married. I am in a long-term relationship. I have no children," to which he simply said, "Woooow." Then he goes on to tell Wilma, "I'm a very simple man, but at the same time deep and complicated with my thoughts, easy-going with people that are not picky, open-minded, very honest, sometimes more than it should be. I'm passionate about almost any kind of music; for me, it's like a kind of expression. I'm enthusiastic about dancing, especially salsa; it just releases your soul. Open to changes, you never know what life has for you, what new lessons you are going to learn, what kind of people you are going to meet, and in which way are they going to touch your heart. Tell me what you know about music. I am a world-class violinist, and you, what are you doing for a living?" Wilma decides to start by chatting about music. "I love listening to music, apart from drum and bass; it gives me a headache. I am not sure if you are aware that classical music helps improve concentration while studying, along with helping to block out distractions while I study. Music helps me put my creative ideas together; it helps me when I am having a dreadful day and just need my own space. I go for a walk and listen to music. I dance like the honey monster, so I will give salsa a miss; people will fall about laughing." The inquisitive star sends back, "😂😂😂 You're a student of which course?" Following on with, "What did you do?" She texted back, "I am a part-time undergraduate studying for a Bachelor of Arts in criminology. I am a national volunteer for a charity promoting events and manning the helpline once a week. I also run my blog promoting positive dyslexia, am a beta tester for assistive technology, and am a consultant for a neurodiverse company aiding in promoting coaching and mentoring people. I also write a variety of articles for dyslexic voices."

    The star reads her message and thinks about what she has said, then texts, "But you said earlier that you don't learn many languages because of dyslexia, but how did you help? Follows on with, "How?" This is a good inquiry, and Wilma loves talking to people about dyslexia. She sends back, "Dyslexia works differently for everyone. Plenty of famous people are dyslexic, like Albert Einstein, Whoopi Goldberg, and John Lennon. It is creative lateral thinking. My brain thinks in pictures; therefore, I use assistive technology to help me. However, I am still not good at learning different languages." It didn't take long to receive, "Tell me more. I only understand the language of violins." Wilma did not know anything about the language of violins or reading music. Wilma looks up the video from the charity made by dyslexia of the dyslexic sperm bank and forwards this to the star.

Wilma adds to the text, "I hope this helps a bit with your understanding of dyslexia." The conversation changes again when he texts back, "How did you earn if it's all voluntary work?" Wilma reads this and thinks about how she will reply, saying, "I am a freelance consultant for a neurodiverse company. I coach and mentor people over Zoom, Microsoft Teams, and Google Meetings. I send in my expenses at the end of the month, and they pay me." He replies, "Wooow, will you be my teacher? There's no tour and concert for now because of the Ukraine invasion 😂😂😂." Wilma knew that concerts were being cancelled due to the war. She was not sure when the issues between Russia and Ukraine were going to be resolved. She sent back a cheeky, "Yeah yeah, I can give you some coaching and mentoring. I will send you a bill; I am not working for anything. 😂😂😂😂." He sends back, "😂😂😂😂," then asks, "So is your man close to you or far?" She looks over at Mr. G sitting in his dog basket typing away on his laptop. She texts him, saying he is close to her; she thinks of her most recent disasters with installing software and adds, "He helps me with my disasters!"

He then opens his heart to Wilma by saying, "You sound very official and strict because of your course of studies. I am single, and I want to meet a woman who can accept me as I am and who I am... I want to be loved again; all my life, I have been single for a long time. But now I want to find the right woman that I can spend the rest of my life with and have a family." It's hard to find someone who loves you when you have the power, money, and fame. As Wilma was studying the relationship between power and money in society, she understood this could be a problem. It was all very plausible so far; time would tell. He then asks, "Have you put yourself into embarrassing disasters?" Wilma laughs at this remark as she has had many disasters. "Disasters? I can trip over fresh air 😂😂😂😂. As for Mr. G, he is my computer geek, and somehow talked me into blogging. I write the blog, and he does all the technical stuff for publishing it. So, when my IT crashes, I ask him for help 😂😂😂." The next text received was, "Wow, you're endowed with many gifts and professions 👏👏👏👏👏." Wilma is glad to have impressed him and adds, "I have been reinventing myself over the pandemic."

The curiosity of the star asks further questions, "What's your blog name?" Wilma replies, "I run 'Dyslexic Tips';" the conversation then moves on. "Okay dear, why did you choose not to give birth?" It is a dreaded question for Wilma; people do not understand infertility and it has more questions than answers. Wilma texted back, "It was Mother Nature that decided that issue." She has an instant response, "Did you still have hope?" Wilma hopes that this is the end of the subject and replies, "I have accepted the fact, it is not a problem for me." He then texts, "How old is hubby, dear?" She thinks to herself, "I am not getting married to Mr. G." While she is thinking this, he says, "You're strong and elegant," she gives nice compliments and texts back, "He is not my husband, and I will never marry him. I got divorced, and I decided not to get married again and live in a loving relationship." After sending this message, she received, "You're not married, let me be your sugar boy 😂😂 just to give you joy and make you happy." Wilma laughs after reading this; she can hear all the jokes about taking on a toy boy and replies, "Oh, I can hear the cougar jokes now 😂😂👯‍♀️👯‍♀️." He mischievously sends back, "Can you manage a crazy violinist like me?" Wilma laughs and loves the mischievous side of the conversation and sends back, "Oh yes, I am not sure you can manage my craziness 😂😂😂😂." She had confused him with this as he sent back, "Why can't I?" Wilma thinks, "I could put you over my knee and spank you!" However, replies, "You have no idea the crazy ideas that go through my head. I am unique and have been informed I am not off my trolley. I have lost the trolley and going through life on a set of wheels 😂😂😂👾💡." At least she can make him laugh 😂😂😂😂. He then asks, "So how romantic are you?" Wilma knows she has run into a bit of trouble here, what is romance? A Yankee candle on the table when you go for a whopper at Burger King? She texts back, "What is romantic? I think a bunch of daisies from the garden with a box of Milk Tray 😂😂😂." She receives, "Don't use criminology terms here." Wilma laughs at his comment; he follows this up with, "Being cool with me, am not a criminal 😂😂." Wilma had been thinking of the Milk Tray adverts while growing up. The man in a black suit skiing down the mountain breaks into your house to deliver chocolates, with the end saying, "All because the woman loves Milk Tray!" She texted back, "Sorry! You probably never saw the adverts with the man delivering Milk Tray. They took the idea from James Bond 😂😂😂." The star asks, "What happened to the man?" He decided to say "Just be romantic," he has set mission impossible, Wilma sent back, "He got lost! I think you might find him in Switzerland eating Toblerone." He must like Wilma's sense of humour and sends back, "Your new man-child wants you to know he is loyal, and he loves you." Wilma thinks they fall in love so quickly and replies, "Awww thanks 🥰." The star then texts, "Let me see your beautiful face, I want to be moved by your beauty." Wilma is thinking, "Oh dear, this guy cannot be serious." He follows on by saying, "If I can't be secured by the young girls, I should be secured by a mom like you. 🥰🥰🥰" Wilma sends a photo of herself; he responds quickly, "You're very beautiful like a brightening star, you look astonishing." Wilma is thinking, "You need to go to Specsavers, pal, for a new set of glasses. Exceptionally smooth!" Wilma says to the star, "You must get some strange requests on social media, I know I have had some strange requests recently." He texted back, "That's normal, dear, anybody can follow you on social media." Wilma is thinking, "No shit, Sherlock." He follows up with, "I don't follow any pages until my media team confirms the page has a legit page." She goes on to tell him, "Oh, I know! I have had some fun; I had Bjorn from Abba a while ago. The profile was correct, but everything on Instagram showed a hugely different story, also kept sending me weird love letters. It had my friends laughing for ages 😂😂😂." He sends back, "😂😂😂😂 cool, what did you have for dinner?" As there was international football on TV, all the guys were at Mr. J's flat with beer, and Wilma had made lots of tapas for everyone. She had sent most of them round for the guys; she was sitting grazing away while watching 'Faking It Tears of a Crime.' She sent, "Tapas, I get the TV to myself tonight, as the guys are watching the football 🏉." She sent a picture of all the tapas she had made. He tells her, "That's cool," and follows with, "You don't watch football with them." Wilma laughs while reading the message and sends back, "No, that is for big Jessies. I am a rugby fan, a beautiful game played by men with odd-shaped balls 😂😂😂." He replies, "😂😂😂."

Wilma decides to ask, "What are your hobbies?" He responds, "Music, travelling, and reading." She asks, "What do you like to read?" He sends back, "Laws and power." Powers? Wilma is confused by the answer and tries to look it up; it is a bit weird. He then said, "Sorry am replying late Judy going home." Ok, that is weird; does he mean just going home? She sends, "What? Austin Powers? 😂😂😂." He sends back that he reads, "Noooo, The Rock Powers 😂😂." Wilma still does not have a clue and says, "Not heard of that one or anything else. Maybe Harry Potter? 😂" She then sends him a picture.

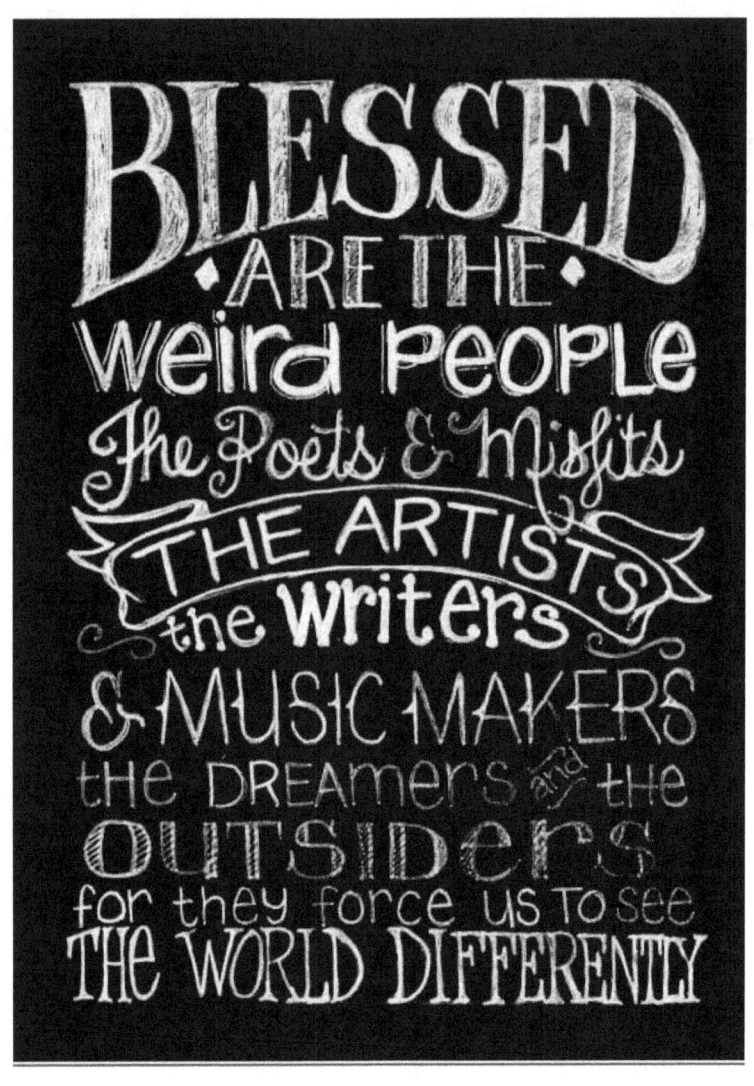

It was a bit quiet, and then she said, "Sorry, I was driving home before." She accepts what he has told her and says, "No problem, safe driving 🙏." She never heard anything for the rest of the evening. The next morning, there was a message saying he was home safely. It was coming up for midday for Wilma;

she was sitting with coffee and biscuits in her cat basket when a message came through, "Good morning." She smiled and sent back, "Good morning, how are you today?" In the Hair Bear Bunch WhatsApp group, the discussion was about how rubbish the football was as Rangers had not won. She sent a message to the star, "I made the correct decision missing the football last night. My homemade tapas went down better than the final score 😂😂😂😂." Within a few minutes, she received, "😂😂😂 I take it they were supporting Rangers, but Frankfurt won, Germany won, we won!" She sends back, "All the Rangers supporters are gutted 😂😂😂😂. They might have better luck on Saturday; I will cheer Hearts on 😂😂😂😂." He inquires, "How was school today?" She was watching the talk on Zoom coming from New Zealand and sent back, "At a virtual conference on neurodiversity and inequalities in the criminal justice system; it is interesting. I know how to have fun 😂😂😂😂." He sends back, "😂😂😂😂 I am about to teach my violin student; you need to become my student at some point!" Wilma thinks it's a bad idea and has bad images coming into her head if she tries to play the violin. Images of someone being poked in the eye with a bow. Then an image of tripping over fresh air; the violin would end up going out an open window and ending up as roadkill on the pavement. She texts, "A bad idea, a violin would turn into and end up broken in my hands. 🦸💡😂😂😂 Do you know I am a wonder woman, I wonder where I left my keys, where I left my purse, where all my money went." He replies with, "😂😂😂😂 How can you break a violin?" She thinks, "That is weird; you broke your Stradivarius in 2008." She says, "Knowing my luck, I would probably trip and fall on top of it. I do have a disastrous stunt career 😂😂😂😂" and adds, "I have even managed to chuck a 25kg bucket of yoghurt over myself. 😂😂😂 He texted back You're funny 😂😂😂😂😂." She follows on with, "I had to give up yoga; the teacher kept shouting 'timber' while trying to stand on one leg 🧘‍♀️🧘‍♂️🤸🧘‍♂️😂" then adds, "I will still take you as my student; I promise it will be easy." "Well, that's a nice invitation that is not going to happen," she replies, "😂😂😂😂 My friends would come just for the entertainment 🧘‍♀️🧘‍♂️. I suggest going axe-throwing, but they said no for health and safety reasons 😂😂😂😂." He sends back, "😂😂😂😂." Wilma goes on to say, "I will stick to blogging and being a student 😂😂😂. I fear bloggers." "Why?" he asks, "Some of them carry inaccurate information or make things up." "That can be true of some bloggers; I have just been editing my new one. I have passed it to the beautiful OrCam fairy; I have been trialling the new OrCam learn for them, and I want to make sure I have not missed anything. Even using text-to-speech to correct everything, it is good to have a second opinion 🙏. Yeah, my experience is that most of them are not like that." She tells him, "I have also been lucky enough to work with a science fiction writer and join their writing class. It helped me change my writing; my blog is a bit of fun. It is also hugely different from writing academically; you're doing well momma." That made her feel old when reading it, "What have you consumed today?" she asks, "Just getting pasta and pesto ready for later tonight 😊." The conversation ended after a few hours. Wilma was feeling mischievous and sent a YouTube video of Danny Bhoy, a Scottish comedian talking about how the orchestra was made, and Scotland was late turning up with the bagpipes.

Wilma was going to meet the Product Manager of Texthelp later that week. He hated the bagpipes and kept telling her they sounded like a cat in a blender. Wilma kept teasing him about his dislike and joked that she was going to find an angry bagpiper to chase him around. She told the star, "I am going to have complaints about bagpipes next week 😂." "Why?" he asked. "So," she tells him, "I am going to an assistive technology conference, and one of the people I have been working with keeps complaining about bagpipers. "He says it's a horrible noise 😂😂😂," he responds with laughing emojis.

At this point, Wilma decides to stir up some mischief and sends the Product Manager at Texthelp a message on LinkedIn, featuring the Red-Hot Chilli Pipers playing "Thunderstruck." She received a large complaint back! Later, she tells the star, "I just had to have some mischief and asked him if he was buying a set of bagpipes next week. 😂😂😂😂 He told me to stop trolling him 😂😂😂😃 followed by, 'Is he still angry about Rangers?' He has got his stories muddled up; she was talking about bagpipes."

She says, "The Hair Bear Bunch are the Rangers supporters, and that is fun for tomorrow evening when we meet up for shenanigans. 😂😂😂😂" and continues, "Friday nights are always pub night and mayhem 😂😂😂😂." She busies herself looking through TikTok while waiting for a response and says, "I see you have started following me on TikTok! Oh dear 😂😂😂😂"

He sends back, "😂😂😂😂." She then inquires, "I can only hope you have not murdered any of your students!" However, he did not send any more text messages that day.

Happy Friday!!

Wilma has finished the majority of her work and sends a text to the star: "Hi, hope you are going to have a great evening with friends that is full of mayhem and laughter 🙏." He eventually answers her text with "Sure and you!" Wilma laughs and says, "I can't wait! My group always starts the evening with a sensible conversation, but it never lasts long 😂😂😂😂."

Sometime later, Wilma is sitting with a pint of cider, engaging in nonsensical banter with the Hair Bear Bunch. The main topic was about the football match scheduled for the following day. They were curious about what tapas she was making for everyone. She had to make some black olive tapenade, as Mr J had commented it was the nicest black olive tapenade he had eaten outside of Spain. They all decided to tease Mr D, who confidently asserted that Rangers would win the football match the next day. Amidst the laughter, Wilma texted the star, "Oh, I have been banned from watching the football tomorrow. 😂😂😂😂" He inquires, "Why?" Wilma responds, "Well apparently, I am a traitor for supporting the wrong side. Love getting them going 😈😂." The Hair Bear Bunch decided to playfully gang up on Wilma, teasing her for causing chaos. She was jokingly accused of living an easy student life, leaving crisp crumbs and salted popcorn everywhere, and allowing red wine boxes to leave red streaks down the fridge. Amused, Wilma texted the star, "Oh yes, the guys say stay single; we women cause nothing but chaos by upsetting a man's routine. Doing annoying things such as letting the box of red wine leave red streaks down the front of the fridge. You can never find stuff because the location has been changed 😂😂😂 The fun I have 😈😂😂."

He asks, "How's your day?" Amidst the laughter and jokes, she replies, "Messy! I realized that I had muddled things up with my assignment. I have spent a lot of time sorting it out. It's all the laptop's fault, nothing to do with the muppet operating it 😂.😂😂😂." She then adds, "The beautiful fairy at OrCam thinks the new blog is great. Wilma blundering around in further education continues 😂😂😂." He responds, "That's cool; you're professional. Aww, thanks 😊." Then inquires, "What have you been up to today?" He mentions being in New York, although Wilma had seen pictures of him standing with the Brooklyn Bridge behind him on Instagram. Despite knowing this, she jokingly says, "Stop talking to me and get out with your friends 😂😂😂" and sends him the message. She thinks he should be going clubbing in New York with his friends.

"😂😂😂 I hope you have a great time with your friends tonight. Try not to play ping pong with your keys while trying to get into your house 🧕🔑😂😂😂😂😂 Also, don't wake up in the morning with a half-eaten kebab plastered to your pillow and face with chilli sauce in your eye 🙏😂😂." The conversation ended for the evening, and Wilma had lots of laughter with the Hair Bear Bunch before heading home with Mr. G. The next day, Wilma had a lecture to help her prepare for her last assignment of the year. She also had been chatting on WhatsApp with her friend Dr Dodgy Shoes, who was working in Munich, telling her he was working hard in the sunshine, though she suspected he was more likely drinking beer and eating pretzels! Later that afternoon, she texts the star: "Hope you are well; I've had a busy morning. That was the last lecture for my second year. Great chat annoying my brilliant friend Dr. Dodgy Shoes. I can only hope I've made enough tapas for this afternoon's football 😃."

"He sends it back 😂😂😂. The Hair Bear Bunch were at Mr. J's to watch the football with beer and tapas. Meanwhile, Wilma was content in her student cave, sipping a glass of wine and watching a program on Ted Bundy. She kept an eye on the football scores via Twitter. When she saw the final score, she knew Mr. D would be over the moon. She then messaged the star, 'Rangers won! Damn it! 🧕💡😂😂😂.' Feeling mischievous, she sent 'Steps - Tragedy.' The Hair Bear Bunch weren't impressed, and she received lots of rude replies, which only made her laugh."

"She adds, 'Shame for Hearts 🙀💡.' He texts back, 'I watched it - Rangers won on extra time. I know; I followed it on Twitter. I have the house to myself; they are watching the football elsewhere 😂😂😂. I have been putting the cat amongst the pigeons and receiving very rude messages from Rangers fans 🤪🤪🤪🤪.' He sends, 'You're among Rangers' fans and you're supporting Hearts. You're stirring the pot! This is true, but we are all friends; we love annoying each other. They will get their own back; I have a wooden spoon and like to stir things 😺😺😺.' He reacts to her stories with 😂😂😂😂. She jokes, 'I did warn you that I am bat-shit crazy 🤪🤪🤪.' A bit later that evening, Wilma sends, 'Oh yeah, and my tapas are dangerous. I have been told off as they make men fat and cuddly as they need to eat them all, #itsatrap 🤪🤪🤪.' He answers with 😂😂😂😂🥲. They didn't talk for the rest of the evening. The following day, Wilma sends, 'Hello, how are you doing today? 🙏 I am fine and you; hope you're cool.' While checking Facebook to see what her friends are up to, she sends, 'Oh, fine. At present, I am trying to find out when my friend from Dr Dodgy Shoes will be returning home to catch up.' Dr. Dodgy Shoes had invited Wilma to Malaga to see his project, the Dyslexic Compass. She was trying to find information for booking flights, etc. She adds, 'He is busy working in Munich at present. I don't believe him; he keeps posting pictures of himself drinking beer and eating pretzels in the sunshine with the bears 🤣🤣🤣🤣.' He replies, 'Oh, that's cool, pretty. Yeah, he travels a lot with his job. He wants me to see a project he has been working on called the Dyslexic Compass in September in Malaga ☺.' Then adds, 'It will be weird meeting him in person; we have talked on Zoom over the pandemic 🤣🤣🤣🤣.' He replies, 'That's cool, I am just about to teach a pupil violin. Please let me know when I can teach you how to play.' She thinks the poor violin will end up murdered and hidden at the bottom of a wheelie bin. She texts, 'I remember trying to learn to play the drums; I do not have the coordination. I understand the technical side, however, playing is another issue 🤣🤣🤣🤣.' Then adds, 'It is a very kind offer; I think I would be the worst violin student you have ever met 🤣🤣🤣.' She didn't hear anything else that evening." Wilma spends the next day studying at the Open University, Open Learn on coaching and mentoring. Later in the evening, she says hello how are you today? He sends back fine and you dear I hope you are well. She replies I am excited about tomorrow's assistive technology conference. I love using writing helper to aid my assignments. I am also getting to see how Talk type works along with a new app called Booost, Scanning Pens and Habitat. I just need an angry bagpiper for the product manager at Texthelp 😂😂😂😂. The next day Wilma gets the bus through to her assistive technology conference. She walked in to find out she was the only person to turn up. There was supposed to be a competition at the end, and Wilma thought she would win a prize for a change. However, this did not happen, they did joke about sending out bloody Marys and oysters as she was the only person to turn up LOL. Wilma showed the prototype of the OrCam learn for aiding dyslexia to everyone, they had heard about it and went around taking pictures of signs and having them read. As she was the only one to be at the conference, it was an early finish and Wilma went for a wonder.

She sends the star a photo and says, "I was let out for the day 🤭🤭🤭," then adds, "I was the only person to turn up 🤭🤭🤭🤭." After having a wander around some shops, Wilma went for her bus home. Later in the evening, while looking through Instagram, she noticed a new picture of the star with his pinkie in a splint. Now, Wilma had been a first aider for years and had seen plenty of sprained and broken pinkies. She sends, "How did you injure your pinkie? 🧐💡." He doesn't reply to Wilma, and it's quiet for a week. While flicking through Facebook, she sees pictures of her friend, Dr Dodgy Shoes, in Munich's square, celebrating a football cup win. So, she decides to send her congratulations. He replies, "I don't follow football." She finds it odd, considering they had discussed football previously. She says, "My friend is in Munich and has posted pictures of football celebrations; I'm not sure what cup they won 😃." He just says, "Oh, I am not into football." Wilma ponders this since he had watched football last weekend. He stops talking to her for a while. It was a beautiful day, and Wilma was walking along the Haberdashery shores and chatting with Dr. Dodgy Shoes. She decides to text the star, "I had a lovely phone call on WhatsApp from my friend at Dr Dodgy Shoes'. He loves travelling but says there's nothing better than coming home to sleep in his bed. While travelling, he never gets around to seeing anything in the country he's visiting because he's too busy working. You might face the same issues at times." Again, she hears nothing. Wilma notices another promotion he's doing on Facebook and Instagram. She texts him, "Well, you say that you're just a violinist. I'd disagree; you're much more entrepreneurial than you give yourself credit for. You inspire many people 🙏." He replies, "Thanks dear, no problem. Take care of yourself 🙏."The next day, Wilma's doing more studying on coaching and mentoring. She decides to put into practice some of what she's been learning and texts the star, "I know you're busy. I was wondering how you'd like to see our friendship develop." He responds, "Sorry, dear, how's work on your side? I've been trying to figure out what's wrong with my assistive technology. It's always a problem when it breaks down. I'm tempted to bury it in a shallow grave in the garden. I must inform the OrCam fairy that I'm still having technical issues 🤦 🤦 🤦. I've had a warm and positive response regarding a campaign on dyslexia and mental health for Succeed with Dyslexia on my LinkedIn account. What have you been up to?" He doesn't say anything else that evening.

The following evening was beautiful and warm, so Wilma and Mr. G decided to go out for a couple of beers. They might as well take advantage of the weather since it usually didn't last long before the rain returned. She was feeling mischievous and sent the star...

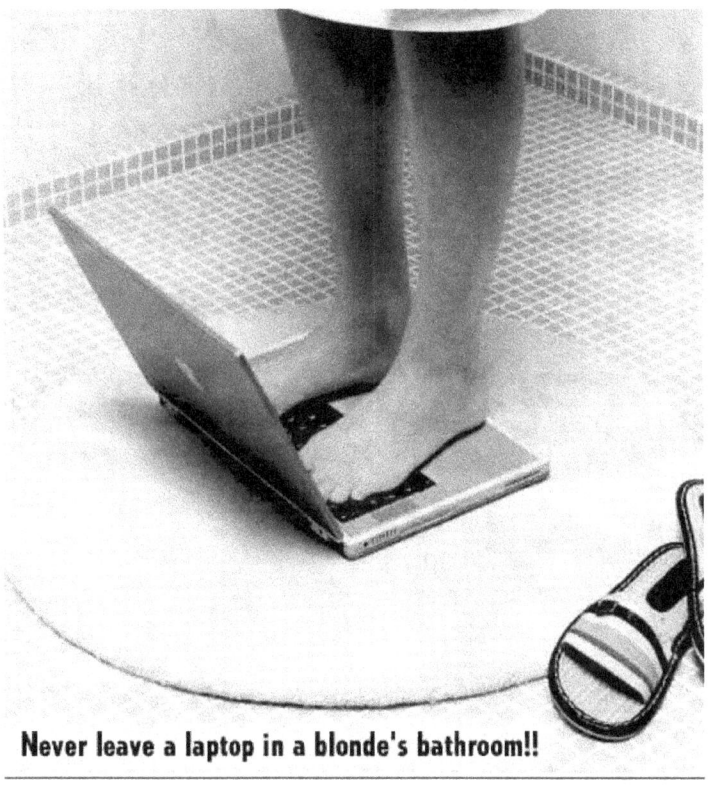

Never leave a laptop in a blonde's bathroom!!

🤣🤣🤣🤣 He replies 😂😂😂😂 She then sends

> I applied for a job at a mental asylum and they told me i have to spend 5 hours with a crazy person. wanna hang out tomorrow?
>
> i got crayons!

Again, he sends it back 😂😂😂

Not only does my mind wander...
Sometimes it fucks off completely...

Wilma asks, "How are you doing?" She's feeling great, relaxing in the sun. It's evening, and the beer garden is empty. The Google meeting with the OrCam representative went well, and the device is finally working! "I've solved my IT issues, and my last assignment is back on track. 😁" He responds, "That's cool! How's your husband?" Wilma shares this with Mr. G, who bursts out laughing and jokingly says, "Tell him this 🤣🤣🤣 I will never marry him! He is his usual happy-go-lucky self! Mr. Grumpy 🤣🤣🤣." She receives a message saying, "😂😂😂 come and marry me." She bursts out laughing again and tells Mr. G, who humorously remarks that he's still looking for a refund, unfortunately, as the place they met has now shut down. She responds, "Nooooooooooooo 🤣🤣🤣🤣 Even kidnappers would give me back. 🤣🤣🤣🤣" then adds, "You must like scary movies 🤣🤣🤣🤣." He sends back, "😂😂😂😂😂😂." The sun was setting, so Wilma and Mr. G decided to head home. Wilma made some nice peppermint tea for herself and Mr. G. She then sent the star a clip of Sheldon singing "Soft Kitty" to Penny in The Big Bang Theory.

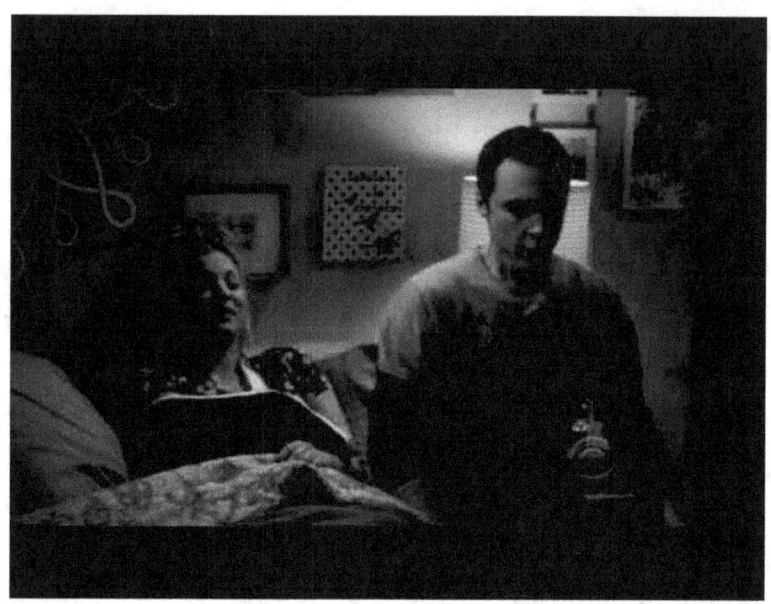

She wished him "Sweet dreams whenever you go to bed xx." He replied, "Thanks, dear. Goodnight." Sipping her peppermint tea, she heard a loud snore emanating from Mr G in his cosy basket. After finishing her tea and the episode of The Big Bang Theory, she headed to bed.

Wilma remained quiet for a while, meticulously assembling her compare-and-contrast assignment for submission and marking. She commemorated the completion of year two by posting a photo on social media and sharing it with the star.

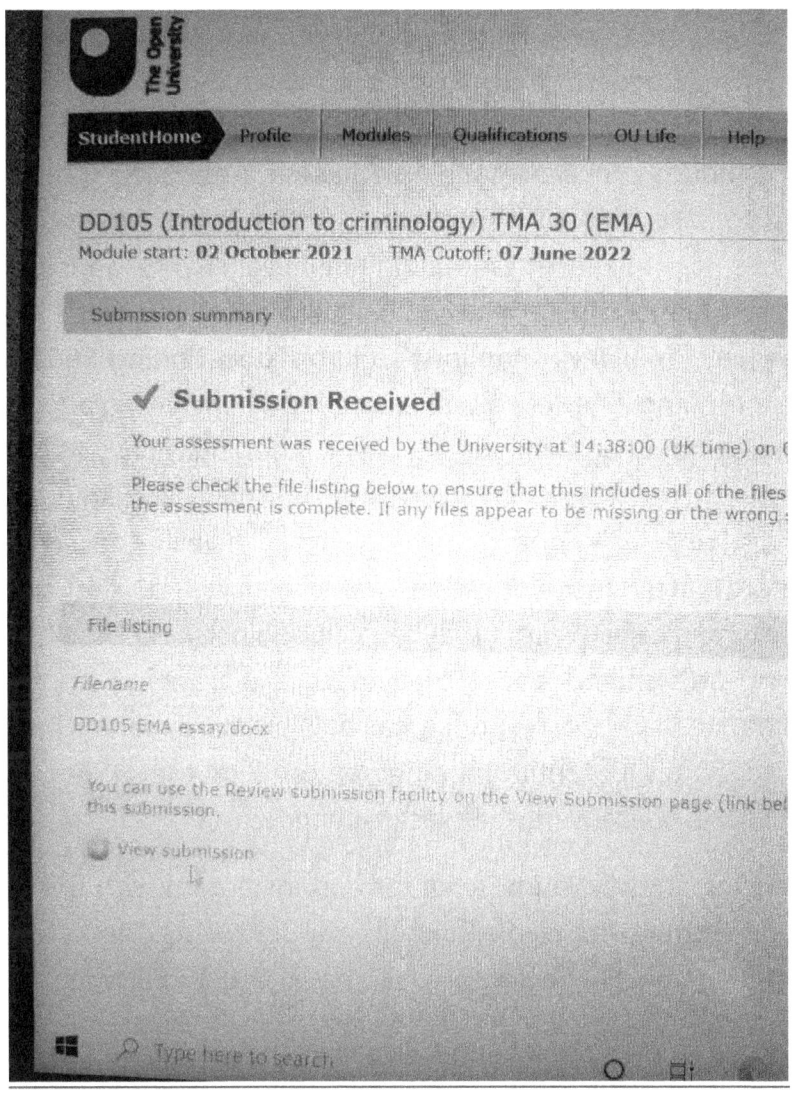

She messaged, "Year 2 is complete, hopefully, I have passed! Now to sign up for my third year, I think I have melted my brain cell 😅." He replied, "Congratulations, that's a big win, you're a scholar." Wilma, not feeling quite like a scholar, replied, "Thanks. I have another 4 years to go, and I might just have a degree. Some days I surprise myself, and I have other days when I wonder why I put my keys in the microwave 🧕💡😵."Seeing the star's busy schedule from his social media posts about concert setups, Wilma sent a message reminding him to take care of himself and allocate time for things he enjoys 🙏. However, she didn't receive any response. One night, while occupied with Mr. G and Mr. D on a project, Wilma watched "The Devil's Violinist" on YouTube, finding Paganini's life intriguing. She sent a text mentioning her viewing and some details about Paganini but got only a laughing reply 😂😂. She then inquired if he enjoyed playing the role of Paganini and if he'd consider another acting role given the chance. Unfortunately, those questions went unanswered. After several weeks of silence, Wilma reached out again asking how he was doing and shared about trialling a new scanning pen from China. However, his response was only a simple "sure." She also joked about potentially being featured in the DSA OrCam brochure. These were their last exchanges.

Later, she saw a photo of him on Instagram with the word 'dildo' next to it. Wilma jokingly thought if he marketed his brand of dildos, he might become a larger millionaire with many satisfied customers worldwide.

The Case of the Man from Instagram: Let's Chat on Telegram

Wilma received another message on Instagram one day saying, "Hi, my darling fan, I have created this temporary page to contact my lovely fans." Wilma texted back a simple "thanks." "Where are you from?" she inquired. "I am from St. Trianians, my friend." "How long have you been a fan?" "Approximately 8 years now!" "Wow, thank you for your love and support so far. I know you are surprised I have reached out to chat with you." She thought, 'Oh, how little you know that I am not surprised at all.' "What is your occupation?" he asked. "I train and support people with assistive technology." "Wow, nice role. I hope your work doesn't stress you and pays you well." "I love what I do. It does get stressful at times, but what job doesn't?" He must have looked at Wilma's profile picture as she had not allowed him access to her account. She received a text saying, "I must say, your beauty is astonishing. Are you married with children?" "Another one who needs to go to Specsavers! Why, thank you! No, I am not married. I don't have any children either." "I would like to know if you have a fan card," he asked. "Well, he is quick at trying to sell something that does not exist," she thought. She returns, "No, and according to your website, there is no fan club." He proceeds with, "There is a fan club which comes with a lot of benefits." Wilma puts on her sceptical glasses. "I will think about it. I have other things going on at present. I'm not always here, and I would like us to keep communicating so we can get to know each other better." "Do you use the Telegram app?" he questioned. "Yes, I do have the Telegram app. Please tell me your number," which he does, and they start chatting on Telegram. Wilma starts the conversation with, "Hi, I found you eventually!" She receives a GIF of a kangaroo with boxing gloves on waving to her, followed by, "It is nice to have you here," and sends a picture of a big bouquet of flowers. "Oh, nice flowers. I wonder where on the internet he found that picture," she thought, but texted, "Nice to meet you!" "So, tell me, what do you enjoy the most about my performance?" She thinks and texts back, "That is a good question as I don't know much about the music industry. I am just an end-user! I am not sure how to judge someone's performance." "I love your sincerity, and I'd like to know more about you!" "Okay, let's see how long it will take to bore him to death," she jokes, and texts, "I am just a loony blundering through life! I am a dyslexic person and aid in supporting a minority community! Dyslexia is perceived as stupidity because of the complex issues. I can read and write very slowly, but I get the big picture of things because of the way my brain works." "You are great, and I don't believe you to be a minority individual. I believe that you are strong, independent, and awesome." "Thank you for your kind words. I know that there are plenty of dyslexic people who are left behind and not supported. I am lucky and do my best to help others who are not as fortunate!" "I am impressed and must say you are lovely, dear! The world needs love, peace, and unity. I want you to be able to express yourself freely here." Wilma thinks about this and what she has been learning in her social science studies and texts back, "It is a beautiful thought. There are too many inequalities in the world to sort out." "That is true.

Let love lead the way." "Where are you living presently?" Wilma thinks that is something you don't need to know and texts back, "In my house." He replies, "I meant the country you live in LOL." She decides to answer this with a sly question of her own, "Why did you get a bat tattooed over your belly button?" He replies, "I love tattoos." "Well, that is the wrong answer, as I am sure it is a transfer that got a fake celebrity on my hands." He then said, "I love your approach and your manners; I would love to chat with you again when I am less busy. Don't forget to write to me when you are free... take care." "No problem, enjoy chilling out. I will text you later, enjoy sweet dreams," she replies. She goes on to listen to ABBA singing "Angel Eyes" before heading to bed.

The following day she receives, "Good morning, how was your night, dear? It feels good to have you again." "Hmmm, I wonder if he has been having strange erotic dreams involving a tin of squooshy cream and a jar of maraschino cherries?" she jokes in her mind. She keeps the conversation clean and texts back, "I had a good night, ready for another day. How are you today? "I am good. What are you up to today?" he asks. "I have a few projects which I have started and need to catch up on." "Okay, dear, I also have a lot to do today. Please write to me when you are less busy; we can talk and get to know each other a bit better. Have a lovely day, kisses and hugs." "You take care of yourself. I know you are busy. Enjoy your day," she replies. Wilma had decided to get out for the day with Mr G as he was on holiday. They decided to have a day out in the city as lockdown did not allow them to go far. Wilma's phone pinged with, "Hello dear, how is your day going?" She texted, "Fine," and continued chatting with Mr. G. He sent back, "I just had you on my mind. Please inform me when you are ready to chat." "Lol, I spend a lot of time chatting online and supporting people; you will be busy organizing concerts." "You are right, but I have my manager to handle anything about my concerts. So, how do you support people online?" "I talk to them about where they are struggling with dyslexia. What reasonable adjustments do they feel they need, maybe a quiet space to fill in their paperwork with some extra time? It works differently for everyone." "My dear, you are doing a fantastic job!" he responds. She sends a screenshot from a follower on Twitter, saying, "Your tweets are on fire. Thank you for being vocal about dyslexia; you have given me the strength to speak up." She added, "I received this message on Twitter yesterday. I am impressed; you are saving lives!" "So, tell me about your relationship life. Are you in any relationship now?" He inquires while she's chatting with Mr. G. "Please let me know if you don't want to talk about your relationship life." "Well, part of what I do is build relationships to support people. What kind of relationship are you talking about?" She already knows the answer but does not want to delve into the whole thing. "I would like to know if you have a special person in your life presently!" She decides to answer, "Well, my best friend is a guy! I don't sleep with him!" He texts back, "You guys are not serious with each other which could lead to marriage." She laughs at the statement, as they had both agreed a long time ago that they would not get married. "I have been married! It's a bad deal from my point of view. I can have perfectly normal relationships with men and not sleep with them. I just like their company. I do get a lot of stick, but I can be just as rude back to them! I enjoy my life and am not bothered about being intimate with someone." "Wow, that means your ex-husband has wronged you that you don't want to settle with another man again? I want to know; will you remarry if you find any man who has true love and care for you?" "No, I will not get married again. I would rather make a whole lot of new mistakes! I am not something which is owned like a piece of jewellery! They are locked away to be viewed by only one person because of their issues." "The ring on the finger changes a lot of things," he says. He then goes on to sell himself, "Well, I am an exciting, thoughtful, and compassionate man with a strong passion for life. I'm optimistic and warm, seeing every day as a new beginning. I've been through a lot and conquered much opposition in life. I would love to meet someone who'll understand how hurt feels and would love to find an honest relationship. I want the love that has been unlocked in my heart to be unlocked by that special lady. Life is special, and I like to wake up feeling excited about what a new day brings, even if it means bouncing off the planets." "Imagine opening your eyes every morning and smiling at the thought of a new day. It's completely different and brings new excitement, and that person you are with feels the same way." Wilma can hear the Vengaboys playing in her head, "Boom Boom Boom!" She thinks, "Life is special, and everyone has complex relationships! Everyone has been hurt in relationships. I do wake up every morning and wonder what life will bring, after I have found my glasses, I cannot see a damn thing without them." "I am an optimist who believes that everything happens for a good reason, and you never know what destiny has for you and someone together." She thinks of baking a special cake and feeding it to him, making sure it is nice and moist! He continues, "I want you to have a fan card, what do you think about it?" "I will stick with the advice your website gives that it doesn't exist. I am a very fun-loving person, but also very sceptical! I'm talking to you directly, and you seem not to believe me." (Oh, she seems to have annoyed him.) "So, you don't feel lonely sometimes? I mean the loneliness of not having a man next to you?" "Lonely at times, yes! I just talk to the Hair Bear Bunch who constantly try to embarrass me with their innuendos! I have my favourite Garfield to cuddle at night, and he is less likely to keep me awake by snoring." He informs her, "I feel lonely a lot of the time. That's why I need to find my true love! A person who will love me as much as I love her. I have a feeling that destiny brought us together for a reason!" She has the sarcastic person in her head shouting, "Oh, my handsome prince, let down your hair, and we can share a true love kiss." She sends the sensible text saying, "We will see how things work out! It is early days. Every relationship takes time! As much as I love watching 'Dirty Dancing,' it's just a Hollywood movie and life doesn't work that way." She sends a YouTube video of Russell Brand having a raunchy phone call on the Graham Norton Show. Russell must pretend to be Aladdin and phone a sex line to see if the person on the line can guess the panto. She adds, "I can be just as dirty-minded as any man." He returns, "I find you so open-minded and fun to be around." She thinks, "I must be with the Hair Bear Bunch," and texts back, "That I am open-minded and just become part of a gang of guys! I love the fun and laughs, even if it is at my expense." "Wow, when is your birthday?" he asks. She responds, "Don't worry about my birthday! Everyone forgets it! Tell me, do you see me like everyone else?" "No, I don't!" he replies. "My star sign? I have a license to do whatever I want. If you must know, you are a Virgo, and I am a Sagittarius. This is not a good match as Sagittarius are free spirits; they enjoy travelling, physically or mentally. They do not like to be pushed around and have their own life to live. Their personality is wild, independent, fun, friendly, outgoing, optimistic, big dreamer, spontaneous, ruthless, creative, and curious. They like freedom and travel. They're philosophers, enjoy being outdoors, and dislike clingy people and constraints." "They try to avoid petty drama and focus on themselves instead. They don't fall in love immediately but are loyal and caring when in love. If you think a relationship will work for you and it will be different, they will walk away as they won't settle in a relationship that makes them unhappy." He reflects on this and responds, "I won't forget, my lady; you are special to me!" She sarcastically replies, "Yeah, right! You will be too busy with Christmas concerts on show. My birthday will be the last thing on your list!" "It's not the way you think, dear unless you don't take me the way I take you. Look, I don't care about my birthday anymore! I love Christmas, and everyone is more concerned about what happens then! I will still listen to Christmas tunes, eat mince pies, and have a glass of wine or seven. Please respect my wishes and leave the subject alone. It's just another day in my life." "I respect your wishes already," he concedes. Wilma changes the topic and asks, "What comedies do you enjoy watching?" He replies, "I watch and listen to all kinds of comedy, what about you?" She laughs at his response and sends a YouTube video of Sheldon singing 'Soft Kitty' to Penny after she has an accident on The Big Bang Theory. He responds, "Hahahaha, I also love playing games." "What games do you enjoy playing?" she inquires. He mentions playing Google Play Mission games and spending a lot on Apple cards due to his frequent playing. She responds, "Okay, that means nothing to me." He responds "Why are you so mean, babe?" he asks. She clarifies, "I am not being mean! I just don't play whatever you are talking about! It's fine, what do you do for leisure? I go for a walk, or do a bit of art and design, cooking." "Beautiful, can you draw a picture of me?" he asks. She replies, "I am hopeless at portraits, but I do try. I am not a good artist," and sends him a couple of drawings. He laughs and compliments her effort, and she responds, "There is always room for improvement, I am sure this is not your cup of tea when it comes to art!" Not She decided to test him, asking, "What sort of art are you into?" He responded with "Human and building portraits." "They are cool! I am more into the impressionist era, personally. I love Vincent Van Gogh, Picasso, etc!" He then abruptly left, saying, "Yes, dear, I will talk to you later. Take care." Wilma, unfazed, decided to listen to Bucks Fizz's "The Land of Make Believe" and replied to his departure with, "Have a good night's sleep! Sweet dreams."

The following morning, she received a picture of a bowl of flowers with a "Good morning, dear" message. She quipped, "Morning, wow, that is an amazing display! How was your night? I hope you slept well!" "It was nice and chilled out, I had a good sleep. What are you getting up to today?" he asked. She responded, "About to go to a rehearsal," adding a reminder for him to take regular breaks. He assured her, "Thanks, dear, of course I will." Knowing how easy it is to lose track of time, Wilma engaged in conversation, "It's easy to get carried away when we are having fun." He asked about her plans, to which she replied, "I will be running my OrCam Learn over some books I need to read." He showed interest, "Oh cool, you love reading too?" "Yes, I love reading books! However, it leaves me exhausted and takes me ages. My OrCam Learn turns text into audio and reads everything to me," she explained, sending a video demonstrating the OrCam Learn laser technology turning full pages into audio and reading. "Wow, that is impressive and less stressful!" he remarked.

Continuing the conversation, she explained, "Yes, they aid many people who are visually impaired, blind, and have learning disabilities like me." He inquired, "Do you have poor vision?" She humorously compared herself to Daphne from Scooby-Doo without her glasses and confessed to being short-sighted, needing glasses for everything. He abruptly shifted gears, asking, "Do you know about crypto trading?" Sensing the direction, she replied, "The only thing I know about Crypto trading is that it goes straight to my spam mail! I guess you have invested in it, right?" He persisted, "So, you don't care about the worthwhile investment and interest that comes with it?" Ignoring his attempts to push the subject, he changed the topic, asking, "Where are you presently? Are you home or out?"

Trying to deflect, she replied, "I am out for a short walk to clear my head and listen to Steps' 'Heartbeat'." He suddenly requested an unusual favour, asking for her help to purchase an iTunes card, claiming it was an urgent and unusual request. Wilma recognized this as a typical fraud and refused, saying, "Sorry, I don't know what you are talking about with your request. I am nowhere near a mall now." She played Jonny Hates Jazz's "Shattered Dreams," signifying her refusal to comply with his request. Scammer: "So, there is no way you can get it for me, please!" Wilma: "Sorry, I can't help you out presently." Scammer: "It's fine. I hope someone didn't upset you today?" Wilma: "Why should I be upset? Just take it easy, okay? When will you be going shopping?" Wilma decides not to disclose her plans and replies, "I have no idea when I will go shopping." Scammer: "I would appreciate it if you could subscribe to a game for me. It's just a favour, my best friend and lover. The amount is more than £300 but I can manage it before I can do it myself, I hope you understand." Wilma: "I don't game, so I have no idea what you are talking about." Scammer insists, "Just help me buy a Stream card from the store." Wilma chooses to ignore the request and responds firmly, "I am also not your best friend or your lover! "After a while, he texts again, "Hello, so what are you to me?" Wilma: "I am getting to know you, maybe the start of a friendship who knows!" Scammer: "So, it's why you find it difficult to assist me with the favour? "Wilma detects the fraud attempt and asserts, "Call me sceptical, but strangers asking people they don't know for Google cards etc. is probably a fraud!" Scammer: "So, you see me as a fraud?" Wilma clarifies, "Well, if the shoe fits, wear it. I'm saying it is untraceable money and plenty of scammers use this while asking for favors! I'm fairly sure that your entourage would have this under control. "Scammer: "I understand you clearly, and my management is working on it already." Wilma, unconvinced, replies, "Time is a great hero in my life! I can assure you I will always check what I can and make my mind up! Good night from me and have a peaceful night x." He leaves her alone for a few days, then contacts her again, "Hi! Hello, how are you today? "The scammer, slightly annoyed, responds, "Helping people is wonderful but you are refusing to help me, why?" Wilma thinks that is because advice costs nothing, unlike a Google stream card. Wilma replies: "Typical! It always comes back to Google Stream or iTunes cards. I have lots of people asking me for them, it makes my life interesting to see how people react when I say no. "Wilma maintains her stance, "I could draft a book about the number of times I have been asked for cards." Scammer: "So, do you also take me the same with all the other people you have met? "Wilma: "No, I am not! What I am doing is sticking to my principles." He leaves her alone for a while, and during that time, she engages in a conversation about recent performances and visiting her parents. Wilma engages in a conversation about the stress of returning to the stage after the pandemic with someone she suspects to be a scammer. Despite the scammer's persistence in seeking help with purchasing cards, Wilma stands firm and doesn't comply, citing her scepticism about such requests due to her studies in criminology and her experiences encountering online fraud. The scammer seems disappointed by Wilma's refusal and implies she doesn't trust or believe in their words.

Wilma explains that she questions people's motives due to encountering numerous fraud attempts online, resulting in some individuals blocking her when she scrutinizes their intentions. After a while, Wilma attempts to reach out again, acknowledging the person's busy schedule and wishing them a pleasant weekend. However, when the person doesn't respond, she decides to block them and move on.

The Scenario Involves Purchasing the Google Stream Card.

"Hello, dear. While browsing my profile, I came across yours and felt a connection. That's why I've decided to reach out through this platform. As my administrator oversees my official account, I wanted to connect with you personally to get to know you better. "Wilma responds with, "Hello and thank you for reaching out. I hope you're doing well. I'm Wilma, and it's a pleasure to make your acquaintance. "Shortly after, Wilma receives a message praising her lifestyle and acknowledging the positive aspects of her career. "It's truly heartwarming to have people on chat recommending and appreciating my lifestyle and professional achievements from around the world. I'm genuinely grateful for the support. "Wilma ponders a suitable response and receives a follow-up question: "Where are you from?" She replies, "Everyone has their unique lifestyle and experiences. Life is what you make it; it's short, and you have an incredible talent. Personally, I could never play the violin. Keep up the amazing work."The person responds, "Thank you for liking my page and the unwavering support. I hope you'll continue to enjoy my music. I'm a busy individual and rarely have time to chat, but I took a moment from my schedule to reach out. Could you share your WhatsApp number? "Wilma replies, "I understand your busy schedule. If you'd like, you can share your circumstances with me." They proceed to chat on WhatsApp, and Wilma traces the number to North America, specifically southeastern Wisconsin. It becomes apparent to

Wilma during their conversation that she's dealing with a scammer. The conversation on WhatsApp began with a typical greeting: "Hi, Wilma. How are you doing today?" The person responds, "I'm doing well, and you?" They proceed with a purpose: "I've been occupied with shows and various engagements, travelling. Thank you for all your support and love; it means a lot. I'm seeking someone I can trust as there are things, I need to oversee without my management knowing. I need a loyal fan to assist." Wilma, sceptical of the claim about secrecy from the impersonated individual's management, responds, "Okay, everyone has their secrets." Curious, she probes further: "What is it that you can't manage yourself?" In response to his inquiry about her location, she improvises and replies, "Texas. "Her phone blinks with a new message, and the person asks, "Do you live with your family?" Wilma responds simply, "Yes, I do. Thanks," avoiding further details. When asked about her age, she randomly chooses "thirty-five." Even though she knows the age of the person being impersonated, she asks, "How old are you?" The person becomes irritated, responding, "I am not here for jokes, okay! "Wilma innocently asks, "What do you mean? What do you think I'm joking about?" Then, the person questions, "Is that you in the profile?" Wilma, aiming to deflect suspicion, replies, "Yes, it's my profile. Do I look old? "The scammer becomes increasingly confused and annoyed. After scrutinizing Wilma's Instagram photos, he comments, "Wow! I just checked your pictures; you look young. I was wrong." Wilma responds with a simple "thanks," not revealing much. The scammer remains suspicious and questions the authenticity of her profile picture. Wilma humorously replies,

"Well, it's not Snow White on my profile picture." She then asks him what age he thought she was, realizing he's trying to catch her out. He admits, "I was totally wrong," commenting that the WhatsApp picture looks older, but she appears younger in other Instagram photos. Describing her outfit in a picture, Wilma responds, "Okay, so I dress weird." He responds with agreement, to which she playfully replies, "I can live with being weird. I hope you're okay with that. "The conversation takes an odd turn as he requests to see how she looks presently. She sends a photo from her phone, mentioning she won't change. He compliments her appearance, admitting he thought she was older due to the WhatsApp profile picture. He then asks if she's married or single, to which she responds that she's currently single. He shares his age (41), prompting her to wonder if he's searching for information online. He proceeds to ask about children, to which she responds negatively. He inquired about her visits to the UK, noting her UK number. Wilma tactfully responds that she's presently studying in the UK. When asked about her profession, she states she helps people with learning difficulties. He revisits her Texan origin and UK residence, seeking clarification. Wilma hopes the conversation takes a different turn and responds positively, "Yes, that would be lovely; it would be nice to get to know you." He then asks, "Have you been married before?" Wilma briefly shares, "Yes, it was a disaster." Hoping to avoid the topic, she doesn't elaborate on her ex-husband, hoping he won't dig deeper. The person empathizes, saying, "Oh, sorry about that," and continues, "I seek true happiness and peace. "Wilma finds it a bit cheesy but plays along, stating, "He's out of my life now. I'm happy he's gone." The person then asks, "Are you a good woman with a good heart? "Wilma, in jest, thinks of a witty response but settles on, "I hope so."

The next question is more direct: "Can I trust you?" Wilma knows the person can't trust her but responds, "Yes, you can trust me." When asked why, he explains his concern about potential leaks impacting his career. Knowing the person texting isn't an international star, Wilma reassures him, "Don't worry, I won't say anything." He thanks her for her confidentiality, and she assures him it's no problem. He proceeds to ask, "How long have you been living in the UK?" Wilma improvises, "A few years now."

The next query arrives: "Do you live alone?" Enjoying the imaginative storytelling, Wilma responds, "I live with a lovely group of friends." He then probes about her thoughts on marriage, to which Wilma bluntly asks, "Why do you ask?" Suspicious of his intentions, she tries to dissuade him, sharing stories of failed marriages. He disagrees, suggesting there are good men out there. Wilma asserts, "It was an unbelievably troubled relationship; I would make different mistakes in my next relationship." He empathizes, reassures her, and expresses hope for her future. Continuing to describe himself, he shares traits like being fun-loving, jovial, passionate, and responsible. Wilma, sceptical of his idealized self-description, plays along, describing herself as a "bat-shit crazy girl who loves life," adding characteristics she believes describe her well. He asks about the time, but Wilma avoids giving specifics, stating it's nearly her bedtime due to an early morning ahead. He says it's late for him as well, asking her to wake him up with a message in the morning. Wilma, feeling it's not her responsibility, wishes him good night, and sweet dreams, and mentions chatting when free.

The next day, Wilma was busy sorting through emails and studying her course in her student cave when her phone flashed with a WhatsApp message: "Good morning, dear. How are you today?" "Doing well, thanks for asking," she replied. He then expressed his complaint about her not waking him up. Uninterested in initiating the conversation, she responded with a simple "Busy! I forgot; it's okay! Hope everything is fine with you over there." Yes, everything is cool, just busy right now! I'll talk to you later. Have a wonderful day, dear," he messaged. Wilma reciprocated the sentiment and returned to her studies, delving into a prosecution case as part of her Open University course.

Later in the afternoon, she received another message: "Hi, dear." Wilma responded with a polite greeting, "Hello, how are you doing?" "I'm all right, thanks. What are you doing?" he asked. Wilma, still occupied with emails, replied, "Catching up with emails." Seemingly observing her busyness, he remarked, "Oh, I think you are still busy." Wilma confirmed, "Yes, it's a busy day."

The conversation paused until later in the evening. While relaxing and watching TV in her cat basket, Wilma received another greeting: "Hello, how are you doing?" She responded positively. He then inquired if she was done with work, to which she confirmed and mentioned relaxing at home watching "The Big Bang Theory. "Expressing his enjoyment in their conversation, he asked about her day. Knowing his real activities from his Facebook page, Wilma couldn't help but notice the discrepancy. He mentioned, "Not much, I've been here waiting to talk to you. "Wilma chuckled inwardly, thinking, "Oh, really?" She responded with a casual, "Cool, I don't know when you are free to talk. We just started talking yesterday. Ha-ha-ha-ha-ha." While checking her Twitter notifications, she encountered an unexpected follower. Shocked to find explicit content on the follower's account, she immediately blocked it and shared the strange encounter with Mr G, showing him the surprising content. Glancing at her Google calendar, Wilma conveyed to the scammer, "Okay, no problem. I'm busy over the next couple of days. What do you want to know?" To her surprise, the person professed strong feelings: "Since the day we met, I've fallen for you. There are no words to express the gratitude I feel in my heart that you've come into my life." Wilma, rolling her eyes at the overly sentimental message, replied, "Oh, thanks, that's sweet. I've been trying to find a way to express my feelings for you." The conversation took an unexpected turn as he continued with cheesy declarations, comparing his affection to public proclamations. Wilma found the expressions as corny as a Boyz II Men song. "I'll make love to you!" He continued with heartfelt promises: "I will be right here beside you any time you need me. I will be with you until I breathe my last breath. I promise to share my life with you no matter what tomorrow may bring. "Wilma, finding the declarations reminiscent of Uncle Fester's vows in the "Addams

Family Values" movie, responded with a simple "Thank you. I really appreciate it." She couldn't help but think this guy might be a couple of sandwiches short of a picnic and replied again with a reserved, "Wow, thanks." Instantly, he asked, "Do you love me too?" Wilma, feeling it was too soon for such sentiments, decided to pull a Dr Evil moment and responded, "How about no, it's too soon. "Sensing the conversation was headed in a direction she wasn't comfortable with, Wilma redirected the discussion, saying, "It's getting late now!" Gratefully, he bid her goodnight, and she sweetly replied, "Good night, sweet dreams."

The following day, Wilma was engrossed in reading and researching female serial killers on her laptop when she received a "Good morning, dear" message. Responding with a simple "Morning!" she was then asked how she was doing. A coffee and chocolate hobnobs beside her, she paused her reading and replied, "I'm doing well, thanks." The conversation seemed normal until the question about his plans for the day arose. Wilma, in a candid moment, shared about her current study of Christopher Barry-Dee's work on the evilest women in the world, wondering if he might mistake her for a criminologist or just a complete eccentric. He responded with a casual "OK, that's great." Then, he abruptly asked for a favour: to get him a £100 Amazon card because he claimed to be out of card downloads for his documents. Wilma, wary of such requests, simply ignored it and continued reading.

She noticed later that he had sent, then deleted, another message. His subsequent messages prodded her about her silence, questioning whether she thought it was good to ignore his request. Wilma, now occupied with washing dishes, took a moment to dry her hands and replied, feigning busyness, "Didn't know what you were talking about, been a bit busy."

Later, she saw another message instructing her to get a card at a nearby store, either Google Play or Amazon. Choosing not to engage, Wilma moved on to making dinner.

In the evening, he reached out again, expressing uncertainty about her ability to acquire the card. He then questioned whether her silence was due to his request for the card. Despite his persistent inquiries, Wilma, feeling uncomfortable with the situation, decided not to respond to his questions and went to bed without further communication.

The next day, Wilma was preparing to go out with Mr. G to celebrate her mum's birthday, which involved arranging lunch. Just before leaving the house to catch the bus, she received a morning greeting from the scammer. Responding briefly, she mentioned her plans to celebrate her mum's birthday and how it would be another busy day. The scammer wished her mother a happy birthday and inquired about where they were planning to go. Wilma knew her mum preferred a nice steak or Italian food but also acknowledged her mum's mobility issues due to arthritis. She politely replied that she wasn't certain yet, mentioning her mum's difficulties with walking due to needing a hip replacement. The scammer empathized and then shifted the conversation back to the card request, asking for her help on her way back.

Later in the afternoon, while enjoying a glass of wine with Mr G and her mum during the celebration, she received another message from the scammer, inquiring about how the birthday was going. Wilma assured him that her mum was happy, but she was elusive about when they'd return home. Feeling mischievous, Wilma sent a picture of a cocktail to tease the scammer, avoiding any specifics about her current location or plans. When he pressed her about getting the card, she brushed off his request, not intending to comply, and hinted she was having a fun time. As he continued to press for the card, Wilma grew irritated and sent cryptic responses, indicating her disinterest. The scammer became impatient, persistently asking about the card and claiming she had promised to get it that day. Wilma, firm in her decision, denied any such commitment. The scammer eventually relented, suggesting she could get it the next day.

Wilma ignored his messages and, upon returning home later that evening, opted to enjoy a relaxing time with a couple of bottles of wine rather than engage further with the persistent scammer. Late on a Sunday morning, Wilma was nursing a hangover when she received a message from the persistent scammer checking in on her well-being. Irritated by his persistence, she decided to ignore the message.

Half an hour later, another message arrived, wishing her a good morning, and inquiring about her well-being. Opting for a trivial lie to avoid further conversation, she fabricated an excuse, claiming to feel unwell due to possible food poisoning and stating she needed rest. Concerned, the scammer inquired about a possible culprit and advised her to visit the hospital. Unwilling to entertain his concern or delve further into the real cause (a bit too much red wine), Wilma dismissed his worries, assuring him that no one had caused her distress and attributing it to a disagreement with seafood, which she claimed she sometimes couldn't tolerate. She mentioned she intended to sleep it off with water. She then took the opportunity to enjoy some peace, watching TV for the rest of the day without any further disruptions from the scammer. The next morning, Wilma initiated the conversation with a casual greeting, but the scammer's immediate response was a request for the card. Irritated, Wilma sarcastically replied that she was indeed still sleeping, which didn't deter the scammer as he persisted with his request for the card. Unwilling to entertain his constant demands, Wilma straightforwardly told him she wasn't planning to go shopping that day. Changing tactics, the scammer attempted to strike up a conversation by asking how she was doing. Uninterested, Wilma chose to ignore his message and focused on her studies. She noticed he had sent another message, promptly deleted afterwards.

Later in the afternoon, while taking a break from studying and watching TV, she received his inquiry about her well-being. Feeling fatigued and needing rest, Wilma responded, mentioning she was still tired and trying to avoid falling asleep. Despite her attempts to convey her exhaustion, the scammer persisted, urging her not to sleep yet. Feeling the weariness, Wilma couldn't help but respond with a big yawn, indicating her struggle to stay awake.

The following morning, while preparing her morning coffee and checking messages, Wilma received a greeting addressed as "Good morning, Wilma Wonka," a playful twist inspired by the character Willy Wonka from Roald Dahl's book. Unimpressed, Wilma responded casually, noting that she'd been called "Wilma Wonka" by friends for years, without revealing her lack of enthusiasm for the nickname. Anticipating his usual request for the card, Wilma brushed off the flattery from the scammer, claiming to appreciate the nickname. As she resumed her studies in her student cave, she ignored his attempts to engage further. An hour later, he presumed she was too busy and asked about her breakfast. Wilma smoothly replied affirmatively, acknowledging his inquiry. Continuing his efforts to charm her, he inquired about her mother's well-being, to which Wilma politely responded that her mother was doing well. Expecting the next question about her plans for the day, Wilma confirmed she wasn't going out and had work to focus on. The scammer persisted with compliments, expressing his fondness for her, and probing about her potential return to Texas. Wilma kept her responses non-committal, stating she was taking life as it wasn't set on any plans yet. As he attempted to steer the conversation back to the card, Wilma sarcastically agreed that she hadn't gone shopping and hinted that acquiring the card wasn't a priority. He then tried to be clever by sending her a link to purchase the card online, which Wilma chose to ignore, despite his excitement about the card's online availability.

Later in the evening, he confronted her, asking why she had stopped talking to him. Wilma, staying firm in her busy schedule, replied that she hadn't stopped but was exceptionally busy and continued to keep her distance for the rest of the day.

The next day, Wilma received multiple messages from the scammer, but she chose to ignore him. His persistence led to inquiries about why she stopped talking, followed by his continued insistence for her to get the card online. Wilma, still focused on her projects, playfully responded, stating she was weird and didn't shop online, emphasizing that obtaining the card was low on her priority list. The scammer reminded her of her previous agreement, which she dismissed, claiming it might have been said for peace's sake. He persisted with nagging questions about when she'd go shopping or use the online link he provided. He claimed the card was necessary to download documents for a crew's streaming card, a story Wilma found incredulous based on her knowledge of technology. When he suggested she ask someone else to get the card, Wilma played along, feigning interest, and claiming she'd research it further, though she had no intention to. The scammer, relentless, continued with attempts to convince her of the card's importance, even resorting to claiming the card she sent him was already used! Wilma, amused by his persistence, decided to prank him further, sending a photo of a used card and claiming it had $100 on it. The scammer, believing her, complained it was already redeemed and tried calling her, but Wilma deliberately ignored his calls and messages, teasing him for his insistence on asking strangers for cards. As he grew increasingly frustrated and demanded answers, Wilma played it cool, laughing off his irritation. Eventually, the scammer, angered, blocked her, signalling an end to their interaction.

Flirting with Thor: A Banter Tale

Wilma was comfortably nestled in her cat basket, sipping on fruit tea, when she received a late-night chat invitation. "Hello, Wilma 😂😎 My dear Wilma, I hope you are well." "I'm good, thanks for asking. How are you today?" she replied. "I'm good. Tell me, have you had your dinner?" "Yes, I've eaten tonight," she responded, adding with a laugh, "I do enjoy food 🤤. What about you?" Wilma, finding the conversation pleasant, inquired, "What sort of food do you enjoy?" "Lol 😂 seems like you might be a lover of food!" he replied. Amused, she texted back, "I love my food this is probably why I am fat 🙊🤷😂 Smiles 😊. I love eating beans a lot." Amused she replied "Well, I don't have any complaints from my friends about my cooking," he replied. Amidst the banter, she teasingly asked, "You like beans, do you fart a lot?" receiving a humorous response, "Ha-ha, lol 😊. Sure, I do but not all the time." Playfully, she quipped, "😂😂😂😂 you might need a gas mask. Hopefully, the duvet doesn't hover above the bed in the morning □😣😂." The conversation continued, drifting to cooking. "Do you enjoy cooking?" she asked. "Yeah, I do all my cooking". He tells her "I'm staying alone, yet I am still hoping for the creator for one loyal one," he shared. Remembering a chat with the hair bear bunch, she replied, "According to my friends, men should stay single; women just muck up your lives. We do annoying things like put things away where you cannot find them 😂😂😂😂. Leave the box of red wine to drip down the front of the fridge 🙊🤷." He flirted, "Ha-ha-ha you are perfect." She retorted, "Yeah, a perfect pain 😂😂😂😂. I cause chaos wherever I go

😂😂😂. "Their banter continued with him expressing a liking for her quirky ways. They exchanged playful remarks about being directionally challenged and enjoying spending time together.

As the conversation progressed, they delved into their lives and occupations. Wilma shared her work as a neurodiverse consultant, helping individuals with hidden disabilities. Wilma, with a smile, asked, "What are your hobbies when you're not travelling?" He shared, "I love going to the gym before heading out to the studio, morning walks, playing my violin, and, of course, singing." Interested but a bit sceptical about the singing part. The star inquired, "What about your hobbies?" "Thankfully, I've been banned from the gym 😂😂😂. I enjoy art, design, cooking, creative writing, walking, and listening to music while out for walks. I love travelling, but I'm not a fan of flying 🙀👽," he responded. Curious about the gym ban, he asked, "Can you tell me why you were banned from the gym?" Wilma explained, "Sure, it's from an accident several years ago involving a badly parked van. I ended up needing one of my legs super glued back together. Repetitive exercises trouble my knee, and I've lost a lot of function in my ankle. Then adds I look like I've been let out for the day if I try running 😂😂😂. "He jokingly remarked, "Oh, and probably you'll be last in the race LOL. "Amid their banter, Wilma shared, "Going through airport security is interesting with all the alarms going off. 🙍👽🚪" He teased, "Lol 🤭 and now you don't even need to walk much, right?" Wilma clarified, "I do enjoy walking; it's good for my mental health. But I stick to flat areas; hills are a challenge now."

Understanding her struggles, he empathized, "Sorry about that, but at least no life was lost in that incident. We thank the creator for that." Wilma acknowledged, "I've adjusted my life, though it gets frustrating. But that's life." He philosophized, "Of course...life is never fair to anyone; just live every moment by staying happy always." Impressed by his wisdom, she agreed, "Yes, absolutely true." Then he asked, "How long have you been supporting my music sweetie?" "Approximately 8 years now. I was housebound recovering from my accident and bored. There's only so much daytime TV one person can watch," she shared. He expressed gratitude, "Wow, I'm grateful and I love you as one of my fans ♡." Wilma bid goodnight, saying, "Well, I'm heading off to bed. I'll talk to you tomorrow 😃🤗." He replied, "It's all right sweet ☺ have a wonderful night's rest 💤." "You too 😃," she responded, ending the conversation for the night.

As lunchtime approached, Wilma received a message: "Good afternoon, my sweet. How are you?" Engrossed in answering calls and emails on the helpline, she replied a bit later, "Sorry for the late reply. I'm well, thanks. How are you today?" he replied "I'm doing great. Oh, what time do you have now 😊? Did you have lunch already 😃?" he asked. "No, not yet. I'll grab lunch once I finish up here. It won't take long; I'm always short on time when it comes to eating 😂," she answered. He responded cheerfully, "😃 😃 I hope you smile all day 😊. I'll have my signature for an endorsement later this evening. It's a big deal for me, and I'm happy everything falls in place 😊♡. What are you planning for the rest of your day, honey 🫠?" She thought wow and texted "Congratulations! That's fantastic news for you. I just finished with the helpline, and my head feels pickled; it's been one of those mornings 🙉🫗. Looking forward to a walk and meeting friends later for a glass of wine 😄," she shared. He sent a picture recently posted on Instagram, featuring himself with Andrea Bocelli. "Great photo of yourself and Andrea 😄," she complimented. Taking a walk while listening to her Spotify a Scottish folk band called "Shooglenifty and Album called Troots," Wilma captured the beauty of the Haberdashery curling pond, the swans gliding with their cygnets, and shared the serene view with the star, saying, "Beautiful day 😄." Impressed, he replied after a few hours, "Oh wow, what a beautiful view 😍. I find most of my music inspiration in places like this—so quiet, natural, and beautiful." Knowing his fondness for nature, Wilma paused her walk to text back, "I know It's nice to clear the head while taking a walk 😍🙏." Sitting on a bench, basking in the sunshine, she asked, "What are your plans for the evening?" "I'll be with my team for the endorsement meeting later," he shared. "Hope you and your team have a wonderful evening filled with fun and laughter. I look forward to hearing about it 😄," she replied. He inquired again about her hobbies, and she responded, "Apart from music 🎶, it's Art and Design, cooking, and creative writing 🫠." He said "Wow, that's nice. I like cooking as well," he added, recalling his experiences cooking and trying dishes like chilli with horse meat during a visit to China. Wilma joined in, "I love slow-cooked chilli, I let it simmer for hours in the slow cooker 😊." He shared a picture of his vegan chilli made in February 2021. As Wilma arrived home, preparing a cup of fruit tea, she received his message, "Wow, cool 😊. We share almost the same qualities. I'm amazed. I don't usually talk to my fans, sweetie, but I find myself comfortable with you from the first time we spoke 😊."Relaxing in her cat basket with tea and a chocolate biscuit, Wilma replied, "I did tell you I was weird 🙀💡😄. He then tells her "I must go now, honey ♡. It's almost time for my meeting with my team. We'll talk later, okay?" Smiling she texted back "Sure. Have a great evening 🙏," he wished her well before signing off.

The following afternoon, Wilma sent a message: "Hi handsome, how was your evening?" She had finished some shopping and a COVID test ahead of her trip to Malaga, picking up a pair of sandals for her time there.

Later, she received a reply: "I'm fine, honey ♡. It's afternoon here for me." She laughed inwardly, noting he didn't mention his previous night's endorsement. He asked, "How are you?" Wilma, waiting at a bus stop, found herself chatting with a stranger about vaping flavours while she waited. Excited about attending the conference and meeting Dr Dodge Shoes in person, she responded to the star: "I'm good, thanks. I've had my PCR test for my flight on Monday. A friend's driving me to the airport in style 😎😄." Curiously he returns "Really? How long will you be away? ☺". She returned "For five days and excited to attend this conference and meet new people 😄," and boarded the bus. She played Culture Club's "Victims" on Spotify, reading his message: "I see you like to meet new people just like me ☺. What time is it now? Have you eaten yet?" Descending the bus and heading home downhill, she confirmed, "Yes, I enjoy meeting new people. It's a privilege to see the work my friend's done in Europe about dyslexia. Then she adds I am proud they earned their PhD! Then tells him It'll be weird meeting everyone 😄 however also interesting 😃." He decides "We'll plan a vacation together eventually 🤭♡," to which Wilma responds, "I like the idea, but we're both busy people. It took me two years to meet some collaborators. Some I may never meet—just waving on Zoom 🙂." He says "Despite being busy, we can spare a few days to meet," Then adds "I wake every morning checking for your messages. No one's made me feel this way since my breakup with my ex 😳💔."Wilma, aware of his highly publicized breakup, replied, "I'm never sure when you're online. I enjoy catching up with you 🙂. You're still getting used to my weird world. I'm Wonder Woman, I just make people wonder 🧑‍🦱💀." Amused, he retorted, "And I'm also a wonder man 🤭. Trust me, I'm equal to the task." He then inquired about family visits, highlighting their importance. Wilma knew he valued family bonds and admitted, "I try to visit when I can 🧑‍🦱💀." He emphasized the fleeting nature of life and the importance of cherishing family. "I do my best to be happy; a day without a smile is a wasted day for me ☺️," He then shared a secret that he is highly disorganised, to which she replied, "I'm dyslexic, spending hours organizing work and implementing strategies to deal with forgetfulness" 🧙‍♀️💀." He admitted, "I hope to work on improving this habit ☹️."

Wilma found it endearing and offered strategies: "I'll share some; they might help or not. No offence if they don't 🙂."

Later, he asked her to share those strategies: "Okay, you can share some strategies with me 😬. I'll try them 😁."He philosophized, "No matter how perfect you think you are, there's always a weak point for everyone on earth." Then inquired, "What are you doing now?" Sitting in her cat basket "Just sitting and watching YouTube 😜," she replied, sharing a

link to "She's Always a Woman to Me,".

After mentioning Billy Joel, he diverted the conversation, asking Wilma, "Tell me, what qualities do you like in a man?" Wilma pondered and replied, "I like a man with a good sense of humour, someone I can talk to about anything. I appreciate when they might not share my interests but support my passions. I enjoy it when they're playful and can make me laugh 😃." "That sounds good 😃. I like being playful too 🙈. It helps me worry less. I want to be the reason behind your smile 😍. I want to wake up to your presence every morning," he responded playfully, she replied, "You can come dressed up as Thor, the god of thunder, playing your violin 🤪😹😺." Amused, he said, "😂 You're very funny and I would rather show off my guitar skills. It's night time for me now, and I'm feeling sleepy 😴. Goodnight from here, honey." Wilma wished him sweet dreams with a message of "sweet dreams xx." The next morning, Wilma noticed it was the star's birthday on Facebook. She sent a cheerful "Happy Birthday" message along with a humorous image. He responded with gratitude but then expressed feeling sad and disappointed for not receiving a birthday wish. Confused, Wilma clarified, "Yes, I did! Look under the picture 😴." After he discovered her message, he thanked her and wished her an impressive day. He expressed his desire for her presence on his birthday and acknowledged their growing friendship. Wilma received her COVID test results, confirming she was fit to fly. Excitedly, she informed the star about her readiness to travel and joked, "I am so excited I could crush a grape 😁." She made sure her essentials were packed, including her laptop and Garfield, as she anticipated a gathering involving Paddington Bear and Hamley Bear. The star continued the conversation, expressing happiness and exchanging pleasantries. He then inquired about a birthday gift, to which Wilma offered a painting she had done. He asked about the painting and hinted at wanting something else as a birthday present. Suggesting a wristwatch, he expressed a desire to cherish it as a token of their friendship. Wilma attempted to evade this by mentioning her tendency to lose wristwatches. However, he insisted he would get the watch and send her a picture with it, claiming it would always remind him of her. Wilma responded diplomatically, acknowledging his gesture, and then diverted the topic by sending a picture of oysters she had enjoyed on her previous birthday. The star didn't continue the conversation that day, keeping Wilma occupied with her travel preparations.

The following day, Wilma's friend picked her up in style to head to the airport, ensuring she travelled safely she wore a sunflower lanyard due to her hidden disability. She posted on Facebook about her trip to Malaga and shared updates with her contacts. Upon landing, she received various messages, including one from the star inquiring about her well-being. As she connected with other friends attending the conference, they all decided to take a taxi together to their hotel. However, since everyone was dyslexic finding the "Exit" was proving difficult. If they ever found the way out it would be time to fly home, LOL. It would have been an updated version of Tom Hanks in "Terminal" It would have been called three dyslexics lost in the airport. Once settled in their hotel, she received a message from the star asking what was new and informing her about his plans for beers and tapas. Wilma enjoyed a few beers and chatting with everyone, along with indulging in beautiful olives, cheeses, oils, vinegars, and fresh bread. She then headed back to the hotel. The next morning, Wilma was up bright and early. She gazed at the sky; it was clear, a beautiful blue without a cloud in sight. She walked down to the pier and took a photo.

Sending it to all her friends, she greeted them with a "Good morning from Malaga," then joined everyone for breakfast and headed off to Babel Idiomas, a Spanish language school where the conference was being held. On the first day, Dr. Dodgy Shoes taught a card game called Barnga, an odd game where people play cards in silence with three sets of rules that Wilma found confusing.

The discussion for the rest of the day revolved around the challenges of dyslexia. Returning to the hotel in the evening, she received a message: "Wow, what a lovely atmosphere! ☺ Good evening from here." She noticed the picture she sent in the morning had a mark saying it was unsent. She quickly texted, "Yeah, Wi-Fi crashed on me! Only just saw it didn't send this morning 🐧💡🤖💡😂." He replied, "Ha-ha, it's okay. I thought you were just waking up now?" Laughing "No, I've had a full day at the dyslexia compass! 😜" Wilma loved the Spanish lifestyle, finding it very relaxing. She expressed, "Hope you're having a wonderful time there... he hinted It would have been nice if we were there together, it would have been lots of fun." Wilma responded, "It's great; I love Spanish culture, and it's lovely and sunny. I think I will see if I can lead people astray for sangria 😂😂😂 Smiles 😊 So, tell me, did you have your breakfast?" Smiling she texted "Yes, I had breakfast, second breakfast, and lunch, and going to eat lots of tapas for dinner, it's a hard life 😂" he inquired about the tapas she was eating that evening, but Wilma, having looked over the menu without understanding it, replied, "Don't know 😂." He laughed, "Oh, you don't want to tell me what you are eating!" Wilma explained, "I don't know what I am ordering; it is all in Spanish 🧕🍷🧑‍🍳🍷." He teased, "Shame that you don't know what you are eating. She admitted So, I am a bit rusty with my Spanish 🧑‍🍳🍷🤭🤭🤭." Wilma explored the shops in Malaga, photographing the beautiful buildings and the large cathedral. Returning to the hotel to freshen up for dinner, she received a message: "😂 Are you done with your meal 😊? Hope you enjoyed it 😊." She replied, "Not arrived yet, I saw the menu this afternoon 🤤." The restaurant was across from the 14th-century Moorish fortress, beautifully lit against the dark skies. They had a sumptuous seven-course meal, one including sharing foie gras, sparking a controversial conversation while accompanied by a few glasses of wine. After returning to the hotel, she received another message: "Hey pretty 😊 what's new? Returning "great dinner, I am stuffed 😊." She sent a photo of the salmon she had and went to bed.

The next day at the Dyslexic Compass, Garfield highlighted the OrCam Learn to everyone. However, while demonstrating the voice recognition software, it decided not to work. The group saw how it read full pages of text, though Wilma wanted to highlight other assistive technologies such as Dragon, writing helpers, and inspirational mind maps but ran out of time. The discussions circled the complexities of dyslexia, and Wilma had some homework for the hotel before heading out for dinner. Settling in her room with a bag of Jamon crisps and a tin of Mahou lager, she received a message: "Good day, my Wilma 🥰! 😊 How is your day going?" She replied, "I'm back at the hotel. I have some homework on aiding people with dyslexia in organizational skills. Then maybe sangria, wine, and more tapas 😃." He joked, "All right, but you will eat more tapas again! You are smart, I can sense that!" Wilma, enjoying the banter, replied, "Loves just grazing on tapas," sending a photo of some tapas she had eaten. He responded, "Yum, they are yummy. So what hotel room are you in? If you receive a knock on the door, it might be me 😎." Wilma chuckled, knowing it wouldn't happen, and said, "Yeah, I have one full day left, and then I need to go home, maybe next time 😁 😎." Her friend expressed deeper feelings, "All right, but it will be great staying together. I must confess that since the first day we started talking, your thoughts have filled my head. You are absolutely amazing..." Wilma, sensing where the conversation was going, replied, "Thank you for such a wonderful warm compliment 😊. You're awesome yourself 😄." The conversation flirted more intensely. Wilma enjoyed the flirting but aimed to keep the conversation grounded. "I enjoy our conversations, and I enjoy reading what you are doing. I am always going to be here when you are feeling stressed, just text when you need a chat. 😁 🙈" She texted Dr. Dodgy Shoes to arrange their meeting; he had promised to buy her a gin and tonic. Having found a lovely gin bar right next to their hotel, Wilma awaited his response. She received a message: "Lol, I understand, you are funny, you know. I will allow you to do your thing 😊. It would be nice if we were walking hand in hand along the streets of Malaga." At this, Wilma laughed the tune from the "Love Boat" popping into her head. Sipping her lager, she gave up on her homework 🍷😍. She texted, "I have already told the group that the dyslexic compass should be advertised as we are officially lost!

I even got lost trying to find the coffee shop where we were meeting for coffee and churros this morning 🧟‍♀️💁. 🤪😂😂😂 😆." He said, "Oh really? You didn't ask questions?" Wilma laughed, admitting she had asked for directions but added, "Yes, but unfortunately, I am never sure if people have told me to go right or left. I could do with having a sense of direction. I just wander about and hope to find the place 🧟‍♀️💁🤷‍♀️💁. I have been told I shouldn't be let out by myself 😂😂😂😂." He teased, "Well, you were trying to be too brave and smart 🤓." Then he scolded her, "I already know you, that's what you were trying to do. You should ask. Come to think 🤔 of it, what will you be saying to yourself when you are walking down the road 🤓?" Wilma, using her wicked sense of humour, replied, "I will be singing 'Oops! I did it again' 😂😂🤗." He chuckled, "Ha-ha, lol 😊." She explained, "I have strategies in place to aid my dyslexia; it works differently for everyone. I still struggle with directions 🤷‍♀️💁." Her friend commented, "But you were just walking as if you knew where you were going to 😎." She replied, "🤭🤭🤭🤭🤭😎😊." Her friend scolded her again, "So maybe next time, you should be more careful, I think ☺. Have you been out for your dinner?" Wilma responded, "Not yet just waiting for the others 😁." He asked, "Oh, how many are you?" Wilma explained, "There are eleven altogether from all over Europe. 🤗. He returns I am just thinking how nice it is in Malaga. Please take a selfie of yourself and let me see you. I want to see how beautiful you are 🐶."Wilma took a selfie in her dyslexia-themed untied T-shirt, black leggings, and sandals, sending it. Her friend replied, "Wow, so pretty 😍🤭🍃🍃. I could not imagine that you are such a sweet-looking woman 🍃🍃 sweet-looking Wilma 😊." Wilma laughed at his flirting and replied, "Crazy Wilma 🤣🤣🤣🤣." He complimented her, "Lol, you are a pretty lady. I credit you for that ♡." She tells him "No, you have the wrong person! Annoyed he returns "Well, I am telling you what I see." She teased back, "I bet you say that to all the girls 😊." He assured her, "Well, I am not what you think. You shouldn't say that I respect every woman." He added, "I going to spend time together with my parents and siblings, Elena, and Alex soon" Wilma clarified, "I have never been looked upon as a supermodel, never been chatted up much." She replied, "I'm just saying I don't have the perception of myself as pretty". He insisted, "Well, I see you as a beautiful woman. I would not tell you if I didn't believe my own words, you know!"

At this point, she received a message on WhatsApp from Dr Dodgy Shoes, indicating it was time to go out for dinner with a few refreshments. She informed her friend, "I am going out now; I will chat with you later 😊." He replied, "All right, take care of yourself out there and be safe too 😊." She reassured him, "I will, don't worry. I have two bodyguards! They don't fancy me; we just work on different dyslexic projects 😊. Take care 😄." She sent him a picture of everyone working on the dyslexic compass, posted earlier on LinkedIn. He responded, "Wow, wonderful team1. She returned they are it has been a lot of work and fun 😁🙏👌." Wilma took a screenshot of LinkedIn and what Dr. Dodgy Shoes had written, then sent it to the star, saying, "What a lovely review of the work done 😁." She moves down the stairs, sits on the couch at the front of the hotel, and waits for Dr. Dodgy Shoes, who is running late. She receives the message, "That's great 😊. She says thank you 🙏. He returns you're welcome 😃 take care 😌." Wilma goes out, watches some football in the Sherlock Holmes pub, talks about what makes a good gin and tonic, and listens to jazz. It was typical that the day they were leaving, Jamiroquai was playing in Malaga for the Andalucia big festival. They all wandered around the bars and enjoyed Aperol Spritzes and tapas before returning to the hotel.

The next day she received, "Good morning, Wilma, and how is your day going?" Wilma, at Babel Idiomas by the time the message was sent, contributed to discussions on improving the website.

Later in the day, she responds, "It has been another momentous day! I am sorry it has ended; I can only hope my input was helpful." She adds, "How has your day been 😁?" Wilma then goes out to buy some wonderful black pudding pate to take home, along with taking pictures of the beautiful lighthouse and beach. Wilma packs her case; she must be at the airport early for her flight home. A message comes through saying, "Wow, it is amazing you have already made an impact on some people's lives. ☺ Good evening from Aachen." The Hair Bear Bunch on WhatsApp informs Wilma that it's raining back home; she sends them pictures of a McDonald's with Mahou beers, saying, "Good evening from Malaga! 😁 How are you doing? Looks like you are having a fun time. "She replies, "I am great! Going for a farewell gin and tonic soon 😋😊. It has been magic; they must not have thought I was too boring, and they are inviting me back in the future 😂😂😂😂 Smiles 😊." He comments, "That's why I said that you are a blessing to them. Laughing she texted Lol, I have said I am the reason they need an extension. I have mucked up their plans by suggesting changes 😂😂😂🤪😂." Wilma laughs, "Hahaha! I am used to getting blamed for stuff 🤪🤪🤪🤪. He tells her you are just so good to them; come to think of it, you make people happy." Her friend reflects, "I will just be happy if one person doesn't face the kind of discrimination, I have faced because of being dyslexic. I am part of a community where I fit in. They accept me as a complete nutter 🤙 👍👍. He tells her my day hasn't been good, but I can still say you cheer me up." Wilma responds, "Everyone faces challenges! No matter how well we plan things, something comes along to muck it up. You take it out on yourself. Well, maybe you just need to chill out, have a nice bath, and a curry with a nice glass of wine 😁 LOL 😝." He expresses, "I need a vacation; I have been stressed at present, and for some time now, I haven't been able to go to the gym and have my morning walk as usual. You don't have to sit and chat with me. You can take yourself for a walk 😁." Wilma encourages, "Sure, right now am doing that, I am on the street of Aachen like this 😎. I came home from Berlin, and I have been at the studio all day. 🎻🎻." Wilma advises, "You to enjoy your me time! It is important to fit it into a busy daily routine 😁 Even if it is just a cup of coffee, and watching the world go by 😁." The star jests, "Well, you should know what I can do 😃 I'm a star, remember 🤓." Wilma decides to give him a bit of a telling-off, "Yeah, I am Wilma who listens to people! Gives practical solutions! It is up to the person if they want to take on board the advice 😁 he returns I am sure that person would listen 🎧 I say you are blessed. She tells him well, I do have a certificate to a level 8 in counselling and psychotherapy 😁 🥃." He asks, "How are your friends?" She replies, "My friends are good! They keep asking when it will start raining here 🤣🤣🤣🤣 no doubt they will make fun of me skiving over here tomorrow night 🤣🤣🤣🤣. I have a hard life just now 🤣🤣🤣 🥃." Her friend acknowledges, "I know you have had great fun 😊 the Spanish way of life is chilled out." She concludes, "Well, I will chat with you later. I need both hands to lift the goldfish bowl of gin and tonic 🥴😵😁🤣 enjoy yourself 🥃💯 😵🥳🍸." As they choose which gin, they want, Dr Dodgy Shoes almost causes a riot with the bartender on the origins of gin. One of the crew, a gin virgin, asks Wilma and Dr. Dodgy Shoes to order an ordinary gin; they both laugh "What is an ordinary gin?" they order the gin virgin an Uncle Tom's Bathtub gin with tonic. After a few hours, they move on to the final meal before heading back to the hotel. The next morning, Wilma is up early, and the taxi arrives early, which makes Wilma panic. She forgets her phone charger and WhatsApp's Dr Dodgy Shoes to retrieve it and post it back to her. She goes through security, wanders around the duty-free, and then heads to Tim Hortons for coffee and doughnuts. She takes a photo of the duty-free and sends it to the star, saying, "Bye-bye from Malaga, time to go home 🙂." As she is getting ready to board her flight home, he tells her that he is sad about the passing of Queen Elizabeth and a photo of meeting her in person. Once she landed and settled to take the bus home she texted. I'm glad you had the chance to meet the Queen. It's sad, but she was an old lady. It had to happen at some point; no one lives forever. Lovely photos of you and the Queen on Instagram! 😁 he returns Thanks a lot, I appreciate it. ♡ 🥲 😀 How are you this evening? Hope you're at home? Wilma was with the Hair Bear Bunch and replied, "No, I'm out with friends; they're telling me about the curry night I missed. I've been showing them all my tapas nights, which were far better 🥴🥴🥴🥴." He asks, "Why are you still outside at this time?" She replies, "No, I'm indoors with friends. It's not as warm as Malaga; we're exchanging curry recipes 🙂🥲🥴🥴😎." "Wow, you always love tasty food," he remarks; this was true, Wilma did enjoy food. The next message she received was, "are they at your house?" Sipping cider she returned "No, I'm at the local hotel just chatting! Just nice catching up and finding out what they've been up to while I was away 😀." "Sure," he says, then continues, "I'll be sleeping over at the studio tonight. I won't be going home because I still have lots of work to do on my latest record... I'm hoping to finish it tonight." She replies, "Well, make sure you have plenty of breaks; don't burn yourself out 🙁." He returns "Sure, but this period has been good though," he reflects, "I'm saying this because, during the lockdown, my team and I never had just one show or concert 🙂. But I thank the creator for what he's still doing; you know I love what I do, I love playing the Violin 🎻🎻." He then explains, "When I play it on stage... I'm always happy playing it, my head will be full of thoughts... so much happiness playing it ☺." She responds, "I understand! It's been a busy productive week for me. I had regular breaks and great discussions! I love what I do; I know how I work." Then, on a serious note, she adds, "Make sure you put some time aside for yourself 😊." He reassures Wilma with, "Yes, 😃," then adds, "It's the weekend, hopefully, I'll be at home tomorrow." She doesn't believe what she reads and adds, "Probably not 🙅‍♀️🤦🤦🤦." He mentions, "I might go see my family in NYC, Dad, Mum," then adds, "Elena has been worried about not seeing me for a long time. I'm also looking forward to catching up with Alexandra; he's a great advisor. Lol 😎. He even came down to visit me in Berlin; I warmly welcomed him, and I love all my family." Wilma smiled and said, "Good for you, enjoy your life and time out! Smiles 😊." He then asks, "So, are you done with swapping your recipes?" She laughs and types, "Lol! You're never done swapping recipes! Unless it's the nutcase that invited me to the dyslexic compass, he's scary in the kitchen 🙅‍♀️ Lol 😆." He tells her "I was thinking that you'll be a great cook,". She tells him the story from Malaga about Dr Dodgy Shoes when he decided to substitute sugar and milk in his tea as he had run out. She texts, "Who puts tea, hot chocolate, and butter together in one cup 🤪🤪🤪🤪 not me 🤦." The says "Ha-ha-ha disgusting food ideas," she adds, "yes, do you fancy lasagna in a pie? 🙅‍♀️🤪🤦." He thinks about this and returns "You want lasagna pie!" She thinks, "Oh dear god no!" he flirts by saying, "Okay 🤦 Yes, sure, I will because it comes from you 😎 🙅‍♀️. Horrified he might enjoy weird foods she returns I need to stop talking about dodgy recipes 🤦🤪🤦 🙅‍♀️ he then says Lol 😂 you are funny, do you know that!" Several people have been saying this to Wilma recently; she says, "So, people keep telling me! I'm trying not to be! 🙊 I had people laughing in Malaga 🤦. I must be the way I tell jokes 🙊." He texted "Again, you are so funny,". Wilma didn't know whether to be flattered or if it was creepy. She answered, "I'm just an ordinary person going through life! He reassures her, "You are cool2 She thinks aww and returns. Thanks for the compliment! 🙏 he says you are always welcome," then asks, "Have you had your dinner?" telling him "Yes, it was nothing exciting compared to to the tapas I was eating in Malaga! However, I still enjoyed my dinner 😊." Happy he says, "That's good," Wilma then headed off to bed for sleep. The next morning, while drinking a cup of coffee, she received: "Good morning, my dear Wilma, how are you this morning? 🌞 Wishing you a happy weekend! 💐 She returns Good morning, hope you have a nice weekend full of laughter planned 😊" He sends, "Yes 👍 I was up a few hours ago and have done my morning exercises, as well as my morning walk." Wilma thinks he's feeling energetic this morning. She texts that her morning hasn't been that exciting, working on questions for a podcast next week and coursework for the year. He responds, "Wow, nice one Wilma ☺" She returns with a thanks 🙏. He politely replies, "You're always welcome." Wilma is thinking of what to buy for dinner and says, "I can feel a Spanish tapas evening for tonight, I'm missing the weather already 😂😂😂." She looks out the window and watches the clouds move rapidly across the sky. She then reads, "How was your night? Hope you had a great night's sleep and are now feeling relaxed 😌" She responds, "Yes, it was lovely to be back in my bed! I didn't have the air conditioning waking me up through the night 😂😂😂😂." He teases, "Lol, you still want to go back 😂 maybe a vacation favourite I think 🤭." Wilma clarified it wasn't a vacation for her; however, she enjoys being home. She mentions staying out of her hometown for months depending on their shows, though she knows it's longer but leaves the subject alone. She tells him, "I love Spain. During lockdown, I went on YouTube tours around the world 😂😂😂😂. I followed James Blink around the tapas bars in Madrid; it was my favourite! I loved looking at the museum full of Picasso paintings when I visited one year 😃." She adds that she was supposed to go to Krakow for a wander around, but the borders were shut due to COVID-19. "That is a shame 🙁," he responds. She remembers the blog she wrote at the beginning of lockdown, looking for Zombies and Daleks at the start, and laughs about it being some weird reality show 🤣🤣🤣🤣. He says he needs to go and start something up, promising to talk later, ending with ♡🍃. She texts, "Dr Who might drop in on you with the Tardis 🤣 no problem, enjoy your day 😁 Stay safe," to which he replies, "I am always safe these days, 😁."

Later, she receives, "How is your day going?" She responds, "My day has been excellent so far. How is your day going? I am glad your day is going well. What did you do, are you at home?" He asks about her activities, mentioning getting some shopping done and heading out to catch up with friends on a beautiful day 😃😃. He asks if she'll be driving, and Wilma finds it hilarious as she can't drive. He adds, "Will you be driving out?" She jokes, "The only thing I drive is people crazy! My friends don't trust me with the remote control for the W11 in case I put it through the TV 😂😂😂😂😂😂." He doesn't understand and asks if she doesn't drive at all. She confirms she doesn't, explaining her friends drive her around or she takes public transport 😁. He asks if she's had lunch, and she confirms she has, having had a chicken and avocado sandwich 🧑‍🍳💡. They did not talk for the rest of the day.

The following day, while Wilma was sitting drinking her coffee in her cat basket, she received: "Good morning, my world 🤍🌍 how was your night? Wishing you a blessed Sunday. She returns Hello, I hope you are enjoying your day. I had a great evening thanks 😊 As usual he tells her You are always welcome 😁 Hope you had some breakfast. Laughing she texted back That is a silly question for a foodie 😂😂😂😂" he returned Lol 😆 I should assume that you have eaten, right? 😎 She says Correct. I am fond of food, maybe a bit too much 😂😂😂😂😂. That's why you love Spain, grazing on lovely tapas, lol 😆. Wilma adored a variety of food and cooked many dishes. He then apologised to Wilma for not sending any other messages yesterday, explaining he was really busy working at the studio 🎙️. She understands and responds, "It's not a problem. I know you're a busy person, and you should never feel pressured to chat with me. I might not always reply in time myself as I have my work to do. 😊🙏" "Yeah 👍 That's right, so tell me how your day is going to be?" He asks. "My day is going well," she says, "I'm writing about organizing skills for dyslexic people for the Dyslexic Compass. I found what they had written very confusing. I also struggled with some of the language used 🧑‍🍳💡." He returns "You're telling me; it seems like they are speaking another language,". She explains they used phrases like "rendering a task insurmountable," which is very academic and not user-friendly. "We want this to be user-friendly for everyone 😄," she adds. "Nice one, then how are you going to translate that?" he inquires. She mentions using short bullet points about the struggles with dyslexia and suggesting simple solutions tailored to aid dyslexia throughout education, emphasizing that there's no one-size-fits-all with learning. "I'll see what they think 🎥💡," she concludes. He reacts positively, and she jokingly asks, "What mischief will you get up to today?" "What is mischief? 🙂" he responds. She wonders about his idea of fun and says, "Yes, mischief! Spend a bit of time sending something silly to annoy a friend! It must be done in the best possible taste 😀😂😂😂😂😂." "You're funny 😊," he responds, then asks if she's really like that 😂. She jests, "Just fall asleep, my friend, you will wake up with bright pink toenails! 🤪😄"

Later, she texts back, "Yes, I love a good practical joke! I have a friend who hates science fiction. I send him lots of YouTube videos such as Red Dwarf, I just get told I need a life 🤪😂😂😂🤪😀." She shares a YouTube video of two Scottish people stuck in a voice-activated lift and mentions using a voice-activated piece of software called Dragon, explaining it dictates what she wants to say for writing, emails, and forms but occasionally struggles with her voice. "I talked about this at the Dyslexic Compass," she concludes.

However, the star had disappeared and did not talk to Wilma until the evening. How is it going over there with you? Wilma was enjoying a pint of cider in the beer garden of her local. She replied It is great thanks! I love the debate with my friends that has started 😃

As Wilma had been discussing counselling, she shared Dr Brené Brown's content again with the star, who responded with, "That's great 😊." Wilma had been watching videos with Oprah Winfrey on the power of vulnerability and expressed her admiration, saying, "I love Dr. Brené Brown's talks 😁. He inquires What do you love about her talks?" Wilma responds, "Her talks are very inspiring. She openly discusses people's vulnerabilities and our relationship with ourselves and others. How we manage good and troubled times. How our judgments towards others through our thoughts can mess things up 😁. I do try not to judge people; however, I do have my days where some people need a high five in the face, with a chair 📷 👾. Lol 😆 nice one ☺." It was late at night, and he said, "You should be asleep now, take care of yourself and sleep tight ♡." The next morning, she finds the late message and responds, "Good morning, thanks. I had a great sleep. Busy day ahead ☐😁."

Later, she receives a message stating, "I have just woken up from sleep, I slept late; I did lots of work last night at my studio...." Wilma, unsure of what he had been doing at his studio, expresses concern, saying, "You should understand when you need a break 🧑‍🦰👩. It's great to be hyper-focused at times, but you can overdo it 🫠." He responds, "Hmmm well, it's just that I need to fire on with my work 😌. However, I had a lot of fun during the weekend, and I did rest well. Tell me, how did your day start?" She replies, "My day has started well, thanks. I'm looking at my calendar; it's a busy week! I have my meeting to be a student ambassador for learning labs today. I'll make sure I take regular breaks in between everything I need to do, or I will get nothing done 🙂." He advises, "Sure, that should be done daily. It is said that all work and no play make Jack a dull boy. You should have a bit of time to have fun, even if it's telling a bad joke with a cup of coffee 😁." She responds, "Well, I am having one now, and then I will be heading to the studio later in the day, coffee with low sugar in it 🍯." Wilma, confused about "low sugar," jests, "Low sugar? 🫢😂😂😂😂 Yeah, definitely 😁." Still puzzled, she says, "Okay 🫢🧑‍🦰👩. Enjoy 😂." He invites her, and she responds, "Nice invite! And I will make yours too. Tell me how you love your coffee, and I will be happy to make yours too 🤓🍯." Wilma sends him a photo of the black coffee she had in Málaga with some churros to dunk in it, promising to make it the same way for him. "Cool 😁. I hope you've eaten your breakfast; I already consumed mine," he says. She replies, "Yes, I have eaten 🤭🤭🤭🤭." He decides to send a picture of him cooking, and when Wilma checks it out later, she discovers it on Facebook, tagged as "vegan chilli time 2 Feb

244

2021." He confirms it's chilli with beans and sweet corn. Wilma shares, "Nice! I like making chilli with chuck steak. Everyone has a different recipe 😬." Wilma, seated in her cat basket reading emails, receives a message asking her whereabouts. She replies, "At work, getting ready to send more emails 🤣." He acknowledges her work, saying, "Oh okay, that's cool. You are doing a lot of work there," and mentions leaving soon for the studio, reminding her to take breaks. She reciprocates the advice and wishes him a good day.

Later, in the evening, Wilma informs the star that she made stroganoff for dinner and sends a photo. He expresses interest, saying he hasn't tried it before. Wilma explains the recipe and offers a vegetarian version suggestion. He expresses curiosity about her return home. She then said, "I am self-employed; I work from home 🐱 💡." He responded, "That's nice. I know it is far better for me to work 😊." He returns "That's Great 👍 I am happy for you that you have everything at your doorstep," she added. "Yes, and it is good for my mental health as I am in a safe environment 😊,". He then asked, "So how are your friends?" She answered, "They are great! I am back, they are teasing me as normal 🤣 🤣 🤣 🤣." "Lol why do they find you so funny 😄?" he inquired. She laughed and sent back, "I don't have sensible conversations with the hair bear bunch; they usually end up being rude 🤣 🤣 🤣 🤣!" She then asked, "How was your chilli last night? I hope you have not exploded LOL." However, he ignored her remarks. Later, she received, "Good afternoon, my dear ☺. How is your day going? Hope it has been great." "It has been incredibly positive! I am being kept out of mischief 😀 💩 💩 💩. I will see what is next on my ta-da list 😁," she responded. "Mischief?" Again, he did not understand, and Wilma said, "You are very practical and disciplined! 💩 💩 💩 💩 How do you mean? 😋 😋" "I enjoy having a bit of fun, send your friends some silly videos. Stick a whoopee cushion under their chair. 😀 get up to a bit of mischief! He responded with You are an amazing person, you always make my mood rise, and it makes me feel special," he explained. She sent a picture of a cast iron sweetcorn tin, saying, "I made chocolate brownies. It said a cast iron tin was the best; this was the only one I had. I don't know why nobody will eat my brownies." "Lol, so you have already made your brownies. They do not even look nice ☺ Where I come from, they look like a big jobbie 💩 💩 💩 I will pass 💩 💩 💩 💩," he commented. "Ha-ha, lol 😊 that image is now stuck in my head. You can think of Mr Hankie the Christmas poo all day now 💩 🙍 💡 💩 💩 Ha-ha-ha tell me what you think about the shape of your brownies 😋 I would advise that you shouldn't make it with that iron tin ☺," she teased. He responded, "Yes, definitely 😁. Tell me, how did you know that you've gone wrong?" She thinks this guy needs a sense of humour. A text arrives saying, "I will just tell you that you are an amazing kind of person, I always feel something good and special here." "Thank you, that is lovely to know 🙏 😊," she replied. He flirted with Wilma again, "You're funny 😊 you always make me think nice thoughts." "Awww, you sweet 😃 😊 😃 you can't imagine how much you take away my worries, your thoughts are in my head honestly," he confessed. Wilma laughed and sent back, "Watch out, they will send the crazy bus with a straight jacket!

Don't keep my crazy thoughts in your head 😂😂😂😂." He sent back, "Well, I can imagine. I believe your thoughts aren't crazy; they are real." "Yes, okay! You will be the first person not to call me crazy when I talk about cute white fluffy vampire bunnies with telepathic powers 🧛‍♀️👻🐰👻," she joked. He decided to be philosophical and said, "Things don't go the way we think; however, if we read deep into it, there will be no more of a reality. We should embrace it and make it good ☺." Wilma thought of some of the discussions she had with Dr. Dodgy Shoes and texted back, "Another philosopher to add to the list 🧛‍♀️👻🐵😂😂 Ha-ha-ha! You are just a special kind of being and knowing you as a person is the best thing. Almost every day I kept looking at the pictures you sent to me." Wilma thought, "I always seem to attract weird people," and said, "Really, 🧛‍♀️👻 I just find that weird, maybe because everyone I hang around with is looking at other women; they tell me about what they find attractive 🐰👻." "You are just so nice... I'm not telling you this because of the way you are, but I must tell you that I like you very much. Well, nothing attracted me more than the way you are as a person; for real, if we could extend our future together, it would be nice 💧☺," he confessed. Wilma knows he is telling her what he thinks she wants to hear and sends back, "It's early days, just take one day at a time. 🙈 Hmm 😊 Well, maybe you don't feel the same way for me.... or you don't just have the time." He has picked up that Wilma is playing it safe and follows on with it, "But you should always remember that it's also good to have a love life too 💝 Normally work is involved ... however you should always remember love is good 😁." Wilma thinks, "Oh, I better not wear that reinforced sports bra that makes the boobies sit like two static bowling balls; I might take someone's eyes out! I also need to get rid of the new forest growing under my armpits." Maybe the granny pants which are supposed to give you a nice figure and roll down your body and you end up with a big doughnut around your bum is also a bad idea. As she is thinking this, she types, "No! Lol, love activities are just something I talk about! It's been a long time 😂😂😂😂😂." She sits in her cat basket waiting for the reply, "Oh really!" Then inquires, "Please tell me about your love life, tell me how it was, hope you don't mind me asking." He wants to open the shuttle doors, switch the landing lights on, and put his cargo in my cargo bay holder. Wilma was used to this sort of conversation and said, "No, I don't mind you asking. I enjoyed my love life; I have complex women's problems 👩‍🦰💡," then asked, "You did ask 👩‍🦰💡." Wilma knew that discussing women's problems often made guys uncomfortable.

Later, she apologized for the late reply, and he responded, "Well, even that won't chase our love away 😊. I would just tell you that you are well-loved; love conquers everything, you know 🥰. Well, I can't run these days 😂😂😂, life in the slow lane for me 🐢." He then said, "Well, you don't need to run, Wilma.... it can be fun making love to you anywhere at home. 🍆🙊" Oh she thinks maybe he is having fun with a blow-up doll presently. Then the Bon Jovi song pops into her head "Bed of Roses". She thinks roses have thorns it might be unpleasant; she would not enjoy a prick in the bum. Wilma's keep the conversation sensible, replying, "As I said before, it is just something I talk about at present. 🙇‍♂️♀️ he explains I once loved someone when I was younger.... it got crashed; however, I moved on, and I am chasing my destiny. Well, honestly speaking, I am still hoping for the creator to provide me with one loyal one; I will be forever grateful to him 🙏🤘♡." Wilma was sceptical about what he was saying, especially about the creator he kept mentioning. She cautiously asked, "So, you don't mind seeing women with disabilities? It can be very frustrating for other people. 🙇‍♂️♀️" He responded, "Well, I know I have never experienced making love to a disabled woman; however, my case is different from others... I would advise you that you shouldn't give up so easily, OK. When I wake up in the morning, I think of you beside me in my arms! Think 🤭 how it feels to be really in love with someone 💟 ☺ Wilma starts thinking does he wake up with "Betty the blow-up doll in his arms?"☺. The choices should be smart, too, you know that 🐚." She thought he was being kind and replied, "I try and make smart choices! I have made some stupid mistakes as well; one of the reasons I will never get married again! 🙇‍♂️♀️" He replied, "No, you shouldn't say that... You keep remembering all the harmful stuff; it is not nice sometimes, even when you are restricted to things you need... I can't imagine going through depression; it won't be nice, come to think of it 🤭 She returns I have been through a nervous breakdown! I understand what it is like to hit rock bottom ☐🤭😫." Then he said, "Then you should also believe that miracles still happen ☺☺😳." Wilma didn't believe in miracles and replied, "If there are miracles, my guardian angel would have been driven to insanity and become an alcoholic 😩. He goes on to tell her Love is an amazing feeling that everyone needs; it is fun between two people always! 😁" She thinks if he has laid "Betty the blow-up doll down on a bed of roses he might need a good puncture repair kit, he also might enjoy giving her the "kiss of life" She tried to change the conversation by mentioning something that was written about her on Twitter. "I was the hardest working, most caring nutter that Dr. Dodgy Shoes has had the privilege to come to know 😊. That's why I told you that being loved, I tell it will be so much fun 😁. Since meeting you, I found life again and new reasons to live. Your smiling face in the pictures you sent means the world to me. Please let me give a gift to my world, by being mine forever😊♡." Wilma's thoughts wandered to possible erotic scenarios, but she kept the conversation friendly, saying, "I will always be a friend 😊😁. I want to show all the joy along with all the good things life offers, which includes love emotions 💝☺️."At this point, she wondered if he had also watched Graham Norton and made a playful reference to Aladdin and the Magic Lamp. He thanked her for the friendship, to which she replied, "You are welcome! He goes on to say I want to say you shouldn't keep that face in the latest photo you sent me. She asks Why? He explains your face isn't bright and happy; you are looking worried." He then inquired about dinner plans and her evening. "What will you be having for dinner? What are your plans for the evening going to be?" he asked. Wilma replied, "It is going to be quiet, going for a chippy in an hour. Then settle down and watch a film 😁." He then tells her about getting his hair done " I've decided not to cut it short anymore!. Wilma has experimented with many different hairstyles in her life, as everyone has their unique style.

Similarly, Jon Bon Jovi has sported various looks including perms, mid-length, and short hair. It's up to you how you prefer your hair. I've had my fair share of bad styles myself! 😂😂😂 He returns Wow, you're incredibly up to date. Wilma laughs at his observation and replies, "Eh nooo! I keep being told to keep up with the young ones." 😂😂😂 he tells her I can't stop looking at your picture; you're just sweet and amazing! 😍🤩 The shape of your eyes, how you gaze through your glasses 👓🙈. Wilma thinks of Austin Powers, "Do I make you horny, baby?" She playfully flirts, "I am baby spice in disguise! I want to be scary spice." His response is, "I don't think you'd suit Scary Spice; you're too cute for that. So, you're Baby Spice because of your sweet smile 🥰♡🖋. You can't hide your beautiful self for long. Tell me, what are you going to eat tonight, Baby Spice?" 🤭😊 She sends a photo with a black pudding supper 🤪🤪. "Sounds yummy 😊☺," he responds. "I'll be driving home shortly, so I won't talk until I'm home 🏠👣🤩." "No problem 🙏," she replies.

Later in the evening, while Wilma is relaxing, she receives a message, "I'm home now 🙂. What are you doing, sweetie?" "I'm just sitting and listening to music 🙂," she replies. "That's cool 😊. You've had a busy day, enjoy chilling out." "I was thinking about us while driving home, how we met and how our friendship has been building 😊. At first, I didn't think I could trust someone so far from me. You make me want to do things I've never done in my life." Wilma wonders if he has an image of her stuffing a big black pudding sausage into her face or maybe enjoying licking the brown sauce off her pickled onions.

However, she responds, "That's nice 😊. I'm tired and I'll say goodnight. I need my beauty sleep. Xxx" "Sweet dreams 😚," he replies. "Sweet dreams, sweetie 😍."

The following day approached mid-morning, and she greeted with a "good afternoon ☀." "Wilma, I hope you're having a pleasant day ☺🥰♡🍫🍫🍫," he responded. Wilma finished what she was doing and replied, "Thanks! How is your day?" He responds "It's good. My team manager and I just got back from a meeting. We've signed up for another endorsement. I'm happy everything is falling into place," he shared. He sent Wilma a photo of himself, and she wondered about the other man in the picture, investigating and discovering it was Kay Gundlack, a shoemaker, in a photo taken on May 22, 2019. Wilma responded, "Brilliant news 😊 Thanks 🙏♡. He told her However, I'm a bit worried." Curiously, she asked, "Why?" "Honestly, I need someone to hold, to feel that love again..." he confessed. Wilma thought about humorous alternatives but responded, "Love is a beautiful, tender, sweet thing I would like to share with you ☺." She tried to comfort him, mentioning the support of the people around him, to which he replied, "Well, it's not the kind of love about which I am talking. I need that loving feeling 💞🥺." She reflected on his feelings, considering various interpretations but responded compassionately, "Nobody is truly alone; everyone is surrounded by people to help them on their journey. I lost my best friend at the beginning of the year. I am grateful for everyone else who supported me through the grief." He expressed his regrets for her loss and continued to talk about feelings, referring to enjoying a dessert together. "I have strong feelings... you should know, tell me how your night was, I hope you slept well 😽." Wilma shared, "I slept well last night! I awoke to find I have lost my voice which is annoying! I've been preparing for a podcast tomorrow since Monday. I need my voice back; I also have the helpline on Friday, a bit frustrated presently." She reflected on her situation and her friend who passed away, sharing memories. He responded empathetically, "Oh, she was an exceptionally beautiful lady. May her soul continue resting in perfect peace 🙏❣️. We go through things which are not easy, and we also think we don't deserve it." Wilma decided to take a walk around the shoreline, typing, "I know she is at peace; it doesn't stop me from missing the fun and mischief we had together 😁." He acknowledged her memories and experiences, expressing understanding.

Wilma sent images of Patsy and Eddie from Absolutely Fabulous on a wine-tasting night in France, referring to it as a

girls' night in, where everyone gets a little tipsy from sampling various wines. She then mentioned memories of enjoying tapas, lots of wine, and laughter during a holiday in Marbella, stating she doesn't manage drinking well. He shared that he drinks occasionally but prefers smoking. Wilma joked that drinking is her only bad habit and shared a humorous anecdote about her best friend's failed attempt to quit smoking. Reflecting on these thoughts, Wilma decided to take a walk while listening to music. He asked about other friends who smoke and teased about "Calamity Jane," a friend prone to accidents after a few drinks. They bantered about leading each other astray and recalled their group's escapades. Transitioning to the present, Wilma mentioned planning coursework and organizing schedules. As she headed home, Alice Cooper's "Poison" played, and she received a text asking about her day. She expressed a dyslexic moment and feeling like she'd forgotten something, possibly related to email attachments. He offered reassurance and suggested taking it easy.

While setting up for a Zoom meeting, he shifted the conversation, sharing his own experiences of forgetting things in conversations. They both acknowledged the frustration and annoyance it brings. Wilma, during a break in her meeting, offered advice on managing forgetfulness and suggested taking breaks and using techniques like the Pomodoro method. He then asked if she'd had dinner, to which Wilma confirmed she had and reminded him to take breaks, especially during long studio sessions. He then asks, "Tell me why you don't feel the same way, that I feel for you?" you don't know how I feel, whenever am talking to you. She thinks oh shit he wants to get philosophical now when I am in a Zoom meeting! I like to take my time, get to know a person, and also how comfortable they feel talking to me. Well, I will advise you to bring back the "fucking love!" Do not keep it at the back of your heart ♡♡ She was surprised by the message and replied well that is a very assertive statement! He returns Yes because you don't talk about being in love. She returns It depends on your definition of love within a relationship. It is a complex subject of loving someone, I loved my best friend but never told them it was unconditional. I hugged them, supported them and was a calming influence for them. 🧑‍🤝‍🧑 I would always listen to their problems and aid them where I could. He sends well, I am now telling you how love is, it is beautiful and enjoyable when you are really in love with the right person ☺ Love should be practised based on what is from the heart ♡ I am really in love with you, I will confess... Just want to gather you in my arms and make your wildest dream come true, we will work things together. She reads it and thinks wow we are in his fantasy land again making hot sticky chocolate sundaes together. He goes on to say, "Do you feel the same for me, my feelings are real towards you!" Each time I fall asleep I always feel that you are by my side at my right hand. She thinks oh dear he has Betty the blow-up doll beside him in again. He continues with I told you that I am constantly looking at your picture, all the pictures you have sent to me. I keep on looking at them repeatedly, you are blessed and beautiful 😍♡ I wouldn't trade you for anything at all, you should be pampered like an egg... I have fallen for you 😊🙈 Wilma is horrified with being pampered like an egg, does he think I am a female humpty dumpty and will break? She returns I have never had anyone want to pamper me like an egg! I have lots of fun and laughter with all my male friends, I know none of them fancy me. They just joke when I say I will start pole dancing, they will say not to start pole dancing due to the floor not being reinforced! Wow this is a first and I am not sure what to say, she thinks maybe he likes cream eggs biting off the top and licking out the fondant centre, she reads on since the very first day we started chatting, I have been feeling something deep down in me. She thinks too much information try your palm and her five sisters. He continued I was thinking it just too early for me to say this to you, but I decided to let the cat out of the bag. You give me a reason to smile always and never worry about If we take our friendship further, I will be so happy 🍬☺ I would love to lie down in you on my bed, with my arms around your waist s and listen to your heart beating like a drum. It makes me feel that there is someone in this world, whose heart beats only for me, I just can't stop loving you, you are a foxy lady. She wonders how many more love letters she will receive about covering her in sushi and eating it off her, maybe she should give up watching sex in the city. She should maybe sit eating guacamole with chips like Samantha while watching the sexy next-door neighbour take a shower. She tries to cool things down Okay you have told me your feelings. I have built many friendships over the years! Even over the pandemic, nobody has said any of these things to me. I am overwhelmed now and need time to process what you are saying. Have the courage to trust love, I believe this time will be amazing, you are correct you deserve some time to trust your feelings. You are just so special to me, she is thinking, I know this is all a fantasy I wonder if he is reading Fifty Shades of Grey and typing from the book, she simply says thank you 🙏 he continues It's a courageous thing to fall in love. You must be willing to trust somebody else with your whole being, and that's exceedingly difficult, along with being very brave. you've captivated ☐ my heart 🖤 You can't run away from this Wilma 🥹😍 She decides to tell him I know it is difficult and brave to be in love, but I also know all about trust issues, I am not trying to run away. In her mind all the innuendos from the great British bake-off were running through her head, such as checking if she has a "Soggy bottom" He wants her to "give his piping bag a good squeeze" However she is sensible and returns It is flattering that are telling me this! That's why I said that I have been longing to tell you, I thought it was too early for us to start discussing this... but can't hold onto it anymore. I would say that you are just a special kind of human that deserves to be loved so sweetly 😍🥰 She thinks he is smooth with the romance and adds I know that you are surprised about this, distance isn't a barrier... When there is trust in a relationship, then that relationship would be a perfect one. I have never had a perfect relationship, lots of different relationships, but never perfect. He starts with the same here, I believe every lovely relationship deserves lots of trust. Trust in the sense that the female and the male won't have any reason to lose the trust they already built. Wilma is sceptical and tries not to be sarcastic with the discussion. He follows on by telling us we're never so vulnerable than when we trust someone - but paradoxically, if we cannot trust, neither can we find love or joy.

The more trust that exists in a relationship, the more you look out for each other. You have your beloved's back, and vice versa. Trust is a small word; it is extremely powerful! It takes time and no one is perfect! Everyone makes mistakes, it always depends on what mistakes you make on whether they can be forgiven or not. Have blind trust in people, and even if that ends up hurting me, I won't change. I will go on trusting people because that's the only way I know to love someone. Eventually, someone that you trust did something unforgivable, which means that person is having trust issues, or doesn't even love you though pretending that's just it. He then sent Wilma a selfie which she investigated later she found the photo was uploaded on Twitter while relaxing in Milano dated 12/09/2017 Wilma didn't trust him she knew he was an imposter, and she used her skills and sent back human beings are cruel people. I don't have your blind trusting nature; I have been stabbed in the back too many times by people I was supposed to trust and be my friends. I trust the people whom I have relationships with and have had for a long time. I don't rush things and I go at a pace I am happy for building trusting relationships 🙏 he texts Yeah, that's right as a brave and smart woman, all these qualities should be applied when trusting someone. He is trying to flatter, and she replies well it takes time and effort, which I have learned through life. I have made plenty of mistakes, however, if you don't make mistakes, you never learn anything 🙏Everyone learns from his or her mistakes, but when the mistake is made more than once or twice then I just know that person is a coward! The thoughts of this are rubbish and careful replies I would not say that a person making the same mistake is a coward. Relationships are complex things, people live with their abusers for years, and they might not know anything different. They have not been given opportunities that other people have received; people can never judge a book by its cover. There are lots of reasons why people stay together good and bad. He texted Yeah; I agree with you on that point. However, with love and understanding, trust in life can be regained, but it takes two to get through this, and you need to be devoted to each other and sufficiently motivated to show each other that there is no need for jealousy within the relationship. Wilma thinks it takes a lot of counselling and everyone gets a bit jealous, she sends I have always found that there is a hint of jealousy. In my opinion, it makes a good relationship work, everyone has secrets, and you can never truly know someone. Relationships take time and a lot of demanding work; even with your band as you all work closely together, it depends on your definition of the subject. He goes back I must confess that you have already stolen my heart, I speak honestly and sincerely 👮 😌 She returns It was not my intention to steal your heart. I just wanted to be a friend and get to know you better 🙏 He keeps on with you stole it away, and I will only tell you to keep it in a well-preserved place so you will be mine forever😌 She thinks the conversation is a bit corny and returns I will keep your heart in a safe place. Pleased he tells her Thanks for that 😀 When you find your true love it's going to be good 🤭 I can't stop thinking about you all night, I have saved your picture on my phone, and each time I look at it... I admire your beauty and think sweet thoughts 💝💝💝. Wilma thinks okay it is time to leave, he needs to play with Betty the blow-up doll which will be messy! He could be listening to the band Heart singing "All I wanna do is make love to you". Thank you I am now going to say good night. I am tired and need to sleep, sweet dreams 😴😴😴 Alright sleep tight my Wilma love ♡🍃 and have a great night's rest! Wilma has her laptop on and drinking coffee when she receives Good morning my love 💗 She replies to him in the afternoon hello, I have had a fun morning making a podcast. It should be interesting as I have an extraordinarily little voice and croaking away like Kermit the frog with a sore throat 😂😂😂😂😂

A few hours later she receives how is your evening going? It is going well thanks, what have you been up to today? 😊 I have been with my team all day; we have been working on set all day. She laughs and returns always working 😂😂😂. I hope you have had fun 😊 He asks I would like you to know more things about my work ☺ Sure I do have fun. Wilma decides to ask, what would you like to tell me about your work? I know truly little about the industry you work in. He is sly and adds ☺ I would like to welcome you into the fan club ☺ what do you think about becoming a member of my fan club? Wilma knew this was fake through investigating the internet and the official site and returns, that must be new, your website said you don't have a fan club 🙊💁 He is sly and tells her Yes, I wrote that there, however, I have a few of my favourite fans whom I like to introduce. We deliver an inclusive card; your passport is tagged in it as well as your name and country. The red flags are out in Wilma's head, hand over my passport details to a stranger, I smell shit! He goes on to say that will make you a qualified member of my inclusive fan club 😊 I don't want many people to know, that I am keeping things low key, you know what I mean because you are smart Wilma 😊 😎 It is very kind of you to offer, I will give it a miss at present, I am too busy with other projects on around me. He tries to convince her that it won't bother her work for seriously you know I have seen how good and kind you are to other people. That is why I invited you to my club because you are close to me. I have discussed this with my management as well as other members of the team, they would love to welcome you 👑 It would give me immense pleasure to welcome you. It would show you how I will fulfil you, show what I have for you, 😋 Wilma thinks that sounds dodgy, I think he is heading back to checking out my plumping and showing me his plunger, and sends thanks that is very kind of you 🙏 😌 Please just accept my offer or have you already accepted? She is diplomatic and sends I will accept your offer when I am ready. 😌 Okay, just tell me when ready, Wilma feels relieved she is off the hook and replies I will do. 😌 he adds I will be waiting for you! Just know that it doesn't stop you from working 😊 😌 She tells him I know it is just something else for me forget what I have done with it. 👥 👤. 👥 👤 👥 👤 I know my failings when it comes to being dyslexic. I drive people mad by having dyslexic little piles all over the house. Then forgetting what information is where 😂 😂 😂 😂 😂 😂 he says Well that means you are completely disorganised and lose things easily 😆 laughing she returns Yeah. Then when I find things, it ends up like a scavenger hunt trying to find where I put them 👥 👤 👥 👤 Wilma sends a silly gif of Snow White in a padded cell saying I am going slightly crazy. He does not say anything, and Wilma presumes he is busy. The next morning, she finds Good Night my Wilma world 💚🌍 She returns the greeting, 'Morning! How are you today?' he returns 'I'm good, just starting my day as usual,'. As Wilma reads this, she thinks, 'I hope he means working out at the gym.' She reads on as he adds, 'Hope you have had a great start today.' Wilma was not having a wonderful day and had, on several occasions, wanted to throw the laptop out of the window. She texted him back, 'I have done nothing but swear this morning! The joys of being a helpline advisor and the technology you use deciding not to work 🤦‍♀️😱🤬🤬🤬 Lol tell me more, what happened?' 'Firstly, I have no voice so I can't use my Dragon dictation software to fill in all my documentation. My spell check has given up and run away 🤦‍♀️ The hubbub system crashed and wouldn't let me take phone calls or return them. I am using a different system now and getting back on track 😊 Fun morning so far 😛.' He returns 'Lol, it started as a stressful day, however, you were persistent and overcame it. She returns I am an expert at breaking assistive technology, or I just bend it to my will, according to people I work with 😂😂😂😂😂 🤩 he says nice one, you are having a wonderful day now hopefully. Hope you've eaten something?' She says 'Well, still have a few things to do once I finish the helpline. It's my friend's birthday today, I brought back blue-labelled vodka. This is currently in the freezer, I think vodka yoga might be practised later this evening 😂😂😂😂 he says Wow, nice, you be careful with what you are drinking tonight. Also, the happiest of birthdays to your friend! 🎂🎉🎁' She laughs 'I will be careful, I don't usually drink vodka, however, it is a special occasion 😊 I am more of a red wine drinker 😊 Wilma sends the star ⭐ I know you are busy and will not disturb you for the rest of the day! 🙏 Enjoy your weekend 😁' he returns 'All right, I will definitely... Just take care of yourself too ☺️🤗 You don't need to worry about me, I will be fine 😊.' Later in the evening, he sends, '100% for sure, hope you are having a great time ☺️.' Wilma is sitting listening to the Hair Bear Bunch disagreeing about politics and replies, 'I love sitting listening to my friends and their debates 😁.' He responds, 'That's cool 😊 funny Wilma 🤭.' Wilma laughs and tells him, 'This lot would start an argument in an empty room 😆🤣🤣.' He replies, 'For real! You're in an empty room?' She is distracted by their conversation and says, 'I can certainly start an argument in an empty room! 🤣🤣🤣🤣' He says again, 'You're alone?' Wilma realized he did not get the quote about argumentative people; she simply sent him, 'Yes! 😆🤣🤣🤣🤣.' She knew he didn't get what she was talking about with his reply, 'Lol for real, you alone in an empty room and you started an argument? 🤡 Hmm 🤔.' He decided to change the subject and sent, 'How is your evening going, taken dinner?' She returns 'It is a great evening so far! Yes, I have eaten 😁.' He tells her 'I am glad you have been sensible and eaten early enough. 😁.'He asks how the birthday party was. 'I am at the party, we are just having a drink and laughing! Thank goodness there is not a karaoke nearby 🤣🤣🤣🤣.' He inquires if she's still out or if she's home. 'I am at our local, I will be at my friend's house later! I already know YouTube will be on and bad dancing to Tina Turner's Proud Mary 💃🎤🤣🤣🤣🤣.'Wilma still had the video of Mr D shaking his ass at her when at Mr Js for a party while Proud Mary was playing. He replies, 'You will be having a fun weekend.' She laughs and replies, 'Oh, I will, as I am dumped tomorrow night by the guys! Suits me, I can watch Dirty Dancing in peace 😁.'" He decides to tell Wilma, 'It hasn't been easy with me today! It has been extremely stressful throughout the day.' She wonders what might have happened, and he says, 'My team and I did loads of work today.' 'I understand. I hope you were able to make a bit of time to have fun! Chill out and enjoy your evening!' 'Yes, I did have fun, however, it was still stressful with the amount of work involved. This is why it has taken me so long to get around to chatting with you. I missed you as well.' She returns 'I understand! I am not far away; you just need to text.' 'Sure, but I just didn't have the time today. Will you be staying out all night? I hope you release what I am working on shortly; I will be busy myself very shortly!' 'No, I will not be out all night. I will be out late. I will be sleeping in my bed at some point or sleeping on the couch 🤣 🤣 🤣' he tells her 'Stop making me laugh, I don't even have the strength for that. I just arrived home now, and I didn't prepare anything for dinner.'

As Wilma had been looking through Instagram, she knew where the international star was at the time. She also thought that he had a lot of driving to do from Athens to his hometown. However, he tells her, 'The house is dry, no stock at home, you know I'm alone.' Wilma is feeling mischievous and texts back, 'Well, just order a takeaway! Be lazy and sit and enjoy a movie 😁.'He returns 'My balance is exceptionally low; I can't order anything.' She is laughing and thinking, 'Oh, you poor wee lamb.' He goes on, 'I don't have anything in my account... If you transfer me some funds, I can order a takeout.' Wilma now knew what she had suspected about the imposter and couldn't help but laugh and send 😂 😂 😂 😂 😂 'You are laughing at me 😳 Why?' She returns 'Well, of course, I am laughing at you. This is a fantasy you have created as Instagram shows the real person is playing in Athens, just now 🫣' He is annoyed and sends back, 'Well, if you think I'm playing in Athens, just take it that way, but I'm serious. I am in a bad mood as well, damn hungry too.' Wilma had no intention of sending him money and texted back, 'Just Google it! The pictures on Instagram from yesterday say a lot as well!' 'I must admit you have been interested to chat with but not the person you claim to be! Do you not think I have not checked what you were telling me, and the dates on the photos you sent me? 😂 😂 😂 😂' He replies, 'Wow, I am not surprised at all. What do you even think of me? You can't be serious about this; tell me you aren't serious.' An evil grin came over Wilma's face, and she typed, 'Yes, I am deadly serious! What do you think about it 😁?' He returns 'How can someone be pretending to be another person, what the hell?' He must have looked up the official Instagram site and knew Wilma had caught him out. She is enjoying herself and texts, 'I am not pretending to be another person! I am a social scientist studying human physiology! Do you want to play some more? 😁'' LoL, you just making me laugh aloud. I already told you that I don't have the strength for all this, and I can't fake my identity. She mischievous returns a text well, have a good rest! I look forward to further conversations 😁. Smiles 😊' She texted him a few days later saying, 'You are incredibly quiet,' however, Wilma never heard from the flirtatious Thor again!"

The Case of 'Do You Want to Meet Skippy Wilma?'

Wilma received a message from the international star through TikTok, with the person waving to her and saying hi. The curious Wilma was sitting in her cat basket watching TV and sent back, 'Hello, how are you?' 'I am good, and you?' 'Nice to meet you, Wilma! Thank you for inviting me to chat with you; everything is cool, just chilling out. Hope you're having a nice, relaxing day.' 'Yes, it can be difficult with the amount of travelling, must do? You will be glad to go home to your own bed at times. I say this as my friends who travel with their work tell me it's great to get home—the love of getting back to that one bed. I know that it is worth it because, without risk, you can't get things done. Thank you so much for caring. What do you do for work? 'My job is a bit weird. I promote positive neurodiversity. It is quite entrepreneurial and covers many areas. 'WOW! I will just say you are an independent woman who strives to do better. I have an excellent job but never find luck in the love part of life, which is so sad. "Thanks, yet relationships are demanding work. Never give up finding the right person; it never happens overnight—that is just Hollywood movies! 'Yes, you are right in everything you see. How has life been with you? Are you married or single?' 'I am single presently. 'Seriously, that is crazy. You're too beautiful to be single. I would think there are a lot of people wanting to ask for a date in your message box.' 'I never really bothered about it as this year got off to a bad start, but things are getting better! My beauty has only come up recently; it has been weird as nobody has talked about my looks. I know that it might sound weird, but it's the honest truth.' 'She decides to ask, how did you cope with the pandemic? ''The pandemic has been rough; however, I remained positive. I couldn't get out of the house and meet up with fans! It is improving now; it's a little good at least a few tours going on.' 'At least you're getting back to something that you love doing; hopefully, you are not finding it too stressful. 'Wilma had seen on social media that Miley Cyrus talked about having a panic attack on stage, and he messaged back, 'Nothing is easy, but it's worth the stress because it has become part of us. Do you have children?' 'I don't have any children. Please don't have sympathy for me; everyone starts asking questions which are too hard to explain. No, I don't have sympathy for your circumstances. I don't have children in the world to go through my stress.' 'Which country is St. Trinian's found?' 'The UK.' 'Shortly after, he inquires, 'That's nice. What are your hobbies?' 'My hobbies are cooking and art and design.' 'That is lovely. Have you ever travelled to other countries before now?' 'Yes, I like travelling. I have not travelled recently because of the pandemic, but I will come back. She had been chatting with Dr Dodgy Shoes and informed the star, 'I might be going to Malaga to see a European project called the dyslexic compass shortly.' 'Where is your favourite place to travel and see? 'Smiles, I love to visit Dubai, but I haven't been for a while because I haven't got a good partner to have fun with while travelling. It's somewhere I have never been. I have a friend who works in the area who calls it the sandpit. Sometimes you just need to go and have fun with a bunch of totally crazy friends.

It's a wonderful place to be. What are your plans after three months of work?' 'My plans are already starting with going back to studying at university to aid in improving people's perspectives of dyslexia.' She misses out on the fact that it is within the criminal justice system. 'That is wonderful. I hope you don't mind having fun with someone a bit crazy with you there.' At this point, Wilma's phone had run its charge, and she was talking with friends. Later, once she had charged her phone, she said, 'Sorry for the delay in messaging you. I was out for a walk and bumped into friends and their kids, and we started chatting.' 'All right, that's cool. How long have you been in the UK?' 'I have been living here for a few years now. I like it in the UK.' 'She decides to investigate by asking, 'Do you find going from living in New York and living in Berlin weird, as it is too unfamiliar cultures?' 'That is a good question, and according to a recent survey, behind its gruff facade, Berlin is a friendly place. Berliners reckon it is easier to make friends, find love, or have fun in the city than New Yorkers do. But they like to keep their relationships IRL, using social media networks and dating apps much less than NYC. Well, I have never used dating apps personally! I have a good friend who has been turned down on Tinder numerous times; you will go out on a date and then be blocked.'" "I also have friends who attract the weirdest people they would ever date. It's about finding out about the person, which is not 20 seconds. Maybe I'm simply weird. When it comes to dating apps, how does this happen? She does not say he agrees with her that finding the right person does not take 20 seconds. Partner, also asks, 'Do you want to be with someone who's going to make you happy?' 'Of course, I want to be with someone who will truly make me happy! I am human; I want to be accepted for who I am. People don't find this easy with my learning disabilities; it makes me stand out from the crowd. I can be fussy, complex, and difficult; people find me hard to deal with, and I accept this. I know this is personal: how do you perceive yourself? Do you perceive yourself as a romantic, good-looking guy who will save the day? Maybe you're just a famous person who enjoys what you're doing for a living; however, this does intrude on your private life?' 'Most things about myself and life are that I never get proud of the things I'm doing, no matter how much fame. I am a normal guy, gentle and soft. I don't care about disabilities, only care about personality. Yes, I want a woman who is caring, loving, and amazing and who can see me for who I am and accept me.' 'As Wilma knows from talking with the Hair Bear Bunch, they all find different things attractive in women and ask, 'So what is firstly attracted to a woman? I am wondering if it is the shape of her body? The size of her boobs? The size and shape of her bum or maybe her legs? As I hang around with a group of guys, they all have opinions on what attracts them to women.' 'I don't care about body; I get attracted by levels of her thinking and maturity.' 'Wilma laughs at this message and sends back, 'Highly unusual, as you need to talk to the person in the first place; there must be something that gets your attraction to the person. My male friends have the attention span of a 10-year-old if they see someone that fancy, ha ha ha. I like a bit of window shopping with eyeing up a guy's bum along with a good look at their legs. Yeah, for real something is there that connects adult souls. Do you have a good mix of friends? Do you hang around with more male company? How do your female friends fit in with your group? I only ask because my best friend passed away recently. I have ended up in an all-male company! They're great, and the conversation is always controversial, intriguing, and very rude! At least I can give them as many rude innuendos as they give me.' 'I will be with you shortly. I have a meeting with my tour management. Give me a couple of minutes, and I will be with you shortly.' 'Seriously! Please don't make promises you are unable to keep. My darling, need to fix up my manager. I can have more time with you and don't want to keep you waiting. I will write to you soon as I'm free xxx. Okay, stay safe in your adventure.' 'Wilma is feeling mischievous and texts, 'If you're going to visit me, do you fancy playing the violin dressed as Thor, God of Thunder?' Just wondering.' 'He replies, 'I am going to rock with playing my guitar.' Wilma smiles and texts back lots of laughing emojis.' 'It was getting late in the evening, and Wilma was watching Great British Menu when she got a message, 'Are you there?'' 'Yes, I am here. I thought you might be sleeping.' 'I have just finished my meeting with my manager.' She decides to inquire, 'So you have plans already for whatever you're doing next?' 'I'm going to be doing some tours in Australia.' Wilma decided she would keep an eye on the internet to see if he was telling the truth. 'The returns are nice; you will be looking forward to seeing Skippy the Kangaroo?' 'Yeah, do you have Google chat?' 'Yes, I have Google chat. Can we chat there, please?' She added the star to her chat and said, 'Hello, how are you doing?' 'I'm fine, thanks. When are you going to work?' 'As it was coming up for midnight and Wilma was getting tired, she replied, 'I am working tomorrow.,' 'He is getting ready for the next set of questions, 'When's your next birthday?'" "In approximately three- or four-years time 😂😂😂😂.' 'Wow, that's cool. You are funny! Can you send some pictures?' 'Yes, I can send pictures. What would you like pictures of? 🤪' 'I want a cute one.' "Wilma decides to be mischievous and looks through the pictures on her phone, which is definitely cute 🤪." It had been a beautiful day when Wilma and Mr. G were out and wandering around. They had ordered a bottle of white wine and just watched the world by; she was smiling with a white top on and a glass of white wine in hand. Wilma decides to assess him with, 'Send me a selfie of yourself 😊.' He does send a photo followed with, 'You are beautiful like a queen!' 'Why thank you. That is lovely of you to say. You are looking braw 😊' Wilma has noticed that the photo sent, the iPhone was an older design, and she can't see the tattoos that are on his forearms. However, it was a lovely shot of them after having a shower. She did like a bit of eye candy and she imagines "Girl will climb up for true love's first kiss. She thinks maybe she has watched Shrek a bit too much and types back, 'Thanks, I am glad you enjoy talking to me 😊 What are you doing now?' 'Oh, nothing exciting, just drinking a cup of coffee 😂' 'That's nice, you are beautiful 😍♡ I keep watching over your picture 📷' She thinks how cheesy and creepy; her mind goes into overdrive with thinking of the song by Rockwell 'Is somebody watching me?' but replies, 'Ha-ha, thanks 😊' 'You're welcome. Do you have documents to travel?' It was early in the morning, and Wilma wondered where this conversation was going and sent, 'What do you mean by documents for travelling?' 'Do you have a Passport and Visa?' 'Yes, I have a passport,' she is curious and receives, 'Okay, that's good. Have you travelled on the Road?' 'What do you mean by travel on the road? Do you ever drive for tourist tours?' Wilma thinks, "I am not trusted with the control for the Wii in case she puts it through the TV. This person wants her in charge of a bus! Seriously, if she tells the hair bear bunch, they will fall about laughing, and the tour bus will be lost in a ditch somewhere. No, I don't drive." "Why?" She thinks of course they are going to ask this, what is the easiest way to say about dyspraxia? "Oh, I know! because I have no sense of direction." "Oh, sorry about that," she thinks. It's to be expected as dyspraxia is the Cinderella of the neurodiverse "Why?" She thinks of course they are going to ask this, what is the easiest way to say community? She also doesn't want sympathy. "Don't be sorry. 😁" She has sent him a picture of the Espresso martini from her birthday party last year. 'Hmmm, I think a picture of yourself will be better! One of the better photos of myself 🙈' he then inquires 'Thanks, I would like to know if you are interested in a relationship? I am happy to make any friendship first. 🙂 I have communicated with different ladies on TikTok; I felt all they wanted was my money, not real love. I'm a music star artist with millions of followers; I need to be with a single woman I can build all my life with,' she thinks, very clever; this person has done a bit of research, time will tell! 'I am not interested in how much of a millionaire you are; I like meeting and getting to know people 🙏' 'Same here. I am very approachable and easy-going. I also have boundaries on which information I will not give out at this point. My trust is earned over time. 🙏' 'That's good to know. I understand. You then want to know; do you live alone or with a roommate?' 'Yeah, I have a roommate. 😊' 'It was Wilma's turn to inquire, so, what do you enjoy doing for hobbies?' 'Hiking, travelling, concerts, music, reading, fishing, and you?' She thinks through all the other discussions that fishing is a new one to add to the list. 'I will get back to you in a couple of hours, I'm expecting another meeting with my music tour with the manager.' Wilma was sitting listening to Enigma playing Sadness on YouTube and replied, 'Okay, no problem. Talk to you tomorrow. I will be going to sleep shortly xxx.'' In the early hours of the morning, he sends, 'Hi dear 💝' After coming downstairs and putting on the kettle for a cup of coffee, she finds the message sends hello and goes to look at all the emails on her phone.

    A short while later she receives, 'Are you up now?' She thinks no, a poltergeist in the house is texting you at present, have you never seen Rent a Ghost? However, she decides to be sensible with, 'Do you not go to bed?' 'Yes, I did not get much sleep. I was thinking about my tour and discussions with my manager, and it was stressful.' 'What was stressful about your meeting?' 'I am going to be playing my violin 🎻 and meet up with some of my celebrity friends to chill out.' She is not sure what is so stressful about that. Wilma just answers with, 'Hopefully, you enjoyed meeting with your friends 😊' 'Yes ✅' She thinks that is great to know he enjoys meeting with friends. He follows on with, 'Though I miss our conversation,' she wonders how long before she starts receiving messages of a sad and lonely prince in need of a shag. He then moves the conversation on with "It's okay, how do you want to see yourself in three months' time?"

"Well, that is a nice easy question to answer. I will be starting my studies again in three months. 😀" Yes, she was getting all the forms filled in on her laptop for starting DD212 theories and concepts of criminology. She was so excited she could crush a grape. Wilma could not believe that her second year had finished, and the third year was not far away. "Okay, that's great." "Yes, it is exciting stuff. 😊 Yes, it is. Do you want to go to Australia with me?" Wilma had done a bit of investigating, and this star was easy to follow. There is no information on their official website. She also noticed on Instagram that the international superstar is on holiday, it looks like they are cycling in the Maldives. She decides to play along by replying, "Wow, what a massive opportunity. When are you visiting Skippy?" "Soon." She thinks that is as helpful as a fart in a wetsuit, "I will not hold my breath for information." She decides to be curious. "Wow, what part of Australia are you visiting? Sweden, okay geography is not great. Where the hell is Sweden in Australia? Try not to be too off-putting with the reply. Unusual, I thought you might be going to Sydney. Maybe if you have time go to Bondi Beach for some surfing. 👰💁" "Yeah, I will visit Sydney." "Nice! Playing in the Opera house?" "Yeah, I am. We going to have a lot of fun together." She has not said anything about arriving; this is an assumption on their part but will lead them on with their conversation. "Most definitely! 😂😂😂😂"Wilma sat down with her laptop and started writing for her blog and looking through documents which she needed to update. A few hours passed when she received, "What are you doing now?" "I am editing some documents. 😊 Really, that's good. Needs to be done. 👰💁 Aren't you going to work?" She thinks, why would they say this after telling you I am editing documents? "I am at work. 😎" She decides to ask, "What are you doing today?" "Writing more songs 🎧, recording more music, playing my violin 🎻 and discussing with my manager how we will move forward with concerts." "Okay, well done in trying to convince me," and she sends, "Nice! I'll be sure to have a fun day!" "Thanks, you too, please can you send me a picture of you." She sends a picture of herself with her Plantronics headset for using her Dragon dictation software while editing documents. "There you go. 😊" "So beautiful. 😍♡" She rolls her eyes and sends back a standard answer, "Thank you for the compliment." "You're welcome. 😊 What do you have for lunch? 🍕🍝🍔" "I made a tuna sandwich with crisps. 😊" He sends over a selfie of himself which was recently realized on Instagram and Facebook, wearing a really cool set of Thomas Stobo sunglasses then inquires, "Do you like this?" "Very cool, you really suit the sunglasses. 😍" Wilma wonders for a second if she had replied that she did not think they looked good on him. "Glad you like it. 😊 Well, a bit of flirting does not hurt anyone, and I certainly do like it. 😊" "Good to hear. 😊 Can we dance together while in Sydney?" She thinks, "We have found another dancer, is this coming from his mother's side? Just must tell him about dancing like the honey monster. 'I would love to be able to dance. I was given two left feet. I hope you don't mind if I stand on your feet a lot. 😂😂😂😂'" "Not at all, that's going to be cool. 🆒❄️ You're exceedingly kind. 😊 But how am I sure we can date?" "That is an exceptionally good question. I haven't thought about it yet. ☐ Please do, as I have noticed the characteristics of a good woman. There, I will keep telling you this fact!" "Why thank you!" "You're welcome. When are you going back home?", "What do you mean about going back home? When are you finishing your work?" She sits and wonders for a minute before saying, "In about 90 minutes. 😃""Oh 😁," that's cool. 👍 He sends over the next selfie of himself wearing the Key Largo t-shirt range. She had received this picture earlier in a different conversation. She decided to comment with "You look lost in thought! 🤔" "What do you mean?" "Yeah, there is always a communication issue," as she has not understood some of the questions, he has asked her throughout their conversation. "What is the easiest way to put deep in thought? 'You're daydreaming, thinking of other things.' 🧐💡" "Yes, great," he agrees with her observation. As he has made her smile, she sends a black and white picture of a woman, with her hands under her chin, saying "Be the reason someone smiles today or the reason they drink! Whatever works. 😁 Nice picture." "Glad you like it. 😃 Yeah, I do. You are beautiful. I will keep repeating this. Listen to my words👂." "Thank you. You told me that earlier today. 😃" She decides to inquire, "Do you have a relaxing evening planned?" "Yes, I do," she answered. "Good, it is important to make some time for yourself. It is good for your mental health. 😃" "Yes, it is." She is wrapping up as she goes to the chip shop for dinner for herself and Mr. G, "Wish you enjoy the rest of your day. 🙏😃"

Much later in the evening, she ends their conversation for the day with "Good night handsome. Sweet dreams. 😴😪😪" "Thank you, I will. 😁" Wilma was still fast asleep, and he sent her a message at silly o'clock in the morning. "Hi, good morning beautiful. I have just returned from tours." She finds the message and is still half asleep. She is wondering what he is talking about saying just returning from tours. She just simply replies "Good morning. 😃 What's up?" "Why would he ask this," she wonders as she tries to wake up and simply replies, "Nothing is wrong. I am simply just trying to wake up. 🥱" "Oh, okay, it is 11:06 here." As she suspects he is in the Maldives, she checks the world clock time. Yes, it is the correct time over in the Maldives. She is still sceptical and replies, "You will be having lunch shortly. I am just having breakfast shortly. 😅" "It's 11:09 PM, maybe he meant AM. Does he suspect she was checking the time? What part of the world could he be chatting to her from," and replies, "I need coffee to wake up. Oh, okay, what are you having for breakfast?" "Bran flakes and banana. 😊" "Yummy. 😊 What do you enjoy for breakfast?" "Pizza 🍕 and coffee☕." "Wow, which is a weird diamond ring on Telegram likes pizza for breakfast, the last time she had pizza for breakfast was recovering from a hangover. It was normal when waking up after a good drink with friends to finish the cold pizza in the morning, Johnny hates Jazz and comes onto her Spotify playing 'Turn Back the Clock.' She replies, "A nice healthy start to the day. Not done that breakfast for a while. 😂😂😂😂😂" Then sends the picture of the spicy pizza she had on Friday. Covered in lots of jalapeño peppers and pepperoni, it was great. The hair bear bunch had mentioned the fact that it was the biggest pizza at the table. It had been the same size of dough as everyone else; it was just rolled out thinner. No one believed her, oh well. They also said no wonder she was fat when she said she also had tiramisu for dessert. 'My lunch last week.' Wow, that's nice." She wonders what other sort of food he enjoys. As it was a picture of a spicy pizza, she asked, "Do you like spicy food?" "Yes, I love it. Do you want to make some for me?" She thinks it will probably never happen but can play along with the game. "I can make you spicy food. 😃 Really, I can't wait." This reply says she has him excited and decides to further the conversation, "I love cooking. The kitchen looks like a bomb site by the time I am finished. I haven't had any complaints from my friends yet. 😃 Okay, that's great. What are you doing right now?" "Making my poster for the #nowrongpath campaign to put on Twitter later. It is a great campaign for school leavers that there is no wrong path for someone's career." "Okay, that's cool. Can you come down to California City 🏙?" Bingo, so that is where you are hiding. This is a bit different from the holiday pictures. She Googled this to find it is southwest of Death Valley and just north of where they keep Air Force One. She also checks out the images of the city compared to the Maldives. How interesting but gives nothing away with the reply to Wilma. "Not at the moment, why? For fun, I want to chill out with you." "She thinks it's great not to blow my cover just yet," and replies "Awww that would be lovely. I am a bit snowed under with work commitments. 👨‍👩‍👧‍👦 When's your birthday?" "February 🎂🎂🎂" "Wow, that's nice. Mine is next month." As she can't remember when his birthday is, she checks Twitter, which he doesn't currently use. She remembers the wonderful time she went out with her friends for her birthday. So, Wilma decides to text: "Doing anything nice with family and friends for your birthday?" She thinks, "Oh dear, I hope he is not expecting me to be there for his birthday. If possibly I have any dear thoughts, I'm not exactly sure what this means." She thinks back to the sudden loss of Princess Twinkle Toes and replies, "Life sometimes takes a funny turn. Nobody can predict what is going to happen. Just enjoy yourself. 😃" "Alright, thanks." Then a sudden thought occurs to her, and she sends, "You will be having lunch shortly. I am just having breakfast shortly 😅 It's 11:09 PM."

She smiles but does not hear from him till the following day when she receives, "Good morning. I hope you are enjoying the nice weather. 😃" "Good morning 🌸🌸 How are you today?" "I am good, and you?" Wilma was looking forward to going for a nice walk later and said, "Yes, everything is good. It looks like it will be a beautiful day. 😃" "Yes, it is." Then he decides to ask, "Why are you not accepting us to be in a relationship? Am I not the perfect celebrity for you?" "Oh, a bit heavy for first thing in the morning but okay," she sends, "Every relationship starts from a gradual process. We have only been chatting for a couple of days. I do have commitments and don't just drop everything! I am happy talking to you. You are rushing me for some reason? What do you mean? I get the feeling you just expect me to drop everything I am doing suddenly. I have been planning a few things for months and I want to see them through. It has taken me a while to get these things in place and I will not suddenly abandon them. This will not stop me from talking to you. Just don't try and rush things. 🙏" "Okay, I understand," she is relieved and sends, "Thank you 🙏 What are you up to today?" "I am promoting my tour and relaxing for another interview." "Yes, he might be doing an interview," she could not be sure and said, "Well, I hope your interview goes well! 🙏" "Yes, dear." "What are you doing now?" Wilma sat replying to some of the people on her Twitter account and promoting #nowrongpath on LinkedIn. She told him, "My Twitter account has gone mad with the #nowrongpath promoting positive dyslexia for a younger generation to believe in themselves and their career choices. 😁" "Oh, sorry about that," she thinks, a weird answer and asks, "Why? You said your Twitter went mad," she thinks you are slightly mad and sends, "Yes, with positive responses to my post. 😁" "Okay, that's good."

The following day late in the afternoon, Wilma receives, "Good morning! Your sweet teddy bear. I am missing you; I can't wait to see you. 'Sometimes I wish there was no alarm clock because that is the only device which wakes me up while I am dreaming of you. Let me wake up next to you, have coffee in the morning and wander through the city with your hand in mine, and I'll be happy for the rest of my little life.' My guiding star! Without you in the few days, I would have been lost in the darkness of the universe. 💟💝❤" Wilma is having an Elvis moment; she can hear him singing "I Can't Help Falling in Love with You." She said, "Good morning. I hope you had sweet dreams and refreshed for a new day. 😁" "Yes, I did! How's your day going? How's London?" "My day is going well. The weather is great presently. I will enjoy it before it disappears. 😁 Maybe go to Hyde Park with my lunch and do a bit of sunbathing for half an hour and just people-watch." "That's good to hear. Are you done with today's work?" "Just about finished. Just putting a few final additions to a document, I am working on. 😁" "Okay, that's good. What's the name of your workplace?" She missed the opportunity to tell him she was working in Harrods! "I have been doing a document for a company called Scanning Pens as I have been testing out their GDPR-friendly pen." 😁 "Sounds interesting." "It is really interesting. It is an excellent product. My preference is still OrCam technology. It is amazing the technology they have developed for blind and visually impaired people. They found it also aids learning disabilities. They have given me the honour of being an ambassador. 😁" "Wow, this is so amazing! Congratulations! 👏👏🎉" "Thank you. 😁" Wilma had been preparing a Caesar salad for herself and Mr. G. Mr. G, of course, grumbled about it because he had been given rabbit food for his dinner and she had not added chips. She takes a photo and sends it to the scammer – a nice Caesar salad. 😊

The following day early in the morning, she receives, "Good Morning. 😊" Then later in the day, she receives, "How are you? How's your day going so far? 💗💗💗" "It is going well, thanks. How is your day going?" "Awesome. 😎 What are you doing now?" "Shopping for dinner. 😁" "That's cool. 😊 What are you going to get for us? Pizza. Do you want your pizza deep-fried?" "That's cool. 😊 I want to ask you a question ❓" Wilma is curious to see where this conversation is going. "What is the question?" "Please tell me what you think? Can you give me a chance to have a better future with you?" Wilma laughs at this and thinks there is no chance but sends back, "We can see what happens. It is early days, just take one day at a time." Wilma thinks she needs a cunning plan and reads his reaction. "What do you mean? Don't rush, just keep talking to me presently." "All right, I will be patient," he says, and then inquires, "How did your work go?" "It was not bad today. I have had worse days at work. How are things going for you? "Everything is cool, well I am not really as I argued with my manager as he has been cheating on me!" Wilma thinks this is not the case but sends an empathetic message, saying, "Sorry to hear that." "Thanks, so much dear. I would like to know when's your birthday?" "It is a while away, don't worry about it just now 😊 Mine is September 4." "Really," she thinks, "you have it on the internet dumbass," but he decides to pursue a different question, "Have you ever been in a relationship with someone before now?" "Yes, I have! Why did you separate and become single?" "He was a total asshole! Some men just behave crazy; women don't deserve to be treated badly." "Thank you 🙏 I had a very terrible relationship with my ex," Wilma knows about the relationship breakdown as she had researched it on the internet and thinks back to the Johnny Depp V Amber Herd case. "Yes, men can be in bad relationships as well. It is just not talked about as much as women in bad relations." He texted "What really impresses you to love someone?" Oh, that is a good question, and she thinks about how to reply and eventually sends, "Time and patience." "That's nice." She smiles and returns, "Thank you 🙏 You are always welcome," then inquires, "What are you doing now?" "Wilma was talking nonsense with the hair bear bunch. I am enjoying time with my friends 🙏." He disappeared and never chatted with Wilma until late in the morning the following day. "Hi, my queen ♡♡♡" "Hello, how are you today?" "I'm fine and you?" "Yes, I am good thanks 😊 What are you doing now?" "Catching up with a few things, such as my emails. 👻💡" "Wow, you are very historical and talented." Wilma was confused by this comment. "What do you mean?" "I think it is beautiful that you are smart and talented," this was followed with "Sorry to ask, how old are you right now?" "Why thank you, that is nice of you to say that 😊 It's my pleasure. It is time for some mischief. I will leave you to guess; a lady never gives her age away. 😀" He argues first, then sends, "I guess my sweet beauty is 37-42."She likes this guess but is not giving anything away with, "Thank you. How did I do, my queen? I want to know if I am in the right area?" She gives an evil grin while typing, "I am not saying anything. 😁""Are you sure?" He must be a bit frustrated, and she keeps him going with, "Yes 😼 😁 You don't want to tell me!" She can imagine his spoon lip coming out and sending back, "No! Why?" "Since you want to know, I am 103 😀" Oh my God! You look amazing for your age!" She says "Glad you like it 👏 Yeah, I love it." He absolutely could not take Wilma's sarcastic thoughts about age as she never heard from him again.

The Case of 'Will You Be My Queen'

Wilma engages with another international star in the fascinating realm of TikTok. Aware that this star doesn't maintain an official presence on TikTok currently, she sits sipping tea in her cat basket and receives a message: "Hello big fan 🫶". Subsequently, he shares a Gmail address; entering Google Chat, she receives a warm welcome to his private space. "Well, this is a nice start," she thinks and replies, "Hello, I hope you are enjoying your day 😃." He responds, "I am! Once more thanks for your love and support towards me. I appreciate it." Wilma smiles and replies, "I am glad to hear you are having a great day. Thank you for joining me on TikTok 😃." She notices on her phone that the international star had been following her TikTok posts and had liked some related to dyslexia. "Wow, that's nice," she remarks, expressing her gratitude. He replies, "You're welcome! It's a great privilege having you here. Hope you're cool with that." "Thank you once more," she smiles, "Yes, I am cool with it. 🙏."

"I would love to know more about you if you don't mind," he continues. Wilma, sensing an unlikely connection beyond social media, decides to engage. He asks about her job and marital status, expected questions that offer her a chance to discuss dyslexia. She responds, "Sure, not a problem. I am a dyslexic person and a student; I blog about dyslexia, which is a neurological glitch that fuels my creativity. However, I struggle with reading and writing. I use a lot of assistive technology to aid me with my studies. I support people with similar issues, and I am not married." Curiosity leads him to ask her age. Instead of a direct answer, she quips, "A lady never gives away her age 😂😂😂😂." When he inquires why, she teasingly responds that everyone tends to guess wrong, which makes her happy as they often think she's younger. He responds with a "really," and she recalls a similar conversation on TikTok where someone had guessed her age completely wrong. "Oh yes! I once had someone guess I look twenty-eight 😂😂😂😂," she shares with amusement. The conversation steers toward hobbies, and Wilma lists her interests—art and design, cooking, walking, swimming, listening to music, and creative writing. When asked about her favourite colour, she cheekily responds with "orange" this time. The international star reciprocates with his hobbies—cooking, swimming, reading, walking on the beach, playing checkers, enjoying comedies, outdoor photography, and spending time with friends. Wilma finds the response cool but isn't entirely sure of its authenticity. The conversation moves to culinary preferences, and when asked about partying habits, Wilma admits she prefers gatherings at friends' houses and occasionally attends a local hangout on Friday nights with a quirky crowd. He inquiries about her family, and she cautiously replies, "My parents are getting older, and my sister lives even further away from them than I do. "Finally, he asks about her likes and dislikes in a relationship. Wilma ponders this as relationships are a tricky subject. Drawing from her experience counselling people, she believes there's no right or wrong answer in this domain, she answers "Everyone has good and bad days. Some things annoy you, and my friends often jest that we women cause nothing but chaos by disrupting a man's routine 😂😂😂😂😂. Well, that's true," she thinks, considering it must have given him a laugh if he agrees with the Hair Bear Bunch. Next, he inquires, "Do you smoke, drink alcohol, or do drugs? Also, what's your favourite food?" Wilma responds, "I do indulge in a bit too much red wine on weekends 🥴. However, I don't do drugs or smoke. As for my favourite food, it's a tough question as I love trying new things, often after watching cooking shows! I think it'd be nice to try making it myself." "Do you believe in true love?" he asks. Wilma thinks love at first sight is a load of rubbish! "It depends on your definition of true love. There are a lot of diverse ways to look at true love," she reflects, and he agrees with her. "What turns you off?" he inquires. Wilma types, "Ignorant people!" He responds, sharing his turn-offs: "For me, it's fake behaviour, lies, deceit, cheating, quarrelling, and argumentative people." She agrees with much of what he says but also knows to tread carefully. "I don't like arguing; it upsets my dyslexia. This makes me frustrated and causes a lot of anxiety and panic attacks. I tend to avoid negative people; it makes my life easier." "What are the five most important things in your life?" he asks. After some thought, Wilma replies, "Good mental health, happiness, having fun with my crazy friends, going on adventures, exploring, challenging myself to learn new things 😊." "What are two things you can't live without?" he inquires further. "One would be my assistive technology to help me organize my disorganized world, and also my cooking utensils 👨‍🍳💡," she responds. "What would you cook for a date at home?" Wilma knows everyone has different tastes and responds, "It would depend on what my date likes. I've been on dates that turned into disasters because of fussiness." She thinks about Bridget Jones's diary and making blue soup. "How do you normally spend your leisure time?" he asks. "It depends; I love being creative," she responds. Then the request comes, "Send me a picture of yourself." She eventually sends one. "If you see somebody you don't know who needs help, would you be of any support?" He likes the photo and compliments her, to which she responds, "It would depend on the circumstances; I would try to find out how to help them." What do you spend most of your money on?" he probes. Wilma now finds it intrusive but decides to reply, "My bills 🙊💡." He probes further, "How much?" At this point, Wilma decides to shut down the conversation with a firm "None of your business!" He then inquires "Would you like to marry?" he asks. Wilma internally screams "Noooooooo!" and firmly responds, "No, I am not getting married. I've been married before, and it's a mistake I don't intend to repeat after my divorce." "Do you talk about your feelings with someone else?" He responds affirmatively, sharing his willingness to listen and support. Wilma responds, "Yes, of course. I have a difficult job that can be heartbreaking at times. Talking to the right people for advice helps." He offers his support, "I have the arms to give you a hug, ears to listen, and a heart aching to see your smile through chat, mail, or phone." "I am delighted to have met you." "Very smooth, whoever you are. Awww, thanks! I'm enjoying chatting with you 😄. I look forward to becoming friends 😄." "Yes, me too. Then I will tell you more about me! I am an honest, kind-hearted, hardworking person who needs the support of a loving woman.

Ideally, I am confident in what I want and who I am. I seek a woman who will love me for who I am, not what I have, someone who can take care of me." "Thank goodness I don't need a dating app! Relationships take time. Only Hollywood has romances that happen in minutes." He responds "Yes, you're right," he responds, knowing he might be saying what he thinks she wants to hear. "Each moment that you and I spend together is so magical that I catch myself smiling for no reason at all." She thinks "He's talking out of his arse, but responds with awww how sweet of you to say 🙏," she muses. "I cannot tell you exactly how I feel, but I hope that you feel the warmth of my love whenever we are together. I look forward to supporting you," he continues. She thinks, "It's okay, I am a dumb fat chickaboo; I have watched Police Academy." "I know you will be busy going back on tour soon," she remarks, acknowledging his upcoming schedule. The first of the love letters arrive, expressing deep sentiments. Wilma finds it overly dramatic and thinks, "Why don't you just break out singing 'No Explanation' by Peter Cetera?" She responds politely, "Cool 🙏. It's lovely getting to know you." He continues with declarations of affection, saying, "Honey, for me, my heart accepts you even though we have not yet met in person. You look so harmless, honey, and I can't wait to meet you in person soon." She chuckles at the "looks harmless" comment and replies with a cheerful, "That's sweet 😊. What time is it in your country now?"

Wilma purposely avoids giving the exact time, simply saying, "It is the afternoon." He responds, "Okay, I will write to you later." She casually replies, "No problem. Enjoy the rest of your day and talk with you later 🙏."

Later that evening, while watching TV, Wilma receives a text saying hello. He asks about her evening and if she's eaten. She jokingly responds, "Yes, I have eaten and had a snooze afterwards 😂😂😂." "Okay, good. I miss you," he says. Wilma thinks it's a bit premature and playful and wonders if he has seen "The Fall Guy" falling flat on his face. "What have you been up to this afternoon?" he probes further. "I'm good, can we talk better?" Perplexed by his cryptic message, she asks for clarification. He continues with a vague inquiry about her current location. She simply replies, "I am at home."

He goes on about feeling closer and more intimate. Wilma responds, "I'm glad you feel comfortable talking with me 😃." He asks about her reading preferences, and she shares that she enjoys various materials. Then, he sends a message expressing how she occupies his mind throughout the day. Wilma finds it intense considering they've only recently started talking. She humorously remarks that while her mind may be occupied, it's with various things, not solely focused on getting to know him. "Yes, you're right. One last thing before I go," he starts. "I've been trying to tell you something, but I've not been able to bring myself to do that." Curious, she asks, "What have you been trying to tell me?" She thinks, "Oh, for goodness' sake." "I think this is the time for me to say I'm in love with you," he declares. She responds sceptically, "Do you fall in love with everyone you chat to this quickly?" Seemingly typing frantically, he insists, "I'm trying to find the words to express the feeling in my heart. I care about you deeply, but I don't know where to start. I guess I will start right here, right now. You are the one I want to be with, the one I want to give myself to. You'll be the last, the one I want for life until the day I die. You are the one God sent from heaven above to be my future wife. You brighten my day, your smile is so bright, and you are the one I wake up to each morning." Wilma chuckles at the dramatic romantic declarations and thinks, "The computer says no." He continues, expressing his longing for her, "I want to be with you; you are alone, your image is painted in my heart. I want you to be the love of my life." Amused, she replies, "You haven't gotten to know me just yet. You might find me incredibly annoying once you get to know me. Everyone has their habits, and they can clash. It takes time to get used to them. You might be extremely uncomfortable with the chaos my dyslexia brings to everyday living!" But he persists, expressing more affection, "You mean a lot to me. I can't even concentrate on my work! You're always in my thoughts! I really love you; I want you to give yourself to me." Amused by his overflowing emotions, she responds with a touch of humour, "I am sure you will have no problem concentrating on your work. She thinks oh dear and responds my friends are used to my chaos, but I've faced a lot of discrimination from others. People have very little understanding of living with dyslexia." He continues with more love-themed messages, to which she responds with practical anecdotes about her life and its challenges, including playful mishaps with Wii games. Then, he delves into philosophical thoughts about love being tested by distance and obstacles. He mentions faith in God, prompting her to mention her lack of belief in religion. Ignoring her comment about religion, he continues showering her with affectionate vows and declarations of eternal love. Wilma sees the intensity of his emotions but maintains a grounded perspective, acknowledging her life experiences and the need for understanding beyond romantic ideals. "During sad times, an angel should come to you, open your eyes, and see who that angel is, for that is your one true love," he says, trying to be poetic. She responds with a humorous quip, "I've already made my guardian angels alcoholics! They're all in rehabilitation after having a nervous breakdown! 🧙‍♀️👻👾👻" Not discouraged, he continues with more declarations of undying love, saying, "The love I have for you is strong and enduring. It's being in love with you that makes me happy. I cannot wait for the day that we can join our lives together." She lightens the mood with a humorous metaphor, thinking, "Okay, he wants to show off his lunchbox; I wonder what size of Subway he offers, a 9-inch or 16-inch?" I hope he takes some chocolate eclairs to finish off the afternoon I do enjoy sucking out the cream. He keeps pouring his heart out, expressing intense emotions and longing for her. Trying to keep it grounded, she responds, "It's sweet that you keep telling me you love me, but considering you've only known me for a short period, just chill out, there's plenty of time 🙏." Undeterred, he continues with more enthusiastic expressions of love and desire, describing future fantasies and their life together. Getting tired of the overwhelming affection, she responds more assertively, "I've already told you that I'm not getting married. Relationships don't move as quickly as that in life. He returns Please take a deep breath and calm down." He responds with understanding, but shortly after, disregards her words by requesting a picture of her. Refusing to comply with his request, she replies, "You will be disappointed. You'll just have a black screen; I am just listening to music in the dark and relaxing 🙏." She sends a clear message by focusing on her activities rather than engaging in romantic conversations. Finally getting some peace, she bids him good night, hoping to avoid further romantic exchanges.

The next morning, he tries initiating conversation again, but she's busy and replies briefly. As he becomes more insistent throughout the day, she responds when she can, trying to focus on her work and not encourage his needy behaviour. Feeling a bit exasperated, she continues her day, answering his queries with brief, distracted responses, hoping he might notice her busyness and tone down his messages. Wilma woke up feeling unwell, dealing with a runny nose, a bad cough, and a sinus headache. Despite her condition, she received a message asking how she was doing. Feeling terrible, she replied, "Hello, I am rubbish today. I've come down with a cold. Spent most of the night sneezing and coughing." When he asked for her picture, she was not up for it, feeling unwell and replying, "No! I'm not sending a picture of me sneezing my head off and snotters everywhere 🤧🤧🤧." However, he persisted with queries about her whereabouts and expressed his happiness at chatting with her again.

Wilma focused on her discomfort, responded curtly, "We didn't stop chatting. I'm just busy working, now I have a sinus headache. Talk to you later." Despite her attempts to disengage, he continued expressing his affection and wishing her a good day.

Later in the day, feeling grumpy due to her cold and headache, she replied tersely when he checked in on her. Even when he expressed concern, she couldn't help but be sarcastic. Despite her cold, he persisted with questions about her well-being and continued with romantic sentiments.

Trying to brush him off, she expressed her frustration with the cold, but he continued asking about her activities and expressing his feelings, completely missing her tone and condition. Even when she hinted at her visit to the vet, he persisted in requesting a picture and expressing his longing to see her. Wilma's attempts to convey her illness and disinterest were met with persistence, and she found herself continuously fielding his requests and affectionate messages despite feeling sick and uninterested in continuing the conversation. Feeling awful, Wilma was not in the mood to take a selfie. When he asked about her whereabouts, she replied while struggling to get ready to visit the vet due to her illness. She told him she'd text later and simply acknowledged his message with a thumbs-up.

Despite her unwell state, he continued with his expressions of love and affection. Ignoring these, Wilma walked slowly to the vet, feeling extremely unwell. After a while, she received another message asking if she was there. She replied briefly and mentioned having a chest infection, although she noticed her auto-correct had played a trick on her.

He persisted in asking for a picture, and Wilma, feeling unwell and exasperated, sent a picture of Beaker from the Muppets to illustrate how she looked at that moment. Confused, he asked what it was, to which she explained it was how she currently looked. He continued insisting on a picture and expressing his love, which irked Wilma, especially while she was dealing with her illness. She firmly stated that she was having difficulties due to her health and was not in a position to take a selfie. His final question about her love for him, after her clear explanation of being unwell, ended their conversation abruptly. Wilma felt relieved that the persistent messages stopped, allowing her to focus on recuperating from her illness without further distractions.

The Case of "From Italy with Love"

Wilma received a message on social media one day from a smooth Italian. The person claimed to be impersonating an international star from Croatia. He sent her a WhatsApp number, which she checked and found originated from Italy. Wilma decided to investigate and greeted him with, "Hello dear, nice to meet you here." He sent a photo of himself, which Wilma tried to find on the internet with little success. She replied, "Nice to meet you, how are you today? I am good, and you? What is your name?" "My name is Wilma," she continued, "Wow, you have a nice name. Can I have your picture?" Wilma, feeling mischievous, sent a picture of Patsy and Eddie from Absolutely Fabulous, saying, "I am the one in the pink." "Wow, you look so exceptionally beautiful," he replied, attaching an emoji of a rose. Then the interrogation began. "Do you have kids? Are you married?" Wilma barely had time to answer, "I do not have kids; I am also not married." The next question was, "What is your occupation?" She replied, "I am an assistive technology trainer." As usual, the person at the other end didn't seem to know what Wilma was talking about and replied, "You have a respectable job. "It was late, and Wilma headed off to bed.

The following morning, she found a message asking, "How old are you?" She replied, "A lady never gives away her age," to receive a response of "Good morning, dear." She answered, "Morning." He started again, "How was your night?" "It was good, nice, and relaxing," she replied. "How was your evening?" "It was nice, thanks. What are you doing now?" "Just chilling with a cup of coffee." He resumed his interrogation, "What is your favourite colour?" She wondered which colour to choose this time and decided on yellow. He followed up with, "My favourite colours are red and white. What is your favourite food and drink?" "I don't have a favourite food or drink as there are too many to choose from," she replied. The next question was, "What do you like doing the most?" She responded, "I like doing lots of things." He told Wilma, "I love going to the beach and playing my cello," though she already knew this from TikTok and YouTube videos. "What are you doing now?" "I am just catching up with my cooking programs. Have a wonderful day," she replied. Wondering where in the world he was, she said, "Have an enjoyable day yourself. "Later in the day, she received another message asking, "What are you doing now, dear? I am chatting with my nutty friends." He decided to ask, "Do you have parents?" She answered sensibly, "Yes." The next thing he wanted to know was if she had siblings. Wilma, keeping her private life guarded, answered, "No, I don't have any siblings." "What time is it over there?" Wilma, not caring much for time, made it up, replying, "It's dinner time." "Dear, do you believe in love at first sight?" he asked, a smooth operator as sung by Sade. Wilma's thought bubble popped up with "What a load of rubbish," but she texted back, "No, I don't. I like to get to know people; it's my preference." "What I want to tell you is not a thing to joke about. If you are not comfortable with it, you can let me know," he said. "I shouldn't have said this, but it has been bothering me for a long time now. I just have to say this with a clear conscience." Wilma could guess what was coming but replied, "What are you talking about?" "I am sorry to say this, but I have fallen in love with you. Can you find a place for me in your heart for me to stay forever?" She thought seriously and typed into her phone, "I have never had anyone fall in love with me that quickly! Yes, dear, will you accept me as your hero?" She responded, "I will accept you as a friend; I don't need a hero." "Why? I am an independent woman," she retorted. He replied, "That doesn't matter. I want you to accept me into your heart." Realizing he was a bit of a nut job, she answered, "It is early days, and I don't know you well enough presently." He persisted, "As time goes on, we can understand each other. Can you create a space in your heart for me to stay there forever?" We'll see what happens; we've just met up. He seems to be seeking someone lonely and asks, "Can you create a space in your heart for me to stay forever, baby?" "Why?" She inquires. He explains, "Because I want to spend the rest of my life with you, darling, forever xxxxxx." She thinks, "Real nut job," and responds, "You don't know me! You might not even like me!" "My dear, the beauty of your heart is more important than the beauty of your face. So, I love you for who you are?" he persists. She thinks he's exceptionally smooth and says, "You can love me for who I am, however, it is shallow to think you know someone after such a brief time. It's okay, but can we be good friends in sincerity and honesty for now?" "Yeah, okay," Mr D concedes. He returns to the subject of motor racing, which bores Wilma. "What are you doing now, dear?" he asks. "Chatting with my group of nutty friends," she replies. Then he asks, "What time is it over there?" Wilma never gives away the time and types, "It is evening time." "Okay, I hope you have a lovely day with friends?" he wishes. "I always have a fun time with my friends, always wholesome fun," she asserts. Wilma heads home and snoozes in her cat basket, receiving a message, "It is nice to have a wonderful time, what are you doing now, dear?" "Well, I have just woken up after having a snooze. What time is it over there?" "No idea. I have not looked. What is the weather like over there?" Wilma looks out of the window and answers, "It is overcast but dry outside. What are your plans today?" "Just texting you, dear. Please enjoy the rest of your evening and take care of yourself," he says. "I will take care of myself, my dear. Good night, sweet dreams," she responds.

The next day, Wilma receives, "Good morning, my dear." "Morning, how are you doing?" she asks. "I am well, thanks. How are you today? What are you doing now? What are your plans today?" Wilma, sitting in her cat basket with her laptop, replies, "I must organize a few important emails along with having some meetings and research, dear." Then he surprises her, saying, "I must tell you that I planned a visit to your place." She responds, "We are both busy people; it might take a while before this happens." He reassures her that it can happen. He sends a message in Italian which Wilma translates using Google Translate, but he deletes it and asks her to look for a hotel, saying, "Honey, go and look for a five-star hotel or any hotel in your country and send me the pictures of the hotel. Do you understand?" Wilma, cautious from past experiences, replies, "Yes, I do understand! I am busy just now; I will deal with your request later." The international star leaves Wilma alone for a while, then returns in the evening with, "Hello, darling, how are you doing?" "I am fine; I have been swamped!" she replies. He pleads, "Honey, please search for a hotel." Unsure of revealing her location, Wilma responds, "I will try, I am not promising anything." He messages on WhatsApp, "Okay, honey. Are you still busy?" "I am just trying to finish a few things," she replies. He insists, "Okay, when you are done, just search for a hotel and send me a picture. You know I love you," and adds lots of love hearts. Wilma finishes her research for her criminology course and responds, "I am just finished. I can't be bothered; I will look at this tomorrow." He comforts her, "No problem, honey, just take care of yourself, okay? And enjoy the rest of your evening, darling xxxx."

The following day, he sends, "Good morning, my love," followed by lots of love hearts. Continuing his mission, he texts, "Honey, can you search for a hotel online now?" Wilma, feeling unwell with a runny nose, types on her phone, "Can you leave it for now? I am loaded with a cold presently." However, he persists, replying, "Honey, can you search for the hotel online now?" Unwilling to argue with the imposter, Wilma goes online, contemplating where they could go and decides on a touristy place he might like. "Ah, let's send this to him," she thinks, inserting a link from Trip Advisor for the Grand Hotel in York. She downloads a couple of photos and adds them to their WhatsApp chat, typing, "Nice." He smoothly responds, "Yes, my love. I love the hotel room," and adds, "Honey, I will be sending you the sum of 50,000.00 euros so you can prepare for my coming over! Along with some other stuff that you think is necessary for me to use. When I arrive, please keep some, and we will spend that together. I don't want to stress you about any of my problems. I want you to be strong for me! Please keep some and use some for yourself for your personal needs. I hope you understand, honey." Wilma's imagination runs wild at the offer of a substantial amount of money. She envisions helping other dyslexic individuals with assessments by funding some through her charity she does volunteering work alongside. She also imagines treating herself to a proper Louis Vuitton handbag without haggling with street vendors, as she did while abroad on holiday. She types back, "Yes, I understand," and returns to her pleasant daydream. He replies, "Okay, give me time to contact my accountant." It doesn't take long for him to return, saying, "Honey, my accountant just contacted me, telling me that the money is ready to be sent to you! However, they can't send it to your bank account because of some legal reasons. I know it's a huge amount of money, and you don't know about our love, so they told me they are going to send you the money soon, honey. Hope you understand, my love. "Wilma, impressed by the smooth approach, curls up in her cat basket with a hot cup of lemon and ginger tea, responding, "Not a problem." Upon insistence about messaging his team management, Wilma finds it irritating. "Okay, honey, this is my team management number. Just click on the message and say hello to my management team now, okay, love hearts," he urges, sending a link to another WhatsApp number. Upon investigation, Wilma realizes it's from somewhere in Switzerland. She decides to ignore the request, sensing it might be a trap. Later, he asks, "Honey, have you messaged my team management yet?" Wilma chooses to ignore it and fetches more tissues for her running nose. Missing the Olbas oil, she couldn't be bothered to go to the shops for a bottle. Over the years, she typically used it on her pillow at night to aid breathing but often woke up with red blotches and cartoon eyes due to accidental rubbing. Attempting to talk to his "sweet darling," the person tries calling her, which could have hinted at the person behind the phone number. Ignoring the call, Wilma continues watching "The Innocent Project" on YouTube. Later in the evening, he reaches out again, "Hello dear, are you there?" She half-heartedly replies, "Yes, why?" He asks, "Have you messaged my team management now?" "No, I have been in meetings. I have a sinus headache and find it hard to concentrate," she responds. Dealing with a pounding headache, Wilma is exasperated by the relentless shooting pain. Despite taking paracetamol, the pain remains constant. To avoid further arguments, she simply says, "Okay." Later, he asks again, "Honey, have you messaged my team management now?" Feeling unwell and frustrated, Wilma thinks about Lily Allen's song, "Fuck You." She responds, "Yes," to silence him. Unfortunately, he continues, "Can you take a screenshot of the message you sent to them?" Deciding not to answer, she receives another message, "Hello, are you there?" He attempts to call and sends, "Honey, has the team management responded to the message you sent them? Wilma chose to ignore the three missed WhatsApp calls sent that evening. Drifting in and out of sleep, she woke up coughing and suspected a potential chest infection.

The following day, she phoned the vet for an appointment, considering her condition. Amidst her discomfort, she received a "good morning my love" message from him. Weakened by her illness, she eventually replied, "Morning. I've lost my voice with this cold. Please stop trying to call me right now. "Persistent with his mission, he continued, "Okay, my love, have you messaged my team management now?" Annoyed and feeling unwell, Wilma snapped back, "Stop hassling me about this. I have more important things to organize. I think this stupid cold has turned into a chest infection." His response urged her, "Honey, just say hello to my team management now, okay?" Fed up and feeling too ill to engage further, Wilma blocked both the Italian number and the WhatsApp management team from Switzerland.

In a surprising turn, soon after blocking these numbers, Wilma received an Instagram request from a stranger, later revealed to be the international star's sister. Curious, Wilma engaged in conversation. "Hello, good evening," greeted the stranger. Curious about this unexpected contact, Wilma replied, "Hello, how are you doing?" They exchanged pleasantries, with Wilma avoiding disclosing her location and mentioning she's from Ireland with beautiful weather. Enjoying the sunshine and music, Wilma continued chatting, acknowledging the star's music but denying any previous conversations with him. The stranger asked about being a fan and the possibility of having a membership card, to which Wilma diplomatically responded, declining any memberships, and expressing a preference for enjoying the music without additional associations. The conversation eventually ended, and Wilma chose to block the person she was chatting with due to scepticism.

The Case of the Guy on Holiday

Wilma encountered an international superstar on Instagram. The interaction lasted several days, an unusual occurrence, prompting her to send a follow request. Due to past experiences, she had refrained from allowing access to her Instagram account. The international star initiated a chat, expressing gratitude for her support on their page with a heartfelt message. Wilma thought, 'This seems typical, let's see how this conversation unfolds,' and replied casually. The dialogue progressed conventionally, asking about each other's well-being and origins. Wilma suspected the conversation mirrored typical scammer tactics as she responded, "I'm doing well, thank you. I'm from St. Trinian's! How about you?" The star replied, "I'm enjoying my holiday. How long have you been supporting me? This is my personal Instagram account, reaching out to fans who've supported me over the years." The familiarity struck Wilma as reminiscent of another encounter with a hacker. Despite this, she continued engaging and replied, "I've been a fan for 8 years! Your career is utterly amazing 😊. I'm happy you're enjoying your holiday."

The conversation continued with the international artist remarking, "Yes, it's pleasant here. You seem nice, Wilma." Recognizing the pattern, she read on as the star mentioned, "I'm not active here due to the nature of my job. It'd be great to get to know you more." Then came the moment when the star asked, "Do you think I can trust you with my personal Google chat? We can text there." Wilma felt a rush, akin to

Janine from Ghostbusters exclaiming, "We've got one!" Employing her counselling skills, she replied, "I understand, you're incredibly busy, running a business. You can trust me," and shared her email. The star responded with a heart emoji and provided their Google chat address, addressing her by name. Validating the email, Wilma found a message waiting for her on Google Chat. Entering the chat, she wondered where this interaction with the star would lead over time.

"Hello Wilma, how are you?" The international superstar messaged her. She replied, "I hope you're enjoying the lovely weather with plenty of sunscreen on 😁. It's beautiful here in the Maldives 😊. I'm just chilling out! What's your plan for tonight? I hope your day's been great!" Meanwhile, Wilma was basking in excellent weather, even warmer than the Caribbean as reported on the news. "The weather's amazing! I'm sipping on cider right now," she typed into Google Chat. She was seated in her local beer garden chatting with Mr. G about his new job. Adding, "After a few drinks, I'll settle in for a film 😁. Hope you're enjoying some cocktails 🍸😂." While glancing at the international superstar's holiday pictures on Instagram, memories of wild times in Marbella for Princess Twinkle Toes' birthday flashed back—a chaotic spree filled with beachside cocktails, tapas, haggling for designer bargains, and carefree moments. He messaged back, "It's nice here. Why are you laughing so hard?" Wilma imagined him reclining in a hammock, relaxed, as she replied, "Just reminiscing about one of my favourite holidays with my crazy friends. It turned into a riot of laughter and cocktails at the beach 😂😂😂😂." She found a picture from that trip, looking sunburnt, and added, "I ended up like a tandoori chicken, despite the sunscreen 😋🙊💁🙈🙉😁. I'm struggling to decide what to have for dinner. Please help!"

The conversation paused momentarily. Then, a text popped up on her phone: "Will you be heading to bed soon?" It was early evening for Wilma, and she wasn't sure about the time difference in the Maldives. She replied, "Not yet it's a few hours away. Are you heading for beauty sleep? 🙏" "I'm wide awake and still here to chat if you are," he responded. Wilma enjoyed the fading sunlight in the beer garden as she exchanged messages. His next text arrived, "Do you live with your family, Wilma? I'd like to get to know them better." She quickly replied, "No, I live with my flatmates 🙏." Auto-correct had turned her response comical, so she added, "I mean, I live with my flatmates. Damn autocorrect 🙊💁." Drawing from experience with purported international superstars, she asked a straightforward question, "What's your favourite part of your job?" His response about travelling and making fans happy resonated as genuine. "That sounds amazing 😊," she replied. Memories of Princess Twinkle Toes' advice—loving one's job and making it not feel like work—flashed in her mind. "My flatmates are close friends supporting each other for years 😄," she added. Wanting to know more, she asked about his other musical interests apart from violin and piano. As the night grew late, she and Mr. G returned home for the dinner she had prepared earlier. Not hearing back from the superstar, she sent a message after her meal, "Guessing you're asleep! Sweet dreams, talk tomorrow 🙏." Heading upstairs to bed, she left her phone and iPad in the snug as usual. The next morning, after her routine coffee-making for herself and Mr. G, she checked her messages and emails. She found a Google Chat message from the superstar saying, "I needed some rest, Wilma. Let's talk more tomorrow. Have a good night's sleep." She thought it was sweet and replied, "I hope you had a good rest 🙏." Sorting through emails and social media, she later received another message, "Yes, I rested well, Wilma. What's your plan today?" Wilma was trying to get her laptop started for work. "I'm just trying to get my laptop updated. It's being a bit stubborn about starting up 🤦💡🤪," she typed. An egg timer kept spinning on the screen, assessing her patience. "I apologize for that, Wilma. Can you manage to set that up?"

"Do you have much to do aside from that? Computers have feelings too 😂😂😂😂😂. I'll just swear at it as it takes its time today 😂😂😂😂." Wilma sat there, gazing at the screen, still thinking, 'Hurry up!' She texted back, asking, "Are you just chilling out again today?" "Yes, I'm relaxing and enjoying the weather 😊☺️. Want to join me over here? It's lovely!" His invitation felt delightful, making her wish she could drop everything and read the next text. "How's the weather over there today?" Glancing out of the window at clear blue skies, she replied, "It's beautiful outside. I might need to grab sunscreen today; I'm planning to go out for a glass of cider after finishing my tasks 😆." "That's nice to know, Wilma. But don't stress yourself out, okay? You seem to like your cider a bit too much!" She thought he might be getting the wrong impression, thinking she was an alcoholic.

Nevertheless, she appreciated his concern for her mental health. Then, she received a text asking, "Why do you always laugh?" Sensing his serious nature, she tried to explain in a text, "I'm just relaxed right now! The beautiful weather, which isn't usual, makes me cherish it. Several things are going well, making me happy. I always try to laugh; it's good for mental health." He replied, "You're nice, Wilma. You should keep laughing if that's the reason 😊😊. I'm glad things are going well. Will you be home all day? When do you usually work?" Reflecting on her work-from-home setup due to the pandemic, she replied, "I prefer working remotely.

Occasionally, I meet up with everyone. My job's complex: most people run away when I start explaining everything I do 🤪." "Really! I'm still getting to know you. How about the people you live with? I hope they treat you well." Thinking of Mr. G and her friends, she replied, "I share the best laughs with my friends. Unfortunately, I lost my best friend earlier this year. We've supported each other through grief." "I'm sorry about that, Wilma. It must have been tough. Are you okay now? Have a drink with your flatmates or still at home?" Laughing at the situation where Mr G was in his office and she was working in the snug, she replied, "I'm enjoying the weather and drinking coffee at the moment 😊." She imagined him sipping coffee on the beach, reminiscing about the roller-coaster feelings from grief. "Yes, it was tough, but each day gets a bit easier! I'm having coffee myself now. Ciders for the evening when work's done 😄." "It must be fun there with you. How many live in the flat? You mentioned sharing it with friends, right?" "Just one flatmate, but we visit friends for occasional parties, play YouTube, and dance—Tina Turner's Proud Mary is always a laugh. It takes twirling to a whole new level of cheesy 😂😂😂😂." She remembered Mr. D's claim that he hadn't danced and playfully sent the video to him on WhatsApp. "You seem to have a lot of fun with your friends. I'm glad you're not bored or lonely there 😊😊. You're fun, and I enjoy texting with you," he replied. "Yes, I do have fun with my nutty friends 😂😂😂😂. It makes life interesting, with fun stories even when things go wrong. Ha-ha 😄," she replied. "I don't have many friends, but I do have lots of colleagues. I'm a private person, always have been," he texted. Curious about his privacy, Wilma thought it'd be intriguing to know more as their relationship developed. Just then, he texted, "What about your children? How often do you see them?" Agreeing on the importance of privacy but also cherishing times with friends, she replied, "I don't have children, it's complex, but I'm fine with it now. I get to play with my friends' kids and return them at the end of the day 😄." He replied, "That's your choice, and it's respectable. You seem genuinely happy. I don't have a family either; I don't worry about it. I am extremely delighted. It's great to have your support ♡. Call me crazy, but I love seeing people happy and successful. Life's a journey, not a competition." "Absolutely! So many mistakes. It's not a race but a journey for everyone. We must enjoy it, making good memories. Dr. Brené Brown is great to watch 😄," she replied. "I don't know what you look like, Wilma. I guess you know what I look like!" "I do know what you look like 😍. It's not hard with social media 🤭." She found one of her favourite selfies in the sun with a glass of wine and sent it with a "hello." "Oh ☺☺☺ You look so beautiful, Wilma; your smile is beautiful 🤩. Thank you for sending me your photo 😊. I'm just an average batshit crazy girl," she responded. The international star sent a picture of himself lounging on the beach. Wilma had seen the same picture on Instagram and texted him, "You look nice and relaxed 😊." She had also watched the Empathy vs. Sympathy video on

YouTube and shared it with him.

"Dr. Brené Brown is incredible 🙌 😊. You take good care of yourself, and that's great. I love being outdoors too. Lately, I've been visiting the beach a lot, enjoying seafood. My job involves travelling and keeping my fans happy, but I haven't

connected with anyone like I am with you now. You make me smile, and you're funny 😇😇. Supporting people is part of my job, and I love it, though it does have its challenges! Communication can be one of the biggest challenges 🧑‍🦯💁. What about your job? You didn't mention anything about it." Then, he sent her this message, which she ran through Google Translate: "Aber ich habe nichts hier. nicht einmal eine Scheibe Brot." Translating it, it said, "But I have nothing here, not even a slice of bread." She found it strange! He continued, "My management told me about so many impersonating me with my name. Have you come across it before?" She responded, "Firstly, I'm a neurodiverse consultant; I coach and mentor people, showcasing strategies like assistive technology to help them achieve their full potential. Yes, I've encountered many impersonators in the last year. I enjoy messing with them. I can't stop them, but I keep them away from vulnerable people who might fall for this nonsense momentarily 🙏 🫣💁. It's saddening, and I never want that feeling with you. I also don't want you to be sceptical about me. Sometimes, I can't help but be sceptical. I'm currently working on a personal goal, studying for my degree. I'm aiming for a Bachelor of Arts, focusing on criminology to address issues in the neurodiverse community. I apply what I've learned about these people. Maybe one day you'll create a proper TikTok account. The number of fake accounts there is unbelievable 🫣💁." He understood and reassured her, "I understand, Wilma. Don't worry; it'll be fine. Are you on TikTok?" "I've been busy, but now I'm here. What are you up to?" she asked. "I'm walking along the shoreline; I'm active across multiple social media sites. I keep my Twitter account for work, TikTok is just for fun." "Ah, I see. Managing all those accounts must take intelligence. Are you walking alone now?" She had Jaki Graham's 'Breaking Away' playing and was admiring flowers growing along the shoreline. "For the rest of my day, I'll be reading new literature in a bit," she replied. While strolling by the water's edge, a father and daughter asked for a picture, which she happily took for them. "I'm on a break now; I'll get back to work later. It's one of my coping strategies for dyslexia. If I read too much, I end up exhausted. So, I chunk tasks to manage my workload 😁." She shared a picture of swans swimming around the pond in the area where she was walking. "🌼 It's beautiful," she remarked. "It's good to know you can work from home, but I don't know much about your job. I hope it's not stressful for you. I don't want to distract you from working." He assured her, "No problem at all. I'll be busy tomorrow, but I'll let you know when I'm free. Right now, I can work at my own pace reviewing assistive technology to help others 👐👐😁." Meanwhile, she had a meeting with learning labs, going through the site, and trying out some quizzes to refresh her memory. He messaged, "Alright when I get on the road, I'll find time to text with you because you're nice 😊. Have you eaten? When will you head back home?" Wondering about the online relationship's longevity as he might travel again, she pondered while Clannad's theme from "Harry's Game" played in her playlist. Once she returned home, she treated herself and Mr G to delicious bacon and cheese on naan bread with chippy brown sauce. "I had a bacon butty before leaving the house 😁😁🙏," she replied. He emphasized, "We'll always keep in touch, Wilma; just keep my address safe to avoid any media scandal." She understood 😊😊😊. "I hope you're enjoying a cocktail; it's necessary on holiday!" she messaged, sending a picture of a big Bloody Mary she had on her birthday. "It looks tasty 😋. Are you alone?" As she glanced around, she jokingly replied, "I'm going to find another partner in crime to cyber-cocktail with 🤣🤣🤣🤣." Puzzled, he asked, "What do you mean, Wilma?" Finding a log, she reminisced about mischief and replied, "My best friend and I loved getting into mischief! She'd be in Spain on holiday, I'd be working, and we'd share cocktail pictures, confusing everyone by tagging each other from various locations 🤣🤣🤣🤣. Our cyber-cocktail sessions became famous among our friends 🤪." He commented, "You must have amazing friends. I like cocktails, but it's been a while 😊." "Cocktails are a holiday treat. I have amazing but totally crazy friends; I fit right in 🤣🤣🤣. I went to one of their weddings at a restaurant called Bed, trying to tag 24 people in bed for a reaction 🤪." Amused, he replied, "Haha! You're very funny, Wilma. I like that 😊😊. Enjoy yourself with your friends; take diligent care of yourself, okay?" She shared a picture of the wedding venue, and he responded, "What a nice restaurant; you know how to have fun 😊." Later, he mentioned being busy but promised to continue texting that night. She found it odd, maybe he was meeting friends there! Instagram later displayed photo shoots and videos made on the beach, indicating a less relaxing holiday.

Later that day, she received a text, "Hello Wilma, how are you tonight? How was your day?" "I'm great, thanks. It's cider o'clock for me now. How's your day going? Are you alone?" she asked. Simultaneously, she was tagged in a Twitter post and checked the article. It was the OrCam technology article she had worked on, and she shared the news with the star. Excitedly, she showed Mr. G the published piece and got a response from the star, "That's nice to know, Wilma. Have a wonderful time with your friend; I'm glad you were advertised, and people can receive the support they need. How long will you be out, Wilma? 😁 Are you going to build sandcastles on the beach 🤣🤣🤣? Go get yourself a nice pina colada 😁." Jokingly, she replied, "I'll do that and find someone to drink with, just kidding. I've only been out for an hour 😁." Mischievously, she sent him a picture of a Pina colada from the internet and joked about having one while at home. He appreciated the suggestion and joked about not wanting to drink alone. He asked what she'd do when she got home, and she teased him about dancing to cheesy tunes, offering a Spotify playlist to assist. Laughing, he said he preferred texting while watching TV, not wanting to dance alone 😊😊. They bantered about dancing like Elmo and starting a cheesy tunes party with Steps'

"One for Sorrow."

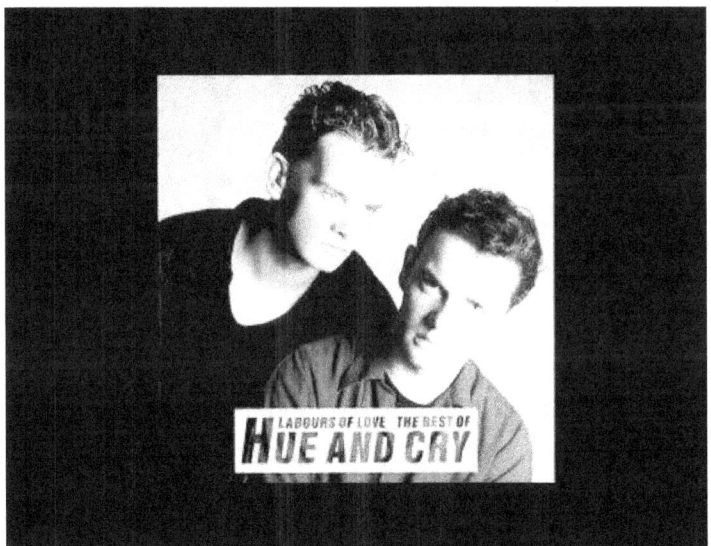

I'd love to sing along, but unfortunately, I can't produce sound! As for the song reference, sounds like a lively one! If you're finding your friends asking about the person you're texting with, it might be a clever idea to have an open conversation with them about it. Transparency can help clear things up and might prevent misunderstandings down the line. The Smokie song's quite catchy, isn't it? I can hear now "Who the fuck is Alice." Wilma's friends just tell her your famous boyfriend just wants to show his big sausage!

"Hilarious 😂😂😂! I'd love to hear you sing 😀. Wilma responds to his question by letting him know that my friends are aware I'm texting you. Then the conversation takes a turn toward talking about famous people I text, but it ends up being quite rude 😂😂😂😂. 'What do you mean, Wilma? I don't understand your last text. Have you been texting with other people before now? I'm not sure if you're using innuendos! You can have a clean but very rude conversation at the same time. The guys will tell me it's not the size of the sausage, it's the weight behind it for hammering it in. Get the crash helmet on, babe; you're going through the headboard tonight!' I have a dirty mind that takes this in another way 🤣. 'I enjoy our conversations, and you seem to be an easy-going person, Wilma. Are you back home now?' 'No, still chatting in the sunshine, about life.' This reminds her of meeting up with my friend for a quick coffee and explaining to the star, 'I have this great friend I met for a quick coffee; we're still chatting three hrs later 🤣💁💁.' It was nice to know he enjoyed chatting with her. Then she received the text: 'It's nice to know. I will allow you to enjoy your time, Wilma. Let me know when you're back home, okay? Bye for now 😊😊.' She found it sweet, caring, and replied, 'I'll let you know when I'm home. Dance to steps in just now 🤣🤣🤣.' Once she arrived back home, she put the kettle on for a cup of herbal tea, sat on her couch with the TV on, and ended up falling asleep. She woke up at the end of the movie, as usual, checked the time on her phone, and thought, 'Time for bed.' She realized, 'Oops, I forgot to say I'm home,' and sent the final text for the night: 'Okay, forgot to let you know when I arrived home. I had something to eat and fell asleep 😂. Oops, I'm off to bed. I'll talk to you tomorrow xxx.'

The next morning, Wilma was up bright and early but had a few things to sort out before jumping on the helpline. She noticed the star had left her a message but was trying to eat her breakfast, tidy up, and get herself ready for a busy day ahead. He had sent her a good morning message: 'Good morning, Wilma 😊 How are you doing today, and how was your night?' Once she was set up, she replied, 'Good morning, handsome. I hope you are well and relaxed 😁.' She sat with her favourite coffee, waiting for the laptop to start up, and quickly checked Instagram and Facebook to see what was happening with her friends. He replied, 'Yes, I am well, and it's a good day as well. What will you do? Have you had your breakfast yet?'

Amused, she replied, 'Yes, I had my bran flakes and banana. I am just getting my laptop set up 😁.' She fired up all the software required to aid her with her dyslexia, including Outlook, Salesforce, and call handling. He responded, 'That's nice to know 😊. Will you be home all day?' Knowing she'd be going for her weekly shopping and then out with friends later, she replied, 'I'll be out later with the hair bear bunch once everyone's done. Busy morning ahead with schools reopening.' Senga had already mentioned she'd have a busy week. Wilma messaged from her laptop in Google Chat, explaining her schedule and her work: 'I'm just setting up the helpline. I'll be busy for the next few hours. I work in a specialized field aiding people with learning disabilities, like my own. I'm an ambassador for OrCam technology! This technology aids people who are visually impaired as well as those with learning disabilities. I posted about this on social media last night to help those going into further education. Please excuse me if I don't answer you straight away; I'll be busy.' Normally, people she talks to ignore the fact that she mentioned being busy. She waited for the reply, expecting the conversation to continue. He texted her back: 'I understand your job better now and read the link you sent me. Your job is complex, and it's nice you can help people. I understand you're busy, and I won't distract you when you work. Don't stress yourself too much, and make sure you text me when you're done with work. Bye, for now, Wilma 😊😊☺.'This reply was a pleasant surprise for Wilma, this was not her normal run-on Google chat and she replied thank you 🙏 I will text you later 😁. After completing everything and then sending friends a quick update in the morning and thought about the hair bear bunch in a few hours. As it was Friday a bit of Katie Perry T.G.I.F was appropriate and sent the link from YouTube

"Friday vibes! 🤘🤘🎸🎸" He texted back, "Thank you, Wilma ☺😊😊😊. Are you done working?" Wilma had a relatively easy day, dealing with substantial issues within the neurodiverse community. She replied, "Yes, finished! It wasn't too bad today 😁." He responded, "I'm glad you had a

wonderful time working, Wilma. How's the weather presently?" Getting ready to head out for shopping, she replied, "Every day is different on the helpline. Thankfully, I have a good support team. The weather is beautiful, looking forward to catching up with the gang later 😊. How's the sandcastle building going?" As she walked, she received his reply: "Everything is fine here with me, just having a wonderful day as well. Good, you'll be out with your friends later 😊. I want you to have a wonderful time as well. Have you had your lunch?" She'd had lunch before leaving and sent him a photo of her homemade Caesar salad. Wilma took the long route along the shoreline to the shop and received his comment: "It looks tasty, Wilma. I want to have a taste now lol." Then he asked, "Are you in your apartment alone now? When do you have to leave the house?"

Already out, she replied, "I'm here texting with you. I don't have much to do until later. We both get along so well. It surprises me 😊." Finding a spot on her route, she replied, "I am just about to go for my daily walk, then get some shopping for dinner, and later, I'll meet the gang. It's not going to be a sensible night; it's summer! I have two guys who like women's breasts, one leg guy, and one who likes the size of their bums 👥💡. I'm glad you're enjoying our conversation 😁."

He replied, "You already have the rest of your day planned out, Wilma. Will you be back home late at night? Who are these guys? Do they live close to you? 😄😄😄" She found a bench and replied, "The Hair bear bunch isn't far away! It's funny how you know they like what you just mentioned. Lol 😄." Sitting on a bench overlooking the shoreline and the multicoloured hills, she replied, "I have worked in a male-only environment for years! They try to embarrass me occasionally! An example would be 'I am going to the toilet; would you like to hold it?' My answer is always 'I forgot my tweezers 😂!'" He quickly responded, "Ha-ha 😂 this is so strange. I just hope you're safe over there with these guys." Wilma laughed, knowing she was safe, and he added, "Do they look at you so much, Wilma lol?" She reassured him, "I am treated as one of the guys! They know I can give as good as I get. They look after me well. 😃"

He replied, "It's ok, Wilma. I just want you to be fine there." Then he asked, "Are you having a boyfriend?" Wilma, thinking this was an expected question, responded, "Yes, I'm fine. I also like to remind them I am studying how to get away with murder 😂😂😂😂! I'll order the digger, lime, and new decking! They've gone on a guys' holiday 😂😂😂😂."He replied, "That's funny, Wilma. I thought you had seen them today, but it's nice to have guys around you 😊😊."

"Hope you enjoyed your salad, Wilma." He decided to send her a picture of a cocktail—she wasn't sure if it was a margarita, but it looked delicious. He asked, "Would you like to drink with me now ☺?" At that point, she was texting her friend about the stressful week, planning a massive jug of mojitos for the evening—she had mentioned that 'wine o'clock' was coming soon. She replied, "Nice! I was just texting my friend about 'wine o'clock.' She's making mojitos tonight 🍹." She referred to the cocktail he sent and talked about "princess twinkle toes" and cyber cocktails. Finding a picture of an Aperol spritz she had once enjoyed, she sent it to the star, saying, "Cheers!"

He quickly replied, "You already told me you'll be out tonight with your friends. I hope you don't drink much 😊. Thank you so much. It's nice that we're both drinking 😊." She appreciated his fondness for cyber cocktails but was unsure about the night's outcome. She recalled past wild moments with her friends and replied, "I end up in worse states when I'm out with the girls 🙈🙊. It's like playing ping pong with myself trying to get in the house 😆."

Thinking about the movie "Absolutely Fabulous" and its adventures, she sent him, "I am meant to behave but there are too many other options!" While picking up her shopping, she received his message, "I smile a lot while we text because you're so funny and seem to crack me up a lot 😊😊. Just let me know when you're busy, OK? I guess you're still out, right?" She replied, "I am just trying to get my shopping. 😆" Standing in the queue to pay, she texted, "I don't get stressed too often 😊."Arriving home and settling in, she relaxed watching TV and replied, "Yeah, home. It has all been put away." He wanted to confirm, asking, "Alright, and what will you do? You still must meet up with your friends, right?" Contemplating the night with her friend Calamity Jane, she thought about their wine-tasting sessions and the antics reminiscent of "Absolutely Fabulous." She messaged back, "Yes, I will be meeting them shortly. I am hoping to chat with my friend Calamity Jane."

She enjoyed talking to this person and received the text back saying funny wine-tasting video 😅😅😅Do have a nice time with your friend my dear 😊😊😊 She wanted him to relax and have a nice night, since she was talking about Absolutely fabulous why not give him a laugh and sent a text with the video link You're on holiday you can watch the film.

"It didn't matter to Wilma if he watched the film or not; it reminded her of fun times with her friends." He replied, "I will see it later on, thank you for sending 😊😊. Are you out now? I don't think I will be out anymore." At that point, the hair bear bunch was ready, and Wilma headed out to meet them all, replying to the star, "Just heading out now 😊." He seemed protective at times and texted back, "Stay safe, Wilma 😊♡." She knew she was in a safe environment and replied, "I will 🙏." Unlike some others she chatted with, this person didn't contact her for the rest of the evening. She had a wonderful time laughing with her friends as they enjoyed the summer evening, but the star didn't text her until the next morning, asking, "Hello Wilma, how are you doing today and how was your night?" Not hungover and casually watching MasterChef Australia, she replied, "Hi, I'm well thanks! Just doing my usual sad act for a Saturday morning, watching cooking shows ☐😂." With no concrete plans for the day and enjoying some free time, the star responded, "Really? That's nice to know ☺. I already drank my coffee and now am sitting and texting with you."

Finding it cute and picturing him in his apartment texting back, she replied, "I hadn't decided what I was doing yet 😂😂😂😂." He asked, "Why are you laughing? Sometimes I feel you laugh for no reason 🙄." Wilma explained that she was simply in a happy place, enjoying uninformed days without strict plans. "I haven't planned anything yet. I usually get told off for not having everything planned all the time. I enjoy being disorganized at times 😁."

Acknowledging her complexity and her tendency to plan extensively, he replied, "That's strange, but it's fine. I just want you to enjoy your day and take care of yourself 😊." Understanding where he was coming from, considering her past experiences, she replied, "I always enjoy and take care of myself. I have been in an unbelievably bad place, but thanks to counselling, I made some changes to my life and things have improved! 😁."

The conversation shifted to acknowledging her improved state, with him expressing, "You seem so happy, and I like that about you. 😊 Have you had your breakfast yet? I don't know what I will do today, but I will read and also watch football." He then asked if she was seeing anyone. Wilma decided to approach the discussion straightforwardly and replied, "I have enjoyed doing more leisure reading since I have my OrCam. It's frustrating when my friends take just a few hours to read a book while it takes me days or weeks sometimes. I'm currently reading 'Confessions of a Sociopath 😊 and 'The Asylum of Terror.' I won the latter in a writing competition with a friend who is an author. I've been attending his writing classes on Zoom during the pandemic 😃. Yes, I am seeing someone." She chuckled to herself, realizing the irony in his inquiry about her seeing a man when Mr. G was indeed a man.

Their relationship had evolved due to her accident, but the bond between them remained strong. Wilma pondered how to explain this to the person she was conversing with and messaged back, "Yes, I am seeing a man. It's a complex relationship, not what you might be thinking. I value his company." He replied, "I understand, but I was just asking. It's fine. I hope it works out well 😊."

Realizing her choice of words might have been misconstrued, she clarified, "It's not a problem. We've both agreed never to get married." The star noticed this and asked, "Really? Why? Are you just friends?" Understanding the intricacies of relationships, she replied, "Yes, we're best friends. We're both divorced. I had an unbelievably abusive marriage, and I don't want to repeat the experience."

Surprised by her revelation, the person she was conversing with expressed sympathy, saying, "Oh, I never knew you were divorced. You must have gone through a terrible experience, Wilma. I'm sorry, but you shouldn't let the past affect your present if you like him." She appreciated this considerate and understanding response, unlike the shallow conversations she had with people posing as the international star.

Reflecting on her bond with Mr G and their shared experiences, she informed the person, "I've talked with him about my experiences; it wasn't a secret. He looked after me when I put myself in the hospital and got my leg super glued back together. We laugh and support each other with our life's challenges." She found comfort in the fact that this person didn't continually express longing or request photos, unlike some others. Encouraged by their genuine interaction, the person responded, "I'm glad to know that you've someone who cares about you over there. It's a nice feeling, and I hope you always feel good because you're nice and also a good woman 😊☺️♡."

Encouraged by the positive exchange, Wilma expressed her gratitude, "Oh, thank you! That's sweet of you to say that. I really enjoy talking with you ☺️." They reciprocated the sentiment, saying, "I also enjoy talking with you and am happy how we get along so well. You've been so nice and real to me ♡."Feeling a sense of warmth and connection, Wilma sent a message reflecting on the joys of laughter with best friends. He responded playfully, "We can be best friends who knows??? ☺️☺️ Just from the few times, I can say I like you and enjoy your company." "Please don't be offended if I get back to work and have less time to write, but I'll always make time for us, OK? 😊😊☺️" Wilma appreciated this considerate gesture and responded, "I won't be offended. I have some spare time now. Once I resume university and start studying, I won't have much time either, especially with assignments. I often find myself in debates over whether I've adequately answered the questions, and referencing can be quite a challenge 😵🥴🙈💁‍♀️🤦‍♀️💁‍♀️." The conversation flowed with the star asking about her return to university. Wilma mentioned, "I'll be back at the beginning of October, but the forums and introductions for the course will open soon." Although the star disappeared briefly from the conversation, it didn't bother Wilma much as they had already spent a good part of the morning chatting.

Later in the day, she messaged, "Sorry, I got busy for a bit, Wilma. What are you up to now?" wondering about his holiday activities, maybe a swim in the sea. She replied, "Out for my daily walk 😊," with Spotify playing "The Waterboys - Whole of the Moon." He responded, "Alright Wilma. Have an enjoyable time 😊. Are you alone or with your friend?" The recurrent inquiries about her being alone made her slightly uneasy, imagining bizarre scenarios. She replied, "I am alone with my friend Spotify 😊."He inquired about her use of Spotify, to which she confirmed and read his response, "That's nice to know. It would be awesome if we were walking together now! Are you in the woods or just walking along your street?" Trying to explain her location, she replied, "Walking along the path beside the shore, just across from the house 😊," and shared a photo of the shoreline. Concerned for her safety, he expressed, "I just want you to be safe. It looks so beautiful and a delightful place to walk. Will you be out for long?" A bit annoyed at the repeated concern, she assured me, "I am watching out for the cyclists! It's my day off, not timing anything 😊."

As she continued her walk, the music shuffled to "Jamiroquai - Virtual Insanity." She sent him the link with a message suggesting, "Just chill out 😊." After a while of no response, a text popped up while she was in the beer garden with her friends, enjoying drinks and keeping an eye on the kids playing. He asked, "Are you back home, Wilma? What are you doing?" She responded, "Out with friends. The kids are playing in the park. What are you doing?" and shared a picture of her cider, saying, "Cheers 😊."He replied, "I was watching a bit of football. I hope you have a wonderful day with your friends 😊😊 We can text when you're back home." Taking a playful dig at football, she teased, "Always football! Bunch of big Jessies! I prefer the sport played by men with odd-shaped balls myself! Roll in January for the rugby starting 😜😂." He chuckled and replied, "Ha-ha I also like rugby and golf, my dear. Right now, I enjoy football. Are you still out and when will you be home? "Later in the evening, as Wilma and Mr G headed home, she informed the star, "Hi honey, I am back home! Listening to Santana 😂." He quickly responded, "I hope you had a wonderful time with your friends, Wilma." She quipped, "I always have friendly conversations with my friends! 😃" Deciding on a simple microwave Rogan Josh for dinner, she replied to the star, "Yes, I had lamb Rogan Josh. Now listening to something that just makes me smile." Living amidst Mr G's guitar collection, she delved into Dire Straits tunes, specifically "A Local Hero" on YouTube, which she shared with him.

Wilma felt cheerful and had a pleasant time watching YouTube. She initiated the conversation by asking the star what makes him smile, but received no response, perhaps because he was busy playing volleyball on the beach or sipping a cocktail.

The following morning, she received a message saying, "Good morning, Wilma. How are you doing today, and how was your night? 😊" She replied, "Good morning! I had a great night, thanks. How are you, and what are you up to today?" He replied that he was fine and already enjoying his coffee. Remembering his love for coffee from previous interactions, she recalled an incident where Mr G had pointed out flaws in a poorly photoshopped picture of the star holding a coffee cup while they were having wine. Curious about her plans for the day, the star asked, "Will you go out today, Wilma?" She hadn't decided on her plans yet and mentioned, "Yes, just made a cup of coffee. Watching a bit of TV now 😃." He expressed his hope for better weather so she could enjoy her day. Asking about breakfast, he inquired, "What will you have for breakfast now?" Wilma replied, "I think I will have some toast with chicken liver pate. I try and meet up with my friends most weekends, depending on everyone's plans." The conversation continued pleasantly, and he expressed his enjoyment in talking to her, adding a playful note about building sandcastles. Unsure of his meaning, she asked for clarification, but the conversation turned to his workout routine. He mentioned finishing his workout and asked if she had eaten and when she'd be going out. Wilma shared her challenges with repetitive cardio due to her previous leg injury. Despite her humorous tone, he expressed concern for her safety, to which she responded playfully suggesting he could do her workout at the gym for her while she watched.

He complimented her humour and their enjoyable conversations, which felt refreshing to Wilma compared to previous interactions. He then asked how she felt about him, to which she cautiously replied about enjoying their conversation and getting to know each other. He encouraged her to ask anything she wished, stating he was glad they were getting to know each other better. Their conversation continued, discussing their reading habits and interests. The star shared his diverse reading choices, and Wilma mentioned her fondness for science fiction, cooking, crime books, and neurodiversity literature to support people. He expressed his interest in online gaming, swimming, and reading about her interests. Wilma and the star continued their friendly banter, discussing hobbies and interests. The star mentioned enjoying activities based on his mood and shared his love for online gaming, puzzles, football, and Mortal Kombat. Wilma recounted a hilarious incident of attempting to play Call of Duty at a friend's house, where she fared quite poorly. The star found it amusing and offered to teach her gaming if they were together, to which she humorously pointed out her clumsiness and sense of direction. After her morning walk, Wilma checked in with the star later in the evening while talking with her friends. She jokingly asked about his beach bum status and shared a funny mishap with autocorrect, mistakenly referring to sushi as fish slices. The star, enjoying his time at the beach, asked if Wilma liked seafood. She jokingly replied with a picture of oysters, claiming she hated being treated to seafood, though she enjoyed it.

The star wished Wilma a lovely day, and she reciprocated the wish, inquiring about his day in the Maldives. He mentioned watching documentaries and asked what she was doing. Wilma shared that she was making dinner while watching the TV series "Red Dwarf." Concerned about her well-being, the star sent a caring message, hoping she wasn't feeling lonely and offering his support. In response, she sent the opening tune of "Red Dwarf" from YouTube.

She was just being a silly Smeg head and received the reply thank you for sending me such lovely videos and I enjoy watching.

Is it freezing outside for you? She laughed at this and replied no it is rather warm just now! How about you're self? 😀🤣🤣🤣

It's cloudy here and it might rain tonight again Wilma. 😊 She thought it would be nice to go out walking in the warm rain over there, then she read the next text I don't know what to do tonight. Am sorry for the late response She thought about how fortunate the hair bear bunch were not around, she knew their response would have a wank! Instead, she put him in St Trinian's School for girls you can watch the movie where I had my training.

"You're only supposed to blow the bloody doors off," he liked it with his reply. "Ha-ha, you've got a lot of clips, Wilma. I guess you're particularly good with the internet, lol." She answered, "No, I just love mischief! 😂😂🤪" He told her, "It's crazy, but I still think you're a good woman." She thought, "You're not wrong there," and texted back, "You were warned! I have been told I am not off my trolley, I have lost my trolley and just going through life on a set of wheels 😂." He then replied, "That's your personality and I like you so much for that. You're real and sincere 😊, that's all I want. I'm not complaining, and I enjoy your company as well!"

"Oh, he is nice to talk to," and said, "Thank you, I am glad you like my craziness 😊 🙏." She decided to ask, "Do you listen to any Scottish bands?" She received the answer, "Not most of the time but sometimes." He then decided to ask, "Are you already in bed now?" Wilma never takes her phone to bed and answers him, "Wow, not many people I talk to listen to Scottish bands as part of their list! Which ones do you like? I will be going to bed in a few hours 😁." She had not picked up he was tired and going to bed himself when he texted her, "Have a good night and sweet dreams, Wilma. We'll text better tomorrow again 😊😴😴." This was not a problem, and she sent back, "Sweet dreams as well. 😁😴😴😴😴." Little did Wilma expect the thunderstorm which started in the early hours of the morning; it was really loud. Now, Wilma loved watching thunder and lightning but not all night, so she felt very tired and grumpy. She was thankful she worked from home and could be grumpy. Early on, she received, "Hello Wilma, good morning to you! How are you doing today and how was your night? 😊 I hope you feel good as well." She texted him back, "Morning! Tired and grumpy. Damn, thunderstorm kept me awake 😴😴 I will write a complaint letter to Thor, God of Thunder, later!" She had just seen Thor on TikTok and had decided to add this remark. She received a message back saying, "I'm sorry you couldn't sleep properly, Wilma," he then added, "Smiles, you're so funny. It's normal for the thunder but I guess it was much yesterday." She thought, "You should have heard it exploding in the sky above the house." Then when she closed her eyes, she could see a massive white light while trying to get back to sleep. He then added, "How's it going for you this morning? 😊" She was checking her Google calendar to see everything which was happening that day. She replied, "It is going to be a busy day. Just been chatting to China to review their translation pen for dyslexia. I have a few Zoom meetings today." She was texting the overseas marking person she was in contact with about the blog on the youdoa pen which had been sent to herself. It was all happening at the same time, and the star texted, "Oh, I see you will have a busy day, Wilma. Will your Zoom meeting last for some hours? Will you start this morning?" Since he had asked, she looked up the calendar. The first meeting was midday. The other meeting was in the evening so she could catch a power nap; she could plan this in. She replied, "I have one at midday and the other one is in the evening. So, I hope to have a power nap this afternoon. 😃." He replied, "Ha-ha then you will be fine when you rest properly. Your work looks strange to me, and I don't understand it so much. But am glad you like what you do and that's the most important thing." The work she did was complex, but then again, she didn't understand his job and replied, "I understand, as a lot of people don't understand what I do. Yes, I love what I do. It is interesting 😃." She knew the conversation would not last as long as it normally did and read the reply sent, "Yes, it's really interesting and nice. Have you had your breakfast yet? I will be having my coffee again soon 😊 I always enjoy my coffee." She replied, "Yes, I have had my bran flakes. I put fresh blueberries with them this morning. I always enjoy my morning coffee. What are you doing today?" As he was on holiday, she wondered what he would reply, and he texted, "I'm not doing much now. I watch TV and text with you. I don't have to work out much today. Good, you've something to eat already, Wilma 😊 I'm sure the weather is better now with fewer thunderstorms." She sent him a picture of a man walking through a river with his umbrella held up saying, "I need to keep my hair dry!" He must have thought she had lost it again and replied, "Smiles, still raining over there?" She looked out the window and smiled watching the rain and replied, "Yes, it is still raining 😂." She received a reply, "You laugh a lot even when you don't have to." She got he was a sensitive profoundly serious person, compared to herself who liked to be goofy. She decided to give him an answer about a bit of her life, "Yes, I laugh a lot. I went through a period where I didn't laugh. I was discussing it yesterday; I went through a time when I needed help. My friend found my texting hilarious because of my dyslexia. They ended up phoning me to help me out. I can laugh at my mistakes, I once sent an email looking for Wellington boots, however, I wrote please can you order six pairs of size 9 yellow Willys 🙈🙊😂." She went to work and didn't hear anything from the star. As she was researching things for her work, she decided to send the star a blog she was asked to do the year before, "I was asked to write this last year!"

Later in the afternoon, she found a message: "I'm sorry I got busy. You should be working now. Don't stress yourself much, ok?" She had fluffed up the first meeting of the day as she couldn't find the link. It had been moved to the next day. She called herself a goat once she worked out where it had gone wrong. She replied later, "I am not getting stressed. Hope you are enjoying yourself and not too stressed yourself 🙏."

Both were late replying to each other, and she received, "Yes, it's nice over here and already evening as well. I won't do much either for the rest of my day." She wondered what would make his day busy; he had finished his message with, "Have you worked?" She answered, "Yes, I have been working. What are you going to have for dinner?" He replied, "I don't know what I will have for dinner yet, Wilma. I will figure it out or make orders for it." She laughed as she didn't expect him to cook his dinner on holiday. He then asked, "Have you also had something to eat?" At this point, she was checking her timing to wrap everything up to make dinner before her Zoom meeting and texted back, "Trying to decide what to cook for dinner. Then go to my Zoom meeting afterwards 😁." He texted her back, "OK, then we can text later in the evening. I will decide on my dinner soon." Wilma smiled and texted him back, "You enjoy your dinner. You might be sleeping by the time I am finished tonight. We do have a bad habit of going over the time with chatting about the subject. Tonight is dyslexia and mental health 🙏."After her Zoom meeting, she ended the evening with the star, saying, "Hope you had a great evening! Good night 🙏." She went to bed and had a great sleep compared to the previous evening. The next morning, she felt a lot better and had a wonderful time at her Zoom meeting. She sent the star, "Morning! How are you today? Hope you are enjoying your coffee 😃." She was going through her normal routine and had MasterChef on the TV while eating her bran flakes when a message came through, "Good morning, Wilma. How are you doing today and how was your night? 😊 It was nice with me, and I hope all is well with you, Wilma?" As she felt good about a few things, she replied, "I had a good night. I always enjoy my Zoom meetings; it is great to be in a safe environment talking to people with similar things. I had a better sleep last night, no thunderstorm 😃." As she was working, she knew it would be another quick chat and he texted, "That's good everything went well yesterday. Am happy you slept well, and you feel good today. Will you be doing much today?" Upon reading this, she decided not to say she had made an error with yesterday's meeting; it had been moved to today instead she told the star, "Yes, I have a meeting with learning labs. I was looking over the variety of assistive technology on this platform and trying some of the quizzes. The stuff they have on supporting mental health helps to know these things when people ask me questions 😃." Then she decided to ask him, "What exciting things do you have planned today?" He replied, "I don't have much planned out and just enjoy it as it goes. Don't worry I will be fine. Where will you have your meeting? It's good you always try to learn and get to know more about what's happening in the world." The pandemic has changed a lot of things. She was used to talking to people over a computer screen and replied, "The meeting was on Microsoft Teams today. The pandemic has given me different opportunities to work with assistive technology companies and talk to them over various platforms. It is nice not to have much planned. I like those sorts of days; I spend a lot of time organizing myself 👩💡."

He replied, "I understand that, and I want you to have an enjoyable time doing that. It will be fine, ok. Always take diligent care of yourself 😊. I want you to be fine always." She understood his concern about mental health being an ongoing issue. She wanted him to know her progress and replied, "I love what I am doing now. I now work in a safe and secure environment, unlike a few years ago. I am off the happy pills; things are improving for me. 😀" She sent him a picture with the message, "Make yourself a priority occasionally, it's not selfish! It's necessary."

Later in the day, he replied, "Thank you for the kind words. I hope you're having a lovely day, Wilma." Excited to share her news after the morning meeting, she texted, "Awww thanks. I am having a momentous day; I was chatting with an assistive technology company on providing help to students and was invited to be an ambassador for them 😀." He replied, "That's nice to know. Did you accept? You have a lot going on with you." She laughed; the team at Texthelp had said she makes others' lives look boring. He went on to ask, "Are you still working now?" She replied, "Yes, never a dull moment in my weird world. Enjoying a coffee break just now. What are you doing at present? I did accept the role of student ambassador for assistive technology 😁." After sending the message, she realized the autocorrect had struck again and sent another message saying, "Assistive, damn autocorrect 🙈🙊." Later in the evening, she received his reply, "That's nice to know and will I say you have got a new job now? Lol." She thought about it; she did cover a lot of areas with neurodiversity and replied, "Lol, I have been working on that over the pandemic, including a couple of videos that are on YouTube. 🙂 You can cover a lot of stuff as a consultant 😄." She then shared her dinner plans, "I made a lovely vegetable frittata for my dinner 😄." He replied, "Smiles, you must have a lot to teach me ha-ha. Good to know you had your dinner already. Will you keep working on it tonight? 😊"She read the message while watching TV and replied, "No, I will not be working tonight. I know my working memory has had enough and it is time to just watch some TV 😄." Since he had mentioned teaching, she thought about the complaints she received from her LinkedIn connections and joked, "Someone else to drive to drink. I can accept that challenge. Someone else to complain that us women just upset a man's routine. Do annoying things such as letting the box of red wine drip down the front of the fridge. Not forgetting you can never find anything because we like to change the location of everything 😈😈😂😂😂😂." He didn't respond further that evening; maybe she had unintentionally upset him with the remarks. Only time will tell.

The next morning, she started her routine and texted the star, "Good morning, how are you today?" After a while, he responded, "Good morning, Wilma. How are you doing today and how was your night? I feel good today." She checked her calendar and realized her dates were mixed up. She thought he must have a few more nights of enjoyment on his holiday. Then she saw his message, "Will you be doing much?" She replied, "I am glad you are well. I am talking with another assistive technology company today. I have an exciting life 😁. What are you doing today?" He replied, "I will enjoy my day and see what I can do. I want you to have an enjoyable time working, Wilma 😊."

She joked, "So what you are telling me is you still haven't invested in a bucket and spade for making sandcastles 🤭🗿💡. I will have an enjoyable time working. Fridays aiding the helpline can be bad for counselling people. If I tell you I don't want to talk it is because I have had a difficult day." The conversation ended there as the star didn't like disturbing her while she was working. As she finished for the day, she texted him, "What mischief have you been up to today?" She thought he might be out chatting up the ladies on the beach. He replied, "I got back to Berlin and rested more. I've not done much, and I don't know what I will do tonight." She hadn't realized he had returned home. She thought about discussions she had with friends who travelled a lot; they loved their jobs but cherished the comfort of their beds at home. He then said, "I will get back to work as soon as possible. What are you doing tonight, Wilma 😊?" She advised him, "Enjoy being back home. I know my friends who travel a lot enjoy getting home to their own bed 😄. Don't undo all the chilled time you have had off by rushing back to work. I am just watching TV tonight 😄." He replied, "That's good to know. 😊😊 I'm good here and just enjoying my evening, Wilma. Are you having your dinner soon?" She replied, "Yes, I am being lazy tonight and making pasta and pesto. I have some nice lemon and ginger ice cream for dessert 😊." He told her, "That's good. You will surely enjoy your dinner. I am not feeling hungry now. I will eat when I get hungry." She replied to him, "I understand that you eat when you are hungry. You might want to try getting some colouring-in books for sitting and chilling out. I know I enjoy sitting with my stencils and making pictures while watching TV 😄." The conversation ended for the evening; she assumed he was back home and perhaps out with his social group.

The next morning, she woke up, started her usual routine, and received an email from Dr. Dodgy Shoes about the event he had discussed with her. She hadn't received any information previously and assumed it wouldn't happen, making her happy. She texted, "Good morning handsome. I hope you had a great evening at home. I have just received some great news. I am so excited I could crush a grape 😄."

While replying to an email, she received a good morning text from him, asking about her night's sleep and her plans for the day. She was excited and replied, "I am glad you slept well. Hopefully, you are enjoying your morning coffee. I do have a lot to do today! I am invited to Malaga to see the opening of my friend's project, the dyslexic compass, on the 5th of September. 😄" She was emailing people she knew about the project, hoping to secure some paid blogs from the event. He responded, "Oh, you will be travelling again Wilma, I hope you have a wonderful time 😊. What are you doing now? I have a meeting coming up soon with my lawyer." She felt discussing his meeting was private and confidential, so she replied, "I am sending lots of emails to assistive technology companies as they want a blog about the dyslexic compass and to showcase their products. I am terrified about going through airport security! One of the problems of having a leg full of metal work. I keep setting off all the metal detectors 🕵️‍♀️💁‍♀️🧟‍♀️💁‍♀️. I hope you have a good meeting with your lawyer 🙏."He responded, "Don't stress yourself working, OK? Of course, I will have a good meeting with my lawyer. Thank you for your care ♡." She found the meeting link on her Google calendar and replied, "Thank you for your understanding 🙏. Talk to you later, going into a team meeting now 👍😊." She received ♡♡♡ and wished him a good day. She was feeling overwhelmed with various projects, and she texted him, "I think I might just go and start doing some cooking. I have organized a lot of good things. My brain is now overthinking everything, and I wonder if I have taken on too much! It is time to do something else for the day." Cooking was her therapy, and she was making veggie chilli nachos. As she pottered around the kitchen, he messaged her, "Smiles, you should enjoy your dinner. I will see if I can make something later or make an order if necessary." Sometimes, she preferred taking a break from cooking and getting take-out. She joked, "Everyone is allowed a night off from cooking! I am a bit worried when going to Malaga and meeting up with my friend for the first time. I have talked to him a lot and he does have some strange tastes. I might end up with duck and banana curry 🥴🥴🥴." She didn't hear anything from him for the rest of the evening. She spent the night watching TV and listening to YouTube on her iPad before heading to bed. Late, she saw a report about an Apple security breach and texted him to update his software.

The next morning, she was up early, heading to the office to set up the helpline. Messages began appearing on her phone, and she realized they were from scammers. Although she usually entertained them, that morning, she was a bit grumpy and not in the mood, attributing it to the early start without her coffee. After grabbing a cup, she set up the helpline, eager for a catch-up with her office colleagues. As she received a message from him asking about her day, she thought it had started better. However, she didn't have much time in the office. "How was your night? She had a good night; she was only tired from an early start. If she had been at home, she would have been sitting and watching TV.

"I hope you're feeling good," she replied when asked about her morning. "Well, weird start to the day with strange love letters 😒 🤣 😄 What the Smeg! My night was nice and quiet. Just watched Point Break again. How was your evening? Is anything exciting today? "She hadn't heard anything and then went to the office; it had been a great morning full of laughs, catching up with everyone. The helpline hadn't been too busy, and the hubbub service was eventually set up. It took two attempts from two dyslexic people and fifty-seven attempts later, but it was up and working. Later, she found a message from the star: "My night was good, and my morning is going well. I have a meeting coming up shortly." She expected nothing less from a businessperson. Then the question came, "Who's sending you love letters, Wilma?" She eventually got around to answering the question, maybe incorrectly. She wasn't talking to Senga, who found it funny, as they had just been discussing an international superstar wanting a large amount of money from Wilma for an orphanage. She said to him, "I get love letters from lots of international superstars! They fall in love within a few minutes and then try to convince me to do them a favour. A fairy tale ending. It can be quite funny at times 😂😂😂." After leaving the office, she sat down and went to text the star, noticing he had read the message. She texted him to wish him a happy weekend; it was Friday, and wine o'clock would arrive shortly. However, the message came back unsent. Maybe she had a poor signal. She tried to resend but nothing happened. She removed the message, checked the signal (which was good), and tried another message, but she couldn't send it. She worked out that he had blocked her, which was a pity as she liked talking to this gentleman. Then, to add to it, she received another cheesy love letter proclaiming she was their queen 👸💡."

Blocked

The Case of 'Welcome to My Weird World'

Wilma received an Instagram message inviting her to chat with someone - just a simple 'hello.' It reminded her of Adele's 'Hello, it's me!' It felt great to have a fan and receive such support. She assured the person of her reciprocal support and thanked them for appreciating her work. Despite not being surprised by this, Wilma responded with warmth, saying, 'AWWW, that's lovely! How's everything? Where are you from, and how's your family?' The person replied, 'My family's great; I'm presently visiting.' During dinner with her parents and Mr G, Wilma took a break from messaging to enjoy the moment, replying to the star later, thanking them for the messages and explaining she was catching up with her family.

The next morning, while making coffee, she received a 'Hello, how are you doing?' Wilma replied, 'I'm fine, thanks for asking!' The conversation remained casual, with wishes for a good day exchanged. Days passed, and Wilma returned home with Mr. G. ABBA's 'Our Last Summer' played as they drove, and Mr. G mentioned Wilma seeming sad and needing a life. Amidst this, Wilma received a message while sitting in her cosy spot, asking what she was doing. She replied, 'Charging my OrCam Learn to read my coursework for the Open University.' The person inquired about her profession, and Wilma explained her role in training people to use assistive technology, particularly for those with learning disabilities like dyslexia, ADHD, and dyspraxia. The conversation briefly paused, acknowledging the

uniqueness of her job, and the person expressed interest in reaching out personally to escape their busy schedule, acknowledging the value of diverse perspectives. They proposed moving the conversation to a safer platform, suggesting Google Chat or Skype. Wilma shared her Google Chat address, and soon, she received a message there. Initiating the conversation, she greeted the person, who responded warmly, appreciating their fans, and emphasizing the uniqueness of Wilma's talent. Wilma thanked them, asking for privacy in their conversation, understanding the sensitivity of the topic given the person's busy life. Expressing interest in friendship, the person conveyed their pleasure in getting to know Wilma better. In response, Wilma playfully hinted at her 'weirdness' and her work in supporting neurodiversity, sharing her firsthand experiences as someone with dyslexia and dyspraxia. She highlighted the importance of assistive technology in her life, mentioning various tools aiding her studies and daily routines. The person expressed admiration for Wilma's journey and her commitment to supporting others like herself. Their conversation took a light-hearted turn, exchanging humorous remarks about dyslexia. Wilma shared an interesting fact, mentioning that individuals with dyslexia often have average to above-average intelligence."
"Unfortunately, the world often overlooks the intelligence of individuals due to the education system's heavy emphasis on reading and writing skills. He was occupied, leaving the conversation for later while Wilma relaxed, watching 'CSI' in her cosy spot. He greeted her warmly, asking how she was doing. She replied cheerfully, mentioning she was unwinding by

watching TV after a busy day. He shared that he had just showered and was relaxing too. Wilma's mind wandered amusingly, wondering if he needed help washing his back, but she asked about his TV preferences instead. When she received no response, she returned to her show.

The next day, he apologized for falling asleep and inquired about her day. Wilma humorously mentioned her knack for starting one show and ending another due to her 'amazing' TV habits, and she shared that her day was going well. He teased her playfully about being tired, to which she welcomed him to her 'weird world' with a mix of humour and sincerity. The conversation continued later, checking if they had eaten and exchanging pleasantries. He expressed delight in their conversation, remarking that she had put a smile on his face. Wilma thanked him warmly, and he asked how she'd feel about meeting in person. She shared her uncertainties due to the ever-changing nature of her life but expressed gratitude for the honour. Her dyslexia sometimes made planning difficult, but she remained optimistic about the future. He mentioned the possibility of meeting after his concert, understanding the need for rest post-pandemic.

The conversation paused until the following day when he checked in again. Wilma humorously shared her typical complicated issues as a dyslexic person and wished him a good weekend. Later, while relaxing with a glass of wine, she mentioned watching 'Harry Potter,' reminiscing about the magical world. He found her amusing and wished her an exciting time. She joked about partying with 'Harry Potter' while he might have fallen asleep.

The next day, he greeted her early, and she playfully mentioned her tiredness from working too much. She encouraged him to take some time off soon. In the evening, while browsing TikTok, Wilma stumbled upon a humorous sketch by Hale and Pace and decided to share it with the star, finding it amusing and worth forwarding."

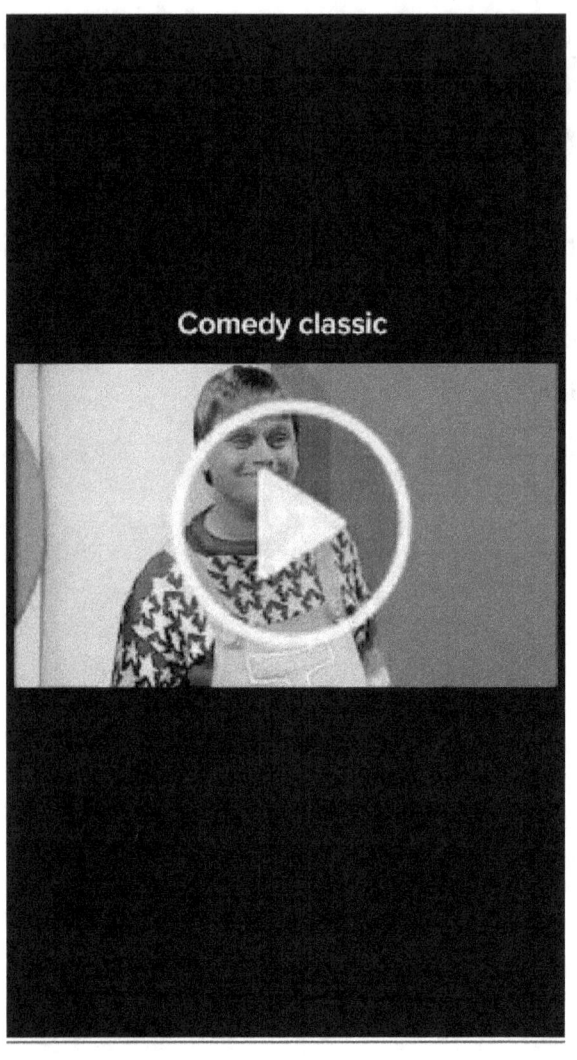

"I found this TikTok video so hilarious—I couldn't stop laughing! He didn't respond until Monday morning, acknowledging the humour. Seizing the chance on #mentalhealthawareness day, I pointed out the benefits of laughter for mental health. We exchanged pleasantries, with me wishing him well on his travels and reminding him to take care.

The following day, he inquired about my day, and I mentioned taking a study break and browsing Twitter. He shared that his day was going great. Then, unexpectedly, he asked my age. I dodged the question with humour, implying I'm perpetually 103 to keep people guessing and often seem younger than I am. He laughed, appreciating the humour and playfulness.

He asked for a photo, so I sent one, and he complimented me. I thanked him, and he followed up by asking if I was single. Curious, I affirmed my single status, prompting his revelation about finding it hard to be alone due to past relationship pains. I empathized, sharing my experience of being bullied and having a nervous breakdown, but finding support and now helping others in similar situations.

He admitted to easily falling in love but struggling with trust and overthinking relationships. Working in male-dominated spaces, he felt accepted but maybe lacked enough female friends for a unique perspective. He mused about trust in relationships and the influence of fame, discussing the complexity of love, imperfections, and Hollywood's role in shaping ideals.

Encouraging him to find contentment within himself and appreciate the people around him, I relaxed listening to ABBA's 'The Piper' on YouTube.

The next morning, he messaged expressing appreciation for our conversation. I suggested a bit of homework—making a list of relationship desires and past mistakes to avoid repetition." "Days later, he initiates contact with a 'hello dear,' and I reciprocate the greeting, asking how he's doing. He expresses that he often thinks of me, and while contemplating lunch options, I reply, wishing him an enjoyable time. Injecting a dose of humour, I share a terrible dad joke about dyslexia and a funny TikTok video by Scottish comedian Danny Bhoy. Later, upon learning of Robbie Coltrane's passing (Hagrid from Harry Potter), I expressed sadness, receiving an inquiry about my day. I respond, mentioning a busy day without stress, and inquire about his sightseeing.

Our conversation continues over the following days, discussing lectures, dinner plans, and entertainment choices. I assure him of being in a safe place while enjoying time with friends. His affectionate messages prompt playful banter from me, including a joke about confusing a Burger King drive-through and sharing comedic content. He expresses fondness and appreciation for our conversations, and I offer a safe space for dialogue. The conversation touches on assorted topics like life's challenges and perspectives. He expresses a desire to meet, but I suggest virtual platforms due to our busy schedules. Eventually, our conversation stops abruptly. I continue my routine, working on dyslexic voice projects and enjoying music while relishing positive feedback on my work. However, he disappears without further communication."

Where the Hell Did You Come from Friend?

Hello dear 💍 This message suddenly came unexpectedly on Google chat. Wilma answered with hello how are you? It had certainly been madding with the number of messages coming to her from TikTok and Instagram at the same time. Even Mr G has been talking about the amount of hacking activity going on at present. He had to stop all the attacks on her website over a fleeting period. The unexpected person talking to Wilma replied am fine dear 😊 How was your day? Wilma was confused but decided to be polite and chat with the person in question. She texted back glad you are fine and had a good day. I have been busy, but it has been a good day 😃 Wilma had been busy organising her studies and going to webinars to keep skills with assistive technology. The person replied to me too, Wilma decided to see where the conversation would go and texted back well, I hope you are taking diligent care of yourself, yes dear, I really like you, you're so caring and lovely 💍 Wilma thought this is weird, I wonder if I have chatted with this person before? Wilma texted back thank you that is nice of you to say so 🙏. The answer was a simple yes. She decides to ask done anything nice today. The person replied I have been relaxing because I will soon have a concert in Mexico. Wilma had known this through following this person over social media. He added and you? Wilma had been chatting to several people on Zoom and Microsoft Teams and answered yes, had a lovely chat with a dyslexic lady today. I look forward to further chats with her 😃 Then added to the text I hope you are enjoying the weather in Mexico 🎷. The pictures on the internet which had been posted were lovely. The band looked like they were having a wonderful time. She receives sure dear. What are you doing now? Wilma liked listening to music to help her to relax before heading off to bed. She texted back just sitting listening to some you tube😂 She received Oh, that's nice Wilma decides to make the person she is chatting with laugh by sending her favourite comedian. Billy Connelly when he was on the Graham Norton Show. He says thanks,

😂😂😂😂 She receives the reply of thanks dear 💗😂. Wilma knew that stars must mingle at many functions as the funny story on the YouTube video went on to describe. Billy talks about when he was dared to put his willy on a plate and

cover it in a salad. He said not to put salad dressing on as you would need a fire extinguisher for your willy. Then you must mingle with important people while holding your salad plate. The outcome was hilarious, and she texted the person now I hope you don't get up to any mischief after watching this 😂😂😂😂 She received the reply no, I won't 😂. Wilma laughed and texted back good! I get blamed for leading enough people astray 😂😂😂😂. Wilma went to bed shortly after sending this message and found this emoji the next morning. 😂

    The next day Wilma received hello. She politely texted back hello how are you today? He replies am fine dear 🤍 I miss talking to you my lovely friend ☺ This confused Wilma again, who is this person? She wondered if this was someone she had blocked in the past and they had kept her email. She replied you have only just started to talk with me yesterday 🤨 The reply she received was no, we have been chatting, for a long time. Hmmm, she wondered if this could be the person who had stopped talking after she had caught them out. It was certainly a puzzle and one she had not figured out yet. Wilma had also seen on TikTok that the star was making a video of one piece on his new album. He was going to play the piece called Danse Macabre and promised it was going to be sexy. Wilma wondered how he would manage this piece sexy as it is a tune about death playing his fiddle at midnight, causing all the skeletons in the cemetery to crawl out of the ground for their annual dancing party for Halloween. The star could not possibly dress up as Thor for Halloween, maybe he had run into Jonny

Depp, as in Sleepy Hollow he would ride past as the headless horseman. Wilma would just have to wait and see what would happen when the video was released. After daydreaming she returned to building a mind map for her assignment; on completion, she would transfer it to her writing helper. Unfortunately, she cannot remember the instructions and trying to find them. Thoughts of help help a damsel in distress came to her mind, I need cunning plan was required! 🙍‍♀️💡 As she was confused by the fact this person had said they had been chatting for a while she replied okay! I am definitely going slightly insane today 🙍‍♀️💡🙊💡😵😵😵. This led to a text coming throw saying how do you mean? Wilma sent back a text trying to explain My weird world is going slightly wonky today! Also, I can't remember chatting for a long time 🙍‍♀️💡🙊💡 So she sends him the short video of the late great Rik Mayall forgetting his lines in Bottom Hooligan's Island.

Then goes on to say this is how my day is going so far 🧠💡 Wilma's brain was going in many different directions at this point! She was busy concentrating on trying to resolve the problem she had with transferring information to writing helper. Thankfully for Wilma, the person had finished talking to her at this point. She contacted her friend in Texthelp for the instructions for transferring her mind map. Then she added it to writing helper. The next step was loading up PDF into writing helper and colour coding notes to aid towards writing her assignment.

Later in the evening, she received a text back saying It is okay, Hello dear 😊. She thought how nice and texted back hello how are you doing? It was a standard answer with I am fine how are you? She replied oh, it has been a busy day. I am getting there slowly but surely😊 She did not hear from him until the next day. Midmorning she receives okay and decides to say hope you are having a lovely day 🙏😁 Earlier in the morning Wilma had been looking through TikTok. A TikTok had posted the video of the international star she was supposed to be chatting with needing help drying his hair. Wilma didn't have this issue as her hair takes approximately fifty seconds to dry. He told her I had a concert today. Wilma was already aware of this fact through Facebook, she replied enjoy yourself at your concert. I hope you have a wonderful time 🙏 There was a simple Yes dear 🍃 Wilma watched parts of the concert that had been posted on social media. In the afternoon she sends you looks like you had an amazing time yesterday evening! Hope you have another great night and enjoy your weekend 🙏 In the evening she receives yes dear, thank you very much 🍃♡. While waiting to go out with the hair bear bunch for a few drinks and lots of laughing, she sees the new video posted by the international star as promised over social media for the last week. As she waited, she texted I am usually a terrible judge of time but just saw your new video very cool ☺ When she watched the video of the Danse Macabre she was disappointed that there were no skeletons in his video. It was a great piece however she failed to see the story behind the music other than him showing off his extraordinary talent. He replies a simple thanks dear ♡☺. As it was a Friday evening Wilma sent to enjoy a few glasses of wine after your concert tonight 🍷🥂 He texts back sure I will. She thinks tell me lies and reads What are you doing now? A bit of creative writing and made a curry for my dinner ☺. She did not expect the answer of WOW that's amazing 😍🤩. She thinks that is nice and weird and texts back thanks, 🙏 and adds just chilling out after a busy week ☺. He sends back you are such a lovely friend 😊☺. She thinks this is nice, however, you don't know me. However, she replied to the star saying thank you. It is lovely chatting with you 🙏 He texts back you're always welcome 😀 Wilma sends the star a picture saying to be the reason someone smiles today or the reason they drink! Whatever works. Receives a reply of thanks again 😀 As Wilma is feeling mischievous and sends a picture of a woman sitting on the couch trying to open a bottle of white wine it said crouching lady, hidden happiness. Yoga is hard and added this will be me shortly 😂😂😂 He sends back you're funny 😊 😂😂. Wilma has been told she is a comedian by several people on Google chat, she simply replies I try 🤪. He tells her to break the bottle 🍾 😂. She thinks I don't want to break the bottle and says I will cry if the bottle breaks! What a sacrifice of lovely wine. I like rescuing wine from shops 😂😂😂 He sends her back Ha-ha, lol 😂😂 Wilma then sends I am thinking of taking this box of wine back and complaining. It said once open this would last six weeks! It only lasted three days. Wilma left her flat with Mr G to go to the local for a few pints of dark fruit cider and catch up with the hair bear bunch. Everyone met in the corner and walked up the hill chatting about how their week had gone. After sitting down with her drink, she looked at her phone and found the message dear am incredibly happy. She thinks aww that is nice and replies glad to hear you are incredibly happy 😀. It doesn't take long to receive some things am lonely I don't have anyone to make me happy 😊 however I find you fun. The hair bear bunch are talking about go-karting at this point, Wilma is listening to them, she already knows how competitive the group are and it would turn into a go-kart version of Top Gear. As the guys are busy discussing who will win go-karting, Wilma replies to the last text with well I am glad you like putting up with my crazy ideas 😂😂😂😂. He ends the chart for the evening with 😊. Wilma turns her attention to the conversation with the hair bear bunch. It goes down a silly route and there was lots of laughter for the rest of the evening. Wilma was sitting on the bus listening to Spotify the next morning. She was going for a wonderful day out in the city and received a good morning from Mexico 😊. Wilma had checked Facebook and had seen photos from the concert the previous evening. She checked the time that was in Mexico. She was trying to work out the time difference with the texts, it worked out to be exceedingly early as it was midmorning while receiving the text messages. She decided to text back good morning what are you doing today? The star tells her It's my last concert in Mexico. Wilma checks the agenda on the official website and this information is correct. She tells him you can have a nice rest for a few days, before starting other projects. Enjoy a bit of sunshine 😁Wilma looks out the window at the sunshine, however, it was slightly cooler than Mexico. The reply she received was yes thank you very much I appreciate 😊 Wilma was looking to go out with Mr G, she had received a voucher for her birthday from friends for champagne and afternoon tea. She was packing her iPad so the QR code could be scanned for the voucher. She texted back with no problem, I am looking forward to a lovely day. My friends are treating me to a glass of champagne and afternoon tea 😊😊 The reply she received was that's sweet 😊 I don't know why I can't stop thinking about you babe 😊. Wilma laughs and thinks he is playing the Prince Charming card. She replies just keep taking the tablets it will go away 😋😁. Wilma was getting ready to disembark the bus and received what tablet? She thinks typical doesn't understand sarcastic comments and texts back It was a joke. Never mind 😂😂😂😂. He decides to say 😄 am serious about my feelings for you dear. I hope you feel the same. At this point, Wilma was far more interested in looking through the shops. She wanted to take several selfies wearing silly hats, which normally embarrassed her friends. Before she started walking, she texted back that it was sweet of you 😊. I will chat with you later. I am away to embarrass my friends by trying on hats 😂😂😂😂

Later in the afternoon sitting with a glass of wine. Wilma decided to send a positive message to the star for his last performance in Mexico. Enjoy life, feel alive, face the crowd, be proud, perform, shine your brightest. Love every minute of it. Amaze them, have a formidable last night 😁🤘

Later in the evening he replied thank you very much dear 😊 Wilma was heading to the bus to go home after a wonderful day and simply replied 😁👍. Wilma saw on Facebook and TikTok Tok the star was heading home. She was unsure if he was heading to New York City or if he was heading back to Germany. She sends a YouTube video of Mark Knopfler playing going home from the film Local Hero.

Wilma simply puts safe travelling 🙏. Wilma left the star alone for several days. She thought it was best as he would be tired and needed a rest along with catching up with his friends. It came as a surprise early in the evening to receive you could not even write me to check on me. Wilma had been busy and had a few moments of wanting to throw the laptop out of the window. She decided this would be a good excuse and texted back sorry I have been trying to write my assignment. It also did not help that my writing helper has developed a glitch and keeps breaking down 🙉💁🙊. I have been driving the lovely team at Texthelp to drink 🙈💁 She sat and wondered how he would take this news; it was not long before she found out with okay and added what assignment? Not wanting to give the game away that she was a social scientist studying criminology and decided to tell him about the assignment and said It was a complex assignment, with three parts to it. Part 1 is about sex workers; do they do this work through choice or is it a social constraint? The second part is about power and inequality following on the discussion part one. Then write a reflection on everything I have learnt 🧑‍🎓💡. The reply was this is your work, she thought that had confused him and replied it is part of my work which is complex 👥💡. He thinks about this answer and says okay, Wilma thinks she might have overdone the explanation and texts back sorry I have a nasty habit of just over-explaining things 🧑‍🎓💡👥💡. How was your journey home? I hope you have caught up with all your washing and ironing. Wilma does not receive a reply and thinks he has gone in the huff, much later in the evening she receives It was all good. Wilma did not what was good and beginning to get tired so simply texted back glad to hear it. I hope you are enjoying some time for yourself 🙏. She wondered what he would tell her and said yes dear. It is hard to be alone, she thinks he is probably sitting with friends or at a party texted back how is it hard to be alone? Wilma waited for his reply which was when I was lonely. Wilma thought about this and professionally replied everyone has periods of being lonely. You can be in a room full of people and still be lonely. Do you think it is because you are missing the adrenaline rush of performing on stage? She knew he would have to think about this and the answer she received was I think so. She smiles okay let us see how he takes this reply that is a natural thing! You have had a wonderful time and want it to go on, a teenage tantrum moment, we all have them 🙏 He thinks about this for a while and sends I still have a concert next year. Wilma thinks to herself you probably have a lot of Christmas concerts coming up, they are always pre-recorded.

She doesn't tell him what she is thinking and texts back that you have plenty of concerts next year. Put yourself in a positive head space. You will be involved in plenty of projects, allow yourself time to chill out 😜. He seems happy about this as Wilma receives yes exactly, Wilma continues with catch up with your friends! Also, catch up with the things you have put off 😜. He decides to assess Wilma with what about you? Wilma was never any good with big plans and liked to plan one week at a time. She tells the star I am busy with plenty of things. My diary goes from empty to too busy in a noticeably brief time 👻💡. He tells her that's nice and follows this with we can still meet anytime we want. Wilma laughs and thinks that is never going to happen. Wilma decides to humour the star with We can meet anytime, we have checked our calendars and found the time. He put surely, we will! She does not want to get his hopes up too soon and answers I do not know about you, but my days just vanish 👻💡. Wilma went to bed shortly after posting this to the star, upon getting up the next morning saw he had not replied to this statement.

A few days later Wilma sent a picture of a Halloween t-shirt saying oooooooooooob !A picture of a dyslexic ghost. He had his sense of humour back at this point and replied 🙀🙀🙀. Wilma was in a playful mood and responded with dyslexic zombies crave Brian's 😂😂😂😂Along with a picture of an empty box which was supposed to have a Chucky doll in it. The picture said Chucky had escaped from his box! Well, that can't be good 🤭🤭🧟‍♀️💡🧟‍♀️💡. He replied later in the afternoon 😂😂. Wilma did not hear anything from the star for a couple of days. Friday came again and Wilma was excited to go out. He had put up pictures of himself in New York City he must be enjoying time to himself. It was also coming up for Halloween. She had noticed that The Lost Boys were on at the local cinema. The cinema in Wilma's town was unique, it was small and had been renovated back to its glory in the 1930s, s. She messaged the star and said Well I hope you have a great weekend. I am going to look out my broomstick, hopefully, the weather is not too stormy as I might fly into a tree. However, I am going to see Kiefer Sutherland as a very cool vampire tonight. I love this retro 80, 's movie Lost Boys. She loved the soundtrack the Lost Boys by Tim Cappello.

Wilma received no reply maybe he was out at a Halloween party himself. As it was the weekend, and the onset of wintertime clocks were going to change. Wilma sends the star a reminder to my dyslexic friends that your cocks go black this weekend. 🤣🤣🤣🤣 The next day the star replies to her in the afternoon. 😂😂😂 I Love it. Wilma then sent a YouTube video of a Scottish comedian called Kevin Bridges to the star. He chats about Halloween in Glasgow when Woodie and Buzz Light Year are chained to a lamppost and Buzz Light Year turns to Woodie shouting you are my favourite deputy before heading to jail.

Wilma never heard anything else from the star that day. The next morning Wilma shared a blue ribbon for dyslexia awareness week. She told the star It is Dyslexia awareness week. We wear blue ribbons to show our support for our hidden disability. I have a busy week ahead and will be quiet 🙏 A few hours later she received okay 👌.

Later in the day Wilma was feeling mischievous and sent a TikTok about accents by comedian Michel McIntyre. You can talk in an Aussie accent to a South African asking if they have found the lost Kola.

😂😂😂😂 He replied to the message the next day with 😂😂 As Wilma was looking through Twitter, she noticed all the jokes about the blue tick. Elon Musk had been talking about charging for owning this official blue tick. A lot of people she followed were outraged by this remark. She sent a picture of a green tick on a black background. She texts the star saying I have a tick on Twitter 😂😂😂. Now the star has an official account and Wilma thought he could not be naive to what is going on. Elon Musk has never been off the news since taking over Twitter. The reply she received did not surprise her as he said, I don't understand. Wilma sent back that apparently Elon Musk is charging everyone with a blue tick on their Twitter account $20 a month 🙊💡 The answer she received surprised her that's great 👍. The mischievous side of Wilma came out and she replied glad you are happy about this news 😜.

Later in the night, she said yeah, I am. Wilma's Twitter account had been growing slowly and she sent it back I am glad I don't have that many people following me to need a tick on Twitter 😁. The reply was that's great 😊 Then he changed the direction of the conversation with have you supported any charity organizations before? Wilma did a lot of charity work supporting organisations that had supported her over the years. She brings about awareness of meningitis a serious illness which acts like a cold, it can leave devasting effects such as loss of limbs, brain injuries and if not caught in time death. Along with bringing about dyslexia awareness and how it works differently for everyone. Wilma replies to the star, yes, I support my charity and tweet about dyslexia. We had an event on Zoom tonight about dyslexia and mental health the bear truth. A momentous event and very emotional about the struggles of dyslexia because you don't fit into an education system 🙊💡 As it was extremely late at night Wilma added to her text I am going to bed. I have another busy day tomorrow 🙏 take care and have a good night 🙏 The star messaged Wilma back which she found the following morning. Why I ask is because my management sent me a letter from the American Heart Association to help raise money to save a kid's Life from kidney disease it's so sad because I am in America now. After reading this message, Wilma sat with a cup of coffee and carefully thought about how she would reply. Wilma put on her counselling head and eventually replied there are lots of charities, I talk about my charity to raise awareness of hidden disabilities. I get stopped all the time to give money to different charities and organisations. If only it was possible to give to all, but this is impossible. it is your personal choice to what charity you give to and bring awareness. If you want to run a marathon in New York to raise money for these different charities, then that is brilliant. It is up to you what you bring awareness to and which charities you support 🙏

Later in the evening the star responded to Wilma's message from the morning are you saying you can't support any charity organizations? Wilma responded with I support charities. I am a volunteer helpline advisor and writer. Supporting people with mental health issues and other areas of their lives. I raise awareness through Twitter, LinkedIn, and Facebook. Wilma had recently received a lovely message on Twitter. She took a screenshot of the message she had received it said your tweets are on fire, thank you for giving me the strength to speak out about dyslexia he asked Is this Twitter. Wilma had received many nice messages about her work in this area and replied yes this was one of the nice messages I received. I have received nice messages from the helpline for listening and signposting to the correct places 🙏. It is really rewarding as a national volunteer to give back to a great supportive charity 🙏 He sent back that is good. Then added I would love for you to join this project. Wilma was suspicious but she was not going to tell the person she was chatting with and sent it back what I am trying to say is that charity work is about something you are passionate about. It is no one's business but yours of how much money you donate 🙏. She was positive the star was trying to rope her into a project. She received are you trying to say I should work on the project alone? This did not sound good, and Wilma decided to text back a passive answer It depends on the project and where you want to take it. He answered that they wanted me to donate and share with friends and family members. Wilma gets more suspicious as this conversation goes on and sends a text back Who? What? Sounds suspect! Within a few minutes, she receives how do you mean? She tries to explain further and sends back I would never force anyone to give to charity. Sharing my charity work with friends and family I still do not ask them to give money. I allow people to give through their own free. Bringing about awareness through celebrity status is an amazing thing. Please do not force people to give money. He replies oh, now I understand am just helping to raise money, I send to them that I can come up with. She thought well you kind of get it she was not convinced and sent back yes; you are just promoting something you are passionate about. It is up to people if they want to donate 🙏 Good luck with your project 😬 He sent back thank you very much. Wilma was glad to hear he was happy, and she had avoided being roped into a project and sent back with no problem. Sometimes it is just having a unique perspective on something that helps 🙏. That is where the conversation ended with this star.

The Case of Unexpected on Instagram

Wilma received the message unexpected on Instagram in German. She receives Hallo guten Tag lieber Van, du sprichst mit mir, dies ist mein privates Konto Ich benutze es, um meine Fans für ihre wunderbaren Likes und Kommentare auf meiner offiziellen Seite zu schätzen Ich neige dazu, nicht auf meiner offiziellen Website zu chatten, also muss ich ein privates Konto erstellen, um meine Fans zu erreichen runs this through Google translate and Wilma replies hello amazingly the message was sent in English a short time later saying good afternoon dear fan you are speaking to me, this is my private account I use it to appreciate my fans for their wonderful likes and comments on my official page. I tend not to chat on my official site, so I need to create a private account to reach my fans how long have you been a fan? I have been a fan for about 10 years now. Thank you for the support. It's my outmost pleasure having you here thanks for your support you have been keeping me all these years, I wouldn't be here if it were not for you my lovely fan. I hope you find joy and happiness in my music? I will have to call you my super fan. I wrote to you confidentially. I hope you will keep it that way. I don't do this my instincts tell me that you are great, I believe with your great support I will continue to go far. What is your take on travelling and what places have you been to? Wilma says I love travelling I can travel anywhere it just takes a bit of imagination I love Spain and I have travelled there. I have lots of good fans from alone around the globe when exactly are you charting from? I would like you to tell me about yourself I can take a few messages here while I am reading my fan page comments. Wilma takes back I am not a dyslexic person I coach people with similar issues to aid them about feeling positive about themselves. Finding simple solutions to challenges which come with being dyslexic as dyslexia is not just a simple reading and writing issue. He then wants to know are you married, and do you have kids? I would appreciate if we could write more on my private telegram, reason is because I reply to comments here on my Instagram, however I have put more privacy settings on my telegram. I can deactivate this private account at any time. I am inviting you to my telegram account as my management will not be happy with me chatting with you, that I have created this please click on the link I have sent you to find and write to me on telegram if that's okay. Wilma replies no problem sent you a message. Wilma moved over from Instagram to Telegram, she has not worked out how to tell the fake addresses now as most people put @ name now. It started of with the usual hello from each other. I have messaged you in confidence and I hope you keep it that way! I don't normally do this however I suspect that you are a nice person. Wilma thinks yeah right and replies I understand that you like your privacy. Alright I hope we can take our friendship from the basis of this platform and turn it into reality. Wilma thinks I have no idea what that means and sends we will see what happens. So, tell me if you came across me in the street what would be the first thing you would do? Wilma responds with I would probably ask you for directions, due to the fact I would probably be lost! Well for me I would probably give you a big hug and then invite you for a cup of coffee or a glass of wine which ever you prefer! Okay that might be weird, He asks what are your hobbies my hobbies are cooking, art and design, walking, listening to music and creative writing. Well, my fun activities include camping, boat cruises, reading ,dancing, traveling swimming and spending time with kids. I love spending time with the motherless baby home every chance I can get. This includes holidays to give the children support in any way I can! What is your favourite colour? Wilma wonders how long it is going to be before he tells her to think of the children!

Later the next morning he sends hello, how are you doing today? hello I am good thanks. He asks again what your favourite colours? It is quite late in the evening and Wilma sends back my day has been great my favourite colours yellow. He is happy and says so tell me more about yourself. Well I'm dyslexic and i.e. the neuro-diverse community by training them with assistive technology. He then sends a message after midnight when

Wilma is in bed she finds that the next morning and it says I want to know more about your life experiences, the kind of person you are, your goals and dreams interests and anything else you want to tell me. At the very least I want you to be friends with someone who is kind honest caring trustworthy and God-fearing

I am finding a lot of peace here I would also like to know are you married with kids? Wilma just sends back I am not married and I do not have children. It was very late at night when he got back to Wilma asking her how she was doing today? I am doing well thank you he is happy and asks how was your day and what religion do you practice? Please if you don't mind could you send me a photo set of yourself? My day was great thank you and I am not religious. He is sad at the thought of Wilma not been religious and asks are you considerate and thoughtful to others? She answers us before going to bed and says yes of course I'm thoughtful and considerate to others. She finds in the morning I want to know more about your life experiences became the person you are your goals and dreams interests and anything else you want to tell me. At the very least I want to be friends with someone who is kind honest caring trustworthy and good feeling I find a lot of peace and that. Well ignores the message until far later in the evening when she is finished all her stuff. The reply was my life experiences living with dyslexia. My interests and dreams are educating people about the discrimination that dyslexic people face. I am looking to improve issues around dyslexia. She never hears anything until the following morning when he sends hello beautiful how are you today Wilma replies assumed to him when he asks well as good is here and what are your plans for today? Well as normal as firing up the laptop for studying and says well as my secure I am just catching up with some studying today you never stop learning. At this he disappears until late at night as it is the weekend, is up late watching YouTube with Mr G. They are chilling out to jazz music and she's in a good mood as her tower for her computer has been wired up. She is excited by this and just needs to sort out software is and webcam for meetings. Excitedly she types back I been setting up my tower it will to have everything ready to aid other people shortly. She goes to bed shortly after this to find in the morning that is great news to hear I hope you don't mind me's asking for you to send me a photo scrap of yourself. She ignores this and then around lunchtime she receives hello beautiful how are you today? Then very well thank you I hope you're having a lovely day she was sitting having a cup coffee on her desk looking at her new computer and setting up various small things that she could as it was such a nice day she planned on going for a walk with Mr G later. All is good at this end so what are your plans for today also see a photograph of yourself Wilma Gibson and sends a photograph. Shortly after he sends you hold the secrets of beauty in this world, if there was competition of the most beautiful woman in the world, you would when you are so beautiful. Two as well as nice of them but nothing you and simply sends thanks for the compliments. If I had a flower for every time I thought of you I could walk in my garden forever you are so beautiful. Where are you from? She wonders should you put some trillions Timbuktu she actually comes from the North Paul and Santa's little helper, however she answers am from the UK. And how are the good people over the are and how is your family doing as well? Everyone is well and enjoying the beautiful weather presently he is happy and goes on to enquire washer interest in men and do you live alone? Wilma sits outside with the pain of cider chatting to Mr G and eventually sends I live with my flatmate. And I enjoy diverse conversations with men. He then asks share something with you? Wilma is curious and wonders what is up to and simply says yes. Could you help me out by going to the store in getting me some steam cards? I need them to update my MacBook to promote some of my CDs on iTunes store and other TV platforms. Please help me dear and just having a little difficulty presently. Wilma thinks there is no chance of that quickly tapes sorry I cannot help you with this issue instantly he says may ask why? Yes it is because I work with assistive technology and with everything I do I never need to use these cards. I am suspicious of why people ask me for them. It is just cash for people and I would never ask a stranger to run to the shops to buy me one he then goes on again I am asking you to help me even if it is a friend to run to the shops and get one for me however you've already said you can tell me with it is okay. Wilma thought she was going to be negative death and simply replies good I'm glad you understand. Okay you have a good D to which it applies the same to yourself. He leaves for a few days and then aid the blue he comes out with hello how are you doing today to which it applies I am doing well thank you.

The Unusual Case of the Best Friend.

This is an unusual case. They had never appeared on Wilma's Instagram page asking to follow her before. Wilma checked out the photo—it was cleverly the same one used on Facebook and LinkedIn. Donning her trench coat and with Berri brandishing the magnifying glass from her Swiss army knife, Wilma set off to investigate. A message popped up on Instagram: "Hello dear." A simple introduction. She replied with a friendly "hello." Then came the customary, "How are you doing, my dear?" Wilma, with her headphones blasting Def Leppard and getting ready to snooze in her basket, sipped her coffee and munched on chocolate hobnobs as she typed, "I'm fine, thanks. How about you?" "I'm doing good, my dear," came the response. Glad to hear that, she typed back on her phone with a smiley face.

The next message read, "I hope you've got your Iconic album already?" Ah, the entrepreneurial pitch. Wilma had encountered these before and proceeded cautiously. It seemed like a pitch to sell a product. Wilma had seen plenty of adverts for the album across social media but, being disorganized, she hadn't ordered it. She replied, "Not yet!" It was mid-November, and Wilma was preparing for her second TMA. She was wrapping up her studies in criminal justice and crime reduction and mentioned, "I'm getting ready to write my assignment for university." Shortly after sending this, she received another message: "Oh, I see. What's your name and where are you from, my dear?" As expected, she replied, "My name is Wilma, and I am from St. Trinian's." "Where?" came the reply. Wilma chuckled at the query. Then followed, "I believe you're a fan." "Yes, I am," she admitted.

The next question was direct: "Oh, that is good. Are you married with kids?" She thought it was an odd question but replied, "LOL, that's a weird question. I'm not married and have no kids." He responded with laughter, "Ha-ha-ha-ha-ha, you're funny LOL." Wilma had heard this a lot in conversations with other scammers. Then he mentioned, "You're a fan of my best friend. I'm his manager and his best friend." Wilma already knew this; she had seen it posted on Instagram and Facebook. It brought back memories of her best friend, Princess Twinkle Toes, and their mischievous adventures before she passed away. Cyber cocktails were always fun. Oh, how Wilma missed the mischief they got up to! She replied, "Everyone needs a partner in crime. Who leads whom astray?" "Ha-ha-ha-ha-ha, you're so funny," came the response. Wilma never found out who led whom astray. "I get to practice being funny. I enjoy leading people astray with my mischief. HA-HA-HA," she remarked, wondering if she had the Count from Sesame Street in her midst. He asked, "You talked about being busy writing assignments for university. Are you a lecturer or tutor LOL?" She thought it was a nice touch that this person was paying attention. She replied, "I am neither. I am a student pursuing my degree. Something I've wanted to do for a while. Despite being dyslexic, I never thought I would achieve a degree. It's a challenge. I also work on raising awareness about dyslexia."

IIt does sound like a lot going on! Yes, I keep busy but manage to have some fun too. Wilma followed this with a joke: "I just saw a dyslexic Yorkshireman; he was wearing a cat flap." Then another one, "Dear grammar Nazis, I'm placing this here specifically to destroy your entire day. Maybe correcting this image is the only thing you'll think about all week." He replied, "Oops! Ha-ha. So, how old are you?" Wilma could have made up an age, but she stuck to her belief that a lady never gives away her age! He responded, "Oh, ha-ha, you're right." Wilma quipped back, "Of course, I am right!"

The conversation then shifted to whether she uses Google Chat. She simply replied with a "yes." He continued, "I believe you've dreamed of chatting with my best friend. He has a private platform on Google Chat where he occasionally talks to fans, but very few people know about this." Wilma chuckled, knowing from the official page that this wasn't true, and replied, "That's nice of him, considering how busy he is." The manager then suggested sharing the private email but insisted on keeping it a secret. Wilma agreed, assuming he'd disclose the information.

"So, my dear Wilma, have you met imposters online pretending to be him?" To evaluate the waters, Wilma replied, "Plenty of imposters. I have one trying to follow me on Twitter now; these accounts usually get suspended in 24 hours. I keep clearing out TikTok, but different accounts keep coming!" The response was a broken heart emoji. Wilma found this unusual and decided to see where the conversation led.

The manager explained that this was precisely why they informed fans about imposters on the official page and clarified that there were no private accounts on Facebook, Instagram, Twitter, or TikTok. Wilma agreed, thinking it was a sensible executive decision. She then remarked, "Even a superstar is entitled to a private life." But as she pondered this, she replied, "It's curious that people pretending to be your friend are drawn to the subject of dyslexia. My TikTok's on dyslexia is liked by these imposters. The world is a strange place." The reply came, "Dreadful things happen to good people."

Reading this, Wilma thought, "No kidding, Sherlock," and then read the question, "Have you had a horrific experience online before?" She decided to recount a bad video call incident: "Yes, once someone pretending to be my friend tried a video call late one night while it was still Hangouts. It seemed real, with movement towards the screen. I saw them sitting before me for about 30 seconds before the camera cut off, but they kept texting me. My brain was working overtime trying to figure it out. Could I have accidentally bumped into your friend?

The next morning, I realized it was a clever scam. They texted saying they had been swindled! They claimed their mother was in the hospital, locked out of their bank account, and asked to borrow money. I was nice but screaming internally, 'Get lost!'" Shortly after this, she received the reply, "Oh, shit. When was that?"

"Did you end up sending him any money?" She laughed, thinking this guy was either crazy or she had been seen as foolish. "I'm not sure when it happened; I find it hard to track time because of my dyslexia. You'd be crazy to think I sent them money. I set boundaries to keep myself safe, especially after counselling people."

Impressed with his response, as she was about to start work, she excused herself from the conversation, saying, "Well, it's been lovely chatting with you. I need to jump on the helpline and sort out other people's problems. I'll catch you later." Later in the day, Wilma messaged, "I'm happy to give you my Google Chat address if you want to enter my weird world. Trust me, it does get weird. Just so you know, I turn down buying Google cards and marriage proposals if that comes up. Enjoy your weekend, and I hope the sales of Iconic go well. Have a blast at your friend's party, drink plenty of wine, and enjoy laughing. "As expected, she didn't hear anything for a few days. Then she received, "Hi dear! How are you doing? I am fine thanks 😊 hope you are having a wonderful day." The manager had sent her an email address for Google Chats, a Gmail address that scammers often use. Wilma checked it out, and it turned up green. The manager asked, "Have you texted my best friend yet?"

Wilma wanted to investigate further and replied, "Yes, I have texted him." When asked about the timing, she responded, "I texted him after you sent me the email address. There might be time differences; he might not have seen it yet. Ha-ha-ha-ha. "The person she was talking to disappeared. Wilma went back to studying. Later in the day, he sent a wave, but she didn't respond.

A few days later, she received another message: "Hello, how are you today? I know you are busy promoting Iconic at present, take care." Wilma had been following the promotion of Iconic on social media. Just after finishing her dinner of homemade chickpea and spinach curry, she received an Instagram invite. The picture was correct, but the information was incorrect. She screenshot the image and passed it to the friend, mentioning that someone must be bored. The response came back, "Ha-ha, definitely. Please block him right now, Charles Noah LOL."

Wilma was about to join a Google Meet meeting when she received the message. She planned to block it after her important meeting. She replied, "Welcome to my weird world! I've received some strange friend requests!" After her meeting, while talking to OrCam, she checked the message asking if she had blocked him yet, followed by a query about adding the best friend on Google Chat. She chuckled internally but replied, "Yes, I've blocked the scammer. As for your best friend, I haven't received a reply yet. He must be quite busy. Maybe you typed in the incorrect email address LOL! I've made that mistake plenty of times thanks to being dyslexic! It has caused some serious and embarrassing moments. Just yesterday, while chatting with my friend Dr Dodgy Shoes on social media, I meant to say, 'wooden cutlery,' but thanks to Grammarly's autocorrect, I posted 'wooden adultery'! Ha-ha! Text me your email address, and I'll pass it on to my bestie. He'll text you when he has some free time."

Wilma sent her address but had a hunch that the person on Google Chat wasn't the best friend. Another request to follow Wilma came through on Instagram, this time from an imposter named Ahmed Sudhada. She responded, "Looks like I'll be busy blocking on Instagram tonight. Another new imposter—Ahmed Sudhada. This is getting worse as the day goes on."

He sent a screenshot of an account, and Wilma noticed it was a dark-mode user. He asked, "Do you follow him? This is a fake account." Wilma wasn't certain if she followed the account shown and decided to investigate later. She replied, "No, I follow the verified accounts with blue ticks. Strangely, I never had any trouble until last year. I've lost track of the number of Keanu Reeves and everyone else. Right now, there's a fake model on TikTok claiming he's in jail, asking for a Google Stream card. All too suspicious—I turned him down and blocked the account." She noticed that the imposter had posted pictures from a recent interview advertised on social media and commented, "Great pictures from last week 😊." "Messages paused for a few days while Wilma was occupied with other projects. She was pleased to receive a message saying, "Thank you, my dear. How are you doing?" Wilma had just received marks for her first assignment, scoring 66%. She replied, "I'm happy with my score of 66% for my first assignment this year 😊 Hope you're having a wonderful day. "Wilma had encountered numerous frustrations while writing the assignment due to her assistive technology breaking down. Not wanting to dwell on the tech issues, she shared, "I faced some tech troubles, but thankfully got it sorted in time. "It was early evening, and Wilma was relaxing when she received a message asking what she was doing and if she had eaten yet. She was chatting with a fellow freelancer about setting up a podcast.

Wilma tweeted her result and got positive feedback. She took a sip of peppermint tea and replied, "Yes, I've eaten, currently chilling out watching Men in Black. Sci-fi geek. Ha-ha-ha-ha! Who's your favourite actor? "Considering all the actors she liked, she answered, "Not sure who my favourite is! Chris Hemsworth could come to my house dressed as Thor; a girl is allowed to use her imagination. He answers Ha-ha-ha-ha! Absolutely! "Then came the question, "Do you live alone?" She smiled at the query, glanced at Mr G in his dug basket typing away, and replied, "No, I live with my flatmate." The response was predictable, "With a male. LOL." Wilma smiled, thinking he'd find her odd, and joked, "I haven't seen RuPaul resembling Santa. As she looked over at Mr G on his laptop, she responded last I checked, he was a man!" The conversation took an unexpected turn, making Wilma suspicious. She commented, "Presently, I'm the only woman among my bat-shit crazy male friends. They'd probably say I'm too annoying. If I were kidnapped, the kidnappers would make a payment on my return!" The conversation halted there that evening. Wilma listened to Michael Bublé's "Everything" before bedtime.

The next morning, she checked her phone for emails and social media updates, made coffee, and headed to Mr. G's office with tea. From going to bed till waking up, she noticed two fake Twitter accounts and a fake TikTok follower. Curious, she texted the best friend and decided to inquire if his best friend might be dyslexic. Knowing that discussing dyslexia in Germany could be sensitive, she wanted to understand why fake accounts were drawn to her work on dyslexia. She had previously made a friend through the star's official Facebook account, discussing the swindles they encountered. They also discussed an interview where the star mentioned being dyslexic briefly. Wilma had seen Hauser and his girlfriend's TikTok videos swimming with dolphins in Dubai but hadn't noticed any outrage. However, she'd heard from friends that swimming with dolphins was an incredible experience. After a few mistyped attempts on Google Chat, she eventually entered the correct information. She messaged, "Hello, my name is Wilma. I've been chatting with your best friend on Instagram. Thanks for the chance to chat with you 🙏. "Eventually, she received a message back, initiating a conversation. The new person seemed confused, asking questions the best friend had already asked. Wilma maintained her responses, realizing it could be a test for authenticity. The conversation turned to personal questions, and Wilma stuck to her principles, not revealing personal details. They exchanged pleasantries and compliments, closing the conversation for the day.

A day later, Wilma received a message while having lunch, continuing their exchange about the star's music. It ended with a playful remark from Wilma about her "bat-shit crazy" side, and she headed out to meet friends for cider and shenanigans. Wilma was settled in her cat basket, engrossed in her Open University coursework when she received a message. He inquired, "What are you doing, my dear? I hope you're having a happy weekend so far." She responded, "I'm studying as I never stop learning. I hope you're having a wonderful time."

Their conversation ended briefly, and a few days later, on Sunday, she reached out to the best friend, concerned about his unusual quietness. She asked if everything was okay and if he had stopped talking to her. He quickly replied, "No, why would I stop talking to you? I find you remarkably interesting." Wilma appreciated the comment but didn't bring up their Google Chat conversation, mentioning she had been busy with other things and asking if he was enjoying some time off.

He expressed frustration with imposters, and Wilma, drawing from her criminology studies, shared insights: "You'll never stop imposters! Unfortunately, it's easy to pretend to be an international superstar. I've found ways to spot them, but a lady never gives away her secrets! Make up false stories, do something out of the ordinary, and use your imagination." He joked, "I'm getting tips from you LOL." Wilma suggested using dyslexic out-of-the-box thinking, even proposing a fake girlfriend or a date with Eddie Monsoon, sending a picture of Jennifer Saunders dressed as Eddie.

He replied, "Oops! Not supermodel enough," and sent Patsy Stone with a bottle of vodka. The banter continued, and Wilma, busy organizing meetings, and training sessions for assistive technology, eventually joked, "I'm not off my trolley, I have lost the trolley and going through life on a set of wheels."

Their conversation shifted back to Google Chat. She noticed Iconic had reached number one in Germany and congratulated him. He appreciated her words of encouragement. Wilma, noticing a Grammarly mistake in her previous message, corrected it and apologized. Days passed without communication, but Wilma was occupied with training sessions and networking in the assistive technology industry. On Google Chat, he asked about the country she lived in. Wilma mentioned Britain and expressed her desire to travel more, despite the pandemic's challenges. She shared her connections to Germany through friends and acquaintances, including one known as "Dr. Dodgy Shoes."

Later, he asked if she had ever had a terrible online experience. Wilma recalled a dodgy video call on Hangouts that turned out to be a scam. She found it scary and lamented how people fall for such scams. As Wilma relaxed in her cat basket with lemon and ginger tea and carrot cake, a message arrived from the star, asking her to share about her unpleasant online experience.

Wilma smiled and replied, "Lol, no, I wasn't swindled! I figured out what they were up to, but my brain was pondering if an international superstar was trying to call me on Hangouts. I did see them for about 30 seconds, and they kept messaging me." He asked, "Oh my goodness, when was that?" Wilma couldn't recall the exact time and continued, "The next day, they messaged saying a loved one was in the hospital, and they needed money because they were locked out of their bank account. Sorry, I can't recall when it happened. Anyway, they promised to repay me, but I refused to help. We had a falling out, but weeks later, they returned, promising to buy a house in the UK and live together. I joked about picking them up from the airport and going straight to the police station. They stuck around for a few months, but one day, I was grumpy, and they dumped me 😂😂😂😂😂" The star replied with laughing emojis, and Wilma continued, "I had an idiot asking me to buy Google Stream cards! I made excuses for 13 days, saying I forgot or didn't shop online. It worked, but I got bored and annoyed the person. People keep blocking me 🙈🙉. Maybe they'll miss someone who falls for these scams if they talk to me!" The star responded with more laughter, and a couple of days later, Wilma received a greeting, "Hey dear, hello, I hope you're well 😃."

    She replied, the next morning, "Yes, I am. How are you?" as she readied herself to study criminological theories and concepts with her OrCam Learn for some reading. He inquired about her plans for the day, and Wilma, observing the weather, joked, "Great weather for studying! I better start my mind map for next month's assignment and answer dyslexia inquiries. Along with checking out more assistive software." However, after her response, he never engaged in conversation again. Wilma eventually decided to block him without mentioning it to the supposed best friend. Wilma then turned her attention back to his best friend on Instagram, asking, "How are you doing?" and receiving a comment about her funny profile picture in response. Wilma changed her profile picture to a bold look and received a compliment from her international stalker. On a busy Friday, she shared a photo of the beer, marking the start of the weekend. However, her social media had been oddly quiet recently, which struck her as bizarre. Discussing this with a friend in Switzerland, they exchanged insights on catching scammers. Wilma messaged the best friend, noting the unusual absence of activity from his fan club. He seemed perplexed but didn't answer her query directly. Trying a different approach, the next day, she asked about his day. The conversation drifted to dyslexia, with Wilma sharing its creative side and a quote about embracing uniqueness. Silence followed during the holiday season, with the star engaging in an advent calendar and Christmas promotions.

Later, she initiated a conversation again, mentioning her engagement with assistive technology and receiving unwanted attention on LinkedIn. When the admirer brought up sitting on a porch listening to Bryan Adams, Wilma humorously recalled a song and explained she was not impressive. The best friend shared her sentiment with a playful denial.

Wilma recalled a hilarious conversation with the hair bear bunch envisioning them in the future as millionaires lounging poolside in Greece. They left her with a bad vision of themselves in "High Visibility vests "and "Budgie Smugglers" with white socks and sandals. It did not scream sexy to her more like "the little shop of horrors". They finished off by singing" I'm too sexy" by Right said Fred. She shared a fun farewell as she headed out with the hair bear bunch for some beers.

Later, she noticed an attempt by an international superstar to follow her on Twitter and shared the screenshot with her best friend on Instagram. Upon the friend's acknowledgement, she playfully mentioned being too busy to oversee the situation immediately, adding a mischievous touch with smiling devil emojis. Days later, while exploring TikTok, she spotted a fake account and reported it to her friend, emphasizing its link to the official account and her quirkiness. A conversation ensued where the best friend asked about a fan ID card, leading to Wilma's humorous remark about having something else to lose and her disinterest in needing a fan card to enjoy his music. On the first of December, Wilma, embracing her Christmas spirit, sent warm wishes for the festive season, which the friend appreciated. While preparing for International Disability Day on December 3rd, she stumbled upon the fact that Itzhak Perlman, a renowned musician, had overcome disability. This struck a chord as her past illness, meningococcal meningitis, was mistaken for polio by her mother. She shared this revelation with the management team, expressing surprise about the friend's teacher being disabled, as it related to her research for International Disability Day. After accidentally breaking the security system on Instagram and receiving numerous requests, she had a light-hearted conversation with the star about their persistent attempts to infiltrate social media platforms. As the best friend would be the next envisioned star as Aquaman leaping from the water and swishing his hair on Twitter, she shared the amusing encounter with his management team. She then offered advice about being cautious with potential hackers, noticing patterns in the fake accounts and maintaining a light-hearted yet informative tone throughout the conversation. It appears Wilma has quite the knack for managing these strange situations! Wilma's interaction with the international superstar's friend continued with a mix of humour and caution regarding scammers. She shared insights into the patterns and behaviours of scammers, emphasizing the ways they manipulate situations to extract personal information or exploit emotions. When the friend seemed curious about her approach, Wilma explained her interest in criminology and her fascination with studying these online interactions. Despite expecting to be blocked for her straightforwardness, she found the friend responding positively, even engaging in conversations about Snapchat. As she continued to observe the friend's travels and updates on Instagram, she noticed an influx of fake accounts trying to follow her, including requests linked to the latest photos shared by the international superstar. Wilma promptly reported these to the management. During her busy schedule, including a mental health course and managing assignments, she kept up the occasional banter with her friend, joking about bugs in computer servers. Despite moments of silence, she'd sporadically reach out with comments on the friend's activities or plans, maintaining a casual rapport. As Christmas approached, she found increased activity on her social media, including messages that seemed automated from supposed celebrities thanking her for likes and comments on their official pages. Wilma seemed to navigate these encounters with a blend of caution and humour, keeping a keen eye on the influx of activity while continuing her engagements with the international superstar's friend. Wilma's interactions, primarily with scammers, continued to be a recurring theme amid the holiday season. She shared standard scam messages with the management, humorously noting the predictable nature of these attempts. Despite the influx of fake account requests and messages, she maintained a light-hearted attitude, even managing to exchange holiday greetings with the international superstar. Wilma seemed to recognize and anticipate the patterns of scammers' messages, conveying their typical nature and promptly informing the management. Amidst her busy schedule and engagements, she balanced these interactions with a playful attitude, exchanging holiday wishes and maintaining a level of curiosity and amusement about the ongoing scam attempts. As she navigated her work with assistive technology, it appeared she kept a watchful eye on the various social media interactions, managing to handle the scam attempts with a blend of humour and vigilance Wilma's commitment to her studies and the use of assistive technology continued to be a significant part of her routine, especially during the holiday period. Despite the serious tone of her studies, she managed to partake in traditional celebrations like Hogmanay, a party with the hair bear bunch involving wine, beer and vodka even sharing good wishes and having a lively time which involved cheesy tunes such as Kenny Rodger's "The Gambler" and Neil Diamonds "Sweet Caroline" This was quickly changed to music from the band Linkin Park and other dance music from the "Ministry of Sound". She encountered a concerning situation on Facebook with a fake email address shared as a means to communicate with the international star. Demonstrating her vigilance, she promptly utilized an email checker tool, which she recommended to her best friend for safeguarding against such fraudulent attempts. Her friend seemed intrigued and asked for more details on how to access this tool. Wilma's proactive approach in addressing potential scams and providing guidance to the best friend highlighted her attentiveness to online security and willingness to help others navigate similar situations. Wilma's been juggling quite a lot between her studies, she is keeping an eye out for scammers and engaging with assistive technology. Despite the difficulties, she's managed to maintain her sense of humour and keep pushing forward. Losing the Princess Twinkle toes a year ago Wilma found it sad to see on the news the passing of Lisa Marie Presley, she could not help but think of all the laughter they had at the time of year. She WhatsApp the "beautiful fairy." discussing OrCam Learn and aiding with a book review. The "beautiful fairy" laughed and told her she would send a copy when it was available to buy on Amazon. She told the "beautiful fairy" to enjoy a great weekend with plenty of wine. Wilma loved some relaxation and an enjoyable time annoying the hair bear bunch with her wacky ideas. After some investigation, she removed several inactive accounts to tighten up her security. Despite the odd conversation with the "Best friend" that followed, it abruptly stopped again. When asked about her favourite celebrities, Wilma listed quite a few names, but the exchange halted once more, leading her to keep an eye on the account's activity. Eventually, when the account migrated to Instagram messages and showed no posts, she blocked and deleted it. It was indeed an odd and interesting encounter for Wilma.

The Case of the Perfect Relationship

Wilma encountered this person on Instagram and decided to investigate by engaging in a chat to uncover any potential fraud. "Hello, how are you doing today? How are the weather conditions over there?" she initiated. "Hello, I am great thanks. The weather is nice but very cold!" the person responded, liking the message. "That is good, where are you from?" Wilma decided to omit mentioning St Trianians for now and simply replied, "I am from the UK; I hope you are having a nice weekend." "That is good, it is my pleasure to communicate with you here. How long have you been one of my fans?" "Oh, approximately 10 years now." "Wow, thank you so much. I want to say thank you for the love, care, and support you have shown me for all these years; you are indeed a super fan," the person said. (Wilma thought, *I have never been told this before*.) "What are some of the favourite tunes of my music?" "Oh, I have plenty of favourites: 'Innovation,' 'Vivaldi v Vertigo,' 'Midnight Waltz,' the Fifth, and others which I cannot spell." "Wow, that is good. What inspiration do you get from my music whenever you listen to them?" "It helps me concentrate while reading. I also like listening to your music while being creative. Are you looking forward to being back on tour?" "Wow, that is amazing. I appreciate you making me who I am today. What do you like about my personality?" "That is a good question. You come across as a very smart guy who is profoundly serious about getting people into music. You just made me smile; you're one of my big fans. Thank you very much for the love and support you have shown me." Wilma delivers the princess twinkle toes favourite saying and texts, "Enjoy life, feel alive, face the crowd, be proud, perform your best, shine your brightest. Love every minute of it," which amazes them. "Thank you very much. Tell me about yourself. What's your job? Are you married? Do you have children and grandchildren? Do you have parents and siblings? How old are you?" "Well, for a start, a lady never gives up her age! I am presently single with no children. I am a freelancer and train people in a neurodiverse community on how to use assistive technology to support them in their studies, work environment, and life." "That is good. You have an excellent job, I guess. Can we be friends with constant conversation? "I love my job! Others might think it is a bit mad. Yes, we can be friends and have a conversation." "Thank you. I see you are a lovely woman, and I like you a lot." "Thank you. Can we talk on other platforms? "Sure, which platform do you wish to talk on?" "OK, do you have a telegram?" "Yes, I do. Please send me your address." "I have found you, and a message has been sent." "Ok." However, there was no phone number with the telegram account; it was @address, and Wilma couldn't figure out where the fake address was coming from in the world. She knew the real star did not have a telegram account from postings on Facebook. The conversation begins, "Hi, how are you this evening?" "Thank you for contacting me here on this platform. How are you doing?" "It is my pleasure. Please, I don't want you to share any of my contact details with anyone, because you know I have to protect my dignity and personality." (Wilma thinks this is standard to start with from scammers.) "I understand and will not share any personal information. To answer your question, I am well, thank you for asking, and thank you for inviting me to chat with you. What is your favourite part of your job?" He tells Wilma to thank her for her understanding. "What are you doing now?" Wilma had the new song from Pink, "Never Going to Dance Again," playing and replied, "I am chilling out listening to music." Ok, that is good. I do appreciate us becoming friends with trust and honesty, what do you think? "What Wilma thinks is, "We will see what tricks you are up to, my friend, and how long till you block me," however, she replies, "Yes, it will be nice to get to know you 😊. So, what do you want to know about me?" She thinks *I want nothing but to distract you for a while.* She asks an easy one for starters, "What are your hobbies?" "My hobbies include music, reading, and spending time with my family. I'm also a fan of watching several television programs. In my spare time, I enjoy playing the violin and piano." (No shit, Sherlock!) "What about yourself?" "They are cool hobbies. I enjoy cooking, art and design, walking, listening to music, and creative writing." "That's amazing. Can I see your picture if you do not mind?" Wilma picks out the selfie she had taken of herself before heading out with all her friends for a party for her birthday. "Wow, you are so beautiful. You must have been the second woman God created after Eve." "God must have lavished abundant time to make such an enchanting, you are so enchanting, highly like a Goddess 😊 (She thinks What a load of rubbish!) Thanks for the compliment!" You're welcome, dear. Please excuse me, can we talk tomorrow? It is late, and I need to sleep; it has been a busy day. I will say good night. "No problem, good night, sweet dreams." "Thank you, same to you." The next morning, a message arrives: "Wake up, friend! It is time to see the beautiful world. I hope your morning is filled full of love, happiness, peace, and harmony. Good morning." "Good morning. I hope you are well and ready to have an enjoyable day. How are you doing today?" "I am well, thanks. I hope your day has got off to a good start." "Yeah, thank you. What are your plans today?" "Studying new assistive technology which has come on the market for training purposes 😊." "OK, that is good. I have started my day already." Wilma knew he would be away practising for his concert at night and remembered to take regular breaks! "You mustn't overdo it and burn out 😊." He answers in the evening, "Ha-ha, how are you doing? "I'm fine. How is your day going? I hope you are taking a break from work 😊." "Sure I am" (she thinks, *liar*). "How was your day?" "It has been good; I have had plenty done on my ta-da list." Wilma had emailed her tutor for breaking down and planning her TMA at the end of the month, as well as looking at invisible harms in theories and concepts of criminology. She found this fascinating, as well as emailed the police to find out about studies for help and support for dyslexia in the criminal justice system. She never mentioned any of this to the star. "What have you been up to today?" "I have been preparing myself for my concert." "Where have you been?" she was in her cat basket trying to run her empire, she sent back, "That is nice. I hope you are feeling prepared for your concert. I have been studying a software called Notion. "She had been asking the person she had a subcontract with about training and how often it was used. He had heard of it but never trained anyone studying with the software. He stopped chatting with her, so she assumed he was playing his concert. The next morning, she received, "Hello dear, good morning." "Good morning 😊. I hope you are ready for another exciting day." "Yes, dear, and you." "Yes, I am, ready for another fun-filled day." Later in the evening, she received, "Hope you are having a good day." "Yes, I am, thinking you. I hope you are having fun." "Yeah, what are you doing right now?" She had Spotify on and singing along with ABBA's "If It Wasn't for the Nights" and answered, "I am cooking my dinner." At this point, she could make up whatever she felt like when replying "Wow, what are you having for dinner?" She was cooking for herself and Mr G and replied, "I am making spinach and chickpea curry." "That sounds delicious. You had dinner already." As he sent this message later, Wilma was in the middle of stuffing her face and messaged back once finished, "Just finished it, absolutely delicious. So, what are your favourite foods and drinks?" "I don't have favourites; I like to try diverse types of food 😊." "That is lovely. What sort of food and drink do you enjoy?" Wilma had to wait till the next morning when he sent through, "Good morning, dear, have a lovely day. I like to eat chicken fries, steak, Burger King, and Taco Bell and drink champagne." Wilma laughed and sent back, "Good morning 😊. I hope you have a wonderful day. Champagne is a lovely treat. I am not sure if it would go well with Taco Bell, but I have never tried Taco Bell." "You are going to love it 😊. How are you doing today? The weather is horrible; I am glad to be working on a project indoors." "That sounds good. Hope you have eaten breakfast?" "Yes, I enjoyed a plate of porridge. I hope you had a nice breakfast." Early in the afternoon, she receives, "What are you doing now?" "I am reading up on information for a project I take part in (It is called the Open University). I am sure you are practising for your next concert." "Yes, I am, but I'm resting a little." She agrees with his statement "Taking regular breaks is good. Take care of yourself 😊." Wilma sent a gif of Eddie Monsoon getting the last bottle of champagne from the fridge, and a new set of bottles comes down like a set of Skittles. "Ha-ha, thank you! Are you happy being single, or do you want a man to put a smile on your face?" After reading this, Wilma just about fell out of her cat basket laughing and replied, "Well, you certainly put a smile on my face with that text." He inquires "Aww, so what kind of man do you love to spend the rest of your life with?" She thinks good question "I do not know what sort of man I would spend the rest of my life with. I have lots of friends who are men, and we always have a good laugh. However, I am not looking for a relationship." "I guess you are okay being single." "Yes, being single is fine. How about you? Do you not enjoy being single?" Wilma never heard anything from him for the rest of the day. For once, she sends the message first, saying, "Good morning, have a lovely day 😊." An hour later, she receives, "Begin a new day of your life like a new chapter, wishing you a wonderful morning and a good day ahead." As it was Friday and Wilma had the helpline, she wished, "Happy Friday! Enjoy your life no matter how hard it may seem. When life gives you a thousand reasons to cry, show the world that you have a million reasons to smile." He sends back, "Being single is not an excellent choice. I'm still looking for the perfect partner. How are you doing today?" She replies, "I do not think that there is such a thing as a perfect partner. This may be why I am still single, as everyone has their faults. I am good and getting ready for another busy day." "Ha-ha, you are not perfect?" "No way am I perfect! He decides to say Hà ha, can you make yourself perfect for a man?" Then adds "A man needs a respectful partner, a lovely and supportive woman." (Wilma thinks, *no way is that happening! What an asshole*) She sends it back, "I am not changing myself for anyone. People can accept me for being the person that I am. "He decides to ask, "Have you ever been married, or have you had a previous partner?" Wilma's brain says here we go again "Yes, I have been married. I am now divorced." He returns "I am sorry to ask." She puts on what she has learned in her course and replies, "Well, he lied, cheated on me, also mentally and physically abusive. I do not judge every man and think they are all as bad as my ex. However, I will not allow a man in a relationship to have that amount of power over me again." "I am so sorry for that; I would like to know what sort of man you need." Wilma smiles, tries this for size, and replies, "It is a tall order, which some men find incredibly difficult. You just must be yourself, someone who is friendly, and I can have a conversation with as well as a good laugh and can take a joke. I can make up my mind over time as I get to know you." "Ha-ha, is that all you want from a man?" Wilma knows he is hinting about impressing her with the size of his aubergine and spicing her life up with it. Wilma sends back, "Yes, is it wrong to just have an enjoyable conversation with a man?" She wonders what he will say "That is a nice idea. Do you know s friendly conversation that could make you fall in love?" Wilma laughs at his comment and types into her iPad, "I have no idea what kind of conversation makes people fall in love." Then follows it on with, "I do know the kind of conversations men have to try and get into women's knickers." That was the kind of conversation Wilma had with the hair bear bunch. He then asks "Ha-ha, do you believe in distance relationships? Do you believe you can find your partner online?" "Yes, I do believe you can build friendships online. I have made several friends online during the pandemic." Thinking about Dr Dodgy shoes, he returns "That is nice. And do you enjoy the conversation with them?" "Yes, of course, I do. That is how we became friends 😊." "OK, I see you as a lovely lady. I only hope that you will forever be a friend." She thinks probably not we will see how long the conversation lasts and return "Thank you. I look forward to growing a good friendship. He texted back Sometimes in life, you find a special friend, someone who changes your life just by being part of it. Someone who makes you laugh until you can't stop, someone who makes you believe that there is good in the world. Someone who convinces you that there is an unlocked door just waiting for it to be opened." Wilma sends back, "The reason someone smiles today or the reason they drink, whatever works. What are you doing now? It's Friday and time for wine o'clock!" He replies, "Ha-ha, I guess you are having a nice time." "Yes, I am. I hope you're enjoying a relaxing evening with your friends." "Yes, I hope you had dinner." As she chats to Mr G she types "Not yet, however, I have already cooked it; just need to heat it. He inquires What did you prepare?" "A chicken red Thai curry." "That sounds yummy. Hope you kept mine as well." She laughs "Sorry, I didn't know if you like spicy food." "I do enjoy spicy food. I would love to taste your food," he says, Wilma sends over a photograph of a dish she cooked of tomato and basil salad. "That looks delicious. I am guessing will taste good." She continues the cooking theme "It was fabulous. Do you enjoy cooking yourself?" "I love cooking, but I don't have much time for it. She inquires when you have time for cooking, are you a recipe book person or do you just make it up as you go along?" He tells her "Sometimes I use a book!" She asks "Cool. So, who are your favourite chefs?" He sends a disappointing "I don't have any favourites." Wilma gets up to mischief, "I thought you would have been a Nigella Lawson fan. Thought you were looking for a domestic goddess," and sends a gif of Nigella Lawson eating lots of chocolate, but she doesn't hear anything from him for the rest of the evening. The next day she receives a message, "Good morning, my dear. It is your choice to either keep enjoying your dreams or wake up and make them come true. Hope you have a lovely day." She yawns and sips her coffee "Morning, have a lovely day." Later in the morning, she receives, "How are you doing today?" She was excited and returned "I am well thanks, watching the rugby later today." "Okay, have a nice day. I will contact you when I'm free." "Cool, take care, remember to take regular breaks while working." Again, Wilma was chatting with Mr G and sipping a dark fruit cider she received, "Hello dear." "Hello! Hope you had a good day." She laughs "Yes, of course. I have. Rugby is a beautiful game played by men with odd, shaped balls." "Ha-ha, I guess you enjoyed watching it?" "Yes, it was a great match. Also, nice weather; and great to be in the pub enjoying drinks with friends. What are you up to this evening?" She sends an Enigma "Return to

Innocence" video and says, "Chill out, my friend." He returns, "Presently, I'm resting before performing again tomorrow. Ha-ha, guess you are enjoying yourself!" The hair bear bunch were on form with the jokes "Yes, I am. Please enjoy your rest, and also enjoy eating some cake. Life is short!" Again, he sends, "Ha-ha-ha, you're damn funny! I like you because you put a smile on my face." Wilma gets up to mischief again and sends "Mahna Mahna" from the Muppet show. Wilma knows it is extremely annoying and ends up stuck in a person's head. That was the end of the conversation for that evening. In the morning, he said, "Good morning, my friend. Make your day unique just like each snowflake." She sends back, "Good morning," followed by a gif of her trying to wake up. Wilma was on automatic pilot, going through all the things that she usually does to get herself organized for the day. She receives, "What are you doing today?" Star then sends, "Hope you're cool!" To which she texts back, "Cool as a cucumber!" Late in the evening, he sends a greeting, to which she replies, "I hope you had a good day." "Yes, dear. And how have you been tonight?" She was just chilling out in her cat basket "I have had a lovely and relaxing evening, thanks!" "That's good. She asks So, what are you up to now?" However, he had disappeared It was unusual for him not to send a nice message in the morning. However, she answers, "Having a cup of coffee before starting another busy day!" He inquires, "Okay, so what are your plans today?" "I have meetings with assistive technology companies and a few training sessions for students. What are you up to today?" "That is good. I am preparing myself for my show later. I'm in Austria now." Wilma checks the internet discreetly to verify his whereabouts. "Nice! I hope you have a great show. I hope you have the time for a bit of sightseeing." "Thank you and have a great meeting today." Wilma shares her favourite saying from the product manager of Texthelp: "Well if I don't break their assistive technology, I will just bend it to my will! He returns Ha-ha. So, what are you doing now? I hope you had breakfast." Wilma was online and chatting through Messenger on LinkedIn with the product manager of Texthelp. They discussed the updated version of Writing Helper, including her issues with Keylight. Their conversation paused until the following morning when she said, "Good morning, dear. How are you doing today?" "Good morning, I am well, thanks. Hope you are well." "Yes, I am. Last night was absolutely magical and classical." She had seen pictures on Instagram "I am glad you had a great evening. What are your plans today?" "I'm preparing myself to go back to Germany today and get ready for tomorrow's concert." Wilma double-checked his schedule and replied, "Have a safe journey back. I hope you have fun." "Yeah, thank you. So, what are you doing today?" "I will be doing some coaching and mentoring on teams today. This is probably not as exciting as your day will be." Wilma was looking forward to her coaching and mentoring sessions but faced a challenge with builders repairing beams damaged by dry rot, causing an issue with power and WI-FI. He mentioned, "Ha-ha, my days are always stressful and busy." Wilma replied, "Everyone has different stresses. Remember, you should always take regular breaks. It is good for you to have five minutes to enjoy a coffee and watch the world go by." Later in the day, Wilma noticed on Instagram that he had posted a photo heading back to

Germany. In the evening, he returned and said, "Hope you're having a good day." "Yes, I have had a good day. I hope your day is going well. Also, I hope your journey isn't too long either." He responded, "No dear, I will inform you when I get there, okay?" "Cool, take care," Wilma sends a gif of Willie Nelson playing to Miss Piggy in the hospital with the Electric Mayhem, singing "On the Road Again," with a message underneath saying, "Enjoy yourself, and yes, I will send you cheesy tunes!" He likes this but does not engage until the following morning. "Good morning, dear. How are you doing today? I hope you are well!" Wilma, quite early and yawning with a cup of coffee, responds, "I thought you would be sleeping after a long journey! I am well and ready for another day." "I slept well enough and I'm wide awake. So, what are your plans today?" "Presently, I am catching up with all my emails before I start planning which webinars I need to catch up with for changes in assistive technology for future training." Then she inquires "Are you getting ready for another performance this evening?" "Yes, dear. Now, I hope you're not stressing yourself out too much." Wilma chuckled and replied, "I am not stressed; I have Google calendars to keep me in check with all my appointments." She glanced at her upcoming week and planned the rest of her day. He then sends "Okay then, hope you had breakfast." Wilma wished he'd stop asking her the same question, "That's a silly question for a foodie! I'm sure you're having a nice breakfast yourself." "Haha, I take it you don't joke about breakfast." Wilma remembered the funny conversations she had with her friends about food and jokingly replied, "I have plenty of amusing food conversations." She shared a clip of Hugh Jackman and Billy Crystal joking about baking innuendos by Mary Berry and Paul Hollywood on the Graham Norton Show. After that, there was no response for the rest of the day. The following morning, she received a cheerful greeting, "Good morning! It's great to know I will spend the rest of the day with amazing friends like you." Wilma, still half-asleep, replied, "Good morning! I'm glad you're going to have an awesome day today!" She wondered if this meant he would text her all day. He continued, "Thank you. How are you doing today? Any nice plans for today?" "I am good, thank you for asking. I have another busy day supporting people," she texted back while on her way to the office. As she was on the bus, Wilma listened to Enya's "Book of Days" on Spotify, enjoying the scenery passing by. Arriving at the office, she grabbed a quick breakfast at McDonald's. On her way, she bumped into some friends but had to hurry to set herself up on the helpline. After finishing her work, she browsed through charity shops, a favourite pastime, before beginning the long bus journey home, listening to Cher's "Love and Understanding." Amidst her travels, she received a message, "Hello, I hope you're okay!" "I am great, thanks! How is your day going?" she responded while being engaged in texting Mr G on WhatsApp. Unfortunately, her phone ran out of charge, and she couldn't reply until later in the evening. Apologizing for the delay, she explained about her phone and added, "My day has been fantastic," sending over a song, Bon Jovi's "It's My Life." He flirted with her, calling her "my pretty," to which Wilma, taking a sip of cider, teasingly replied, "Happy! How are you, handsome?" However, she was taken aback when he referred to her as a goddess. Shocked by the comment, she couldn't help but imagine the hilarious reactions she'd get from her friends if she shared this." However, she maintained the conversation on a sensible note, replying that it was good! She enjoyed catching up with people she hadn't seen for a while. She then asked, 'What have you been up to today?' His response was, 'I've been relaxing all day and thinking of you.' Wilma couldn't believe this for a second and replied with a light-hearted 'ha-ha.' She added, 'I hope you're chilling out with some wine; it was Friday!' Wilma always enjoyed 'wine o'clock' with her group of friends, the Hair Bear Bunch. He replied, 'You always seem to have a good day.' Recognizing that wasn't entirely accurate, Wilma replied, 'Not always, but I am always cheered up by having a bit of fun.' He then asked, 'Do you live alone?' Wilma responded, 'No, I don't live alone; I have a flatmate.' When he inquired about her family, parents, and siblings, Wilma kept it concise, saying, 'My family is like any other—argumentative yet supportive when needed. However, every family is different, and I'm not sure if your family is the same.' After being asked about hobbies and what makes her laugh, he replied somewhat curtly, 'You have asked me that before.' Wilma decided to probe further and mentioned how his family making him laugh sounded lovely. He replied, 'Ha-ha, I do things in private, so I don't involve my family, but I do love them.' Wilma understood his guardedness and replied, 'Everyone has a private life, as long as they have a good laugh with their friends. If you're happy with your life, please live long and prosper.' Feeling mischievous, Wilma teased, 'Ever done vodka yoga?' and shared a GIF of a person bending over backwards, clearly attempting to stir some humour. She noticed his suspicion when he replied, 'Why did you ask? We all have a good laugh with friends, I have gone out with my friends and brought back some famous stories! They are always told when sober and just make everyone laugh! It is nothing personal; I'm just trying to find out what you think fun might be. You might be a serious karaoke person who loves winning every competition!' Wilma lightened the mood by sending a clip of Patsy and Eddie tasting wine from Absolutely Fabulous, mentioning a 'girl's night out with my group!' His response was, 'You're absolutely amazing!' Wilma was taken aback and thought, 'Really?' She responded politely, 'Thank you. I just hope it made you smile.' Then came a reply that caught Wilma off guard: 'I can see you are a perfect match for me.' She felt horrified and thought, 'For goodness' sake! I have never been a perfect match for anyone! I'm just a plain, ordinary, disorganized person. I am not a goddess, just someone who enjoys having fun and a drink with friends. And I also fart like a trooper!' She responded sharply, 'I think it would be nice to have you as mine. What do you think?' Wilma didn't like where the conversation was going and replied, 'What do you mean? I am not a pet! Please just be yourself.' He responded, 'Ha-ha, I never said you'd be a pet.' Feeling uncomfortable, she replied, 'It sounds weird. It just sounds extremely creepy! I want normal things like everyone else!' To illustrate her point, she sent over the trailer clip of Stepford Wives starring Nicole Kidman, Bette Midler, and Matthew Broderick. Tired and uncomfortable with the conversation, she decided to call it a night and sent a simple 'Good night and sweet dreams.'" "He was up before Wilma on Sunday morning and sent a message, 'Every morning brings you new hopes and new opportunities. Don't miss any of them while you're sleeping. Good morning.' Wilma made herself a cup of coffee, settled in her favourite spot, and put on 'My Kitchen Rules Australia' before reading her messages. She replied with a 'morning,' followed by a fabulous Otis Redding song, 'Sitting on the Dock of the Bay!' She added, 'A great chilled-out way to start the day is to have a formidable day.' He seemed to have some time to chat and asked, 'How are you doing? I hope you slept well.' Sipping her coffee, Wilma replied, 'Yes, I slept well.' He inquired, 'So, what do you hope to get up to today?' Wilma hadn't decided how she wanted to spend her Sunday yet usually keeping it as her creative day. She responded, 'I will see what today brings.' He seemed content and said, 'That's amazing. What are you doing now?' Wilma mentioned she was enjoying her morning coffee while watching cooking programs. She knew Mr G called it her 'bitching kitchen,' but she found it entertaining. He replied, 'I guess you are a good cook.' Knowing her fair share of kitchen mishaps, she replied, 'I try to make nice food; however, everyone has a few disasters in the kitchen.' She sensed he was being polite and responded with a 'thank you, that's exceedingly kind of you.' He teased, 'I hope to evaluate your cooking one day. Ha-ha!' Wilma knew that would never happen and replied, 'Well, we will see what happens.' Then she added, 'I have a friend who says I make the best black olive tapenade.' Suddenly, he announced, 'I have something to say, and I can no longer keep it to myself.' Wilma anticipated what was coming, thinking he might declare his undying love. Instead, he said, 'I love you so much and since last night, I dreamt about you! I would love to spend the rest of my life with you. What do you think?' Surprised and sarcastic in her thoughts, Wilma couldn't have predicted this. He followed up with, 'I am profoundly serious about this, babe. I just can't keep this to myself anymore. There is a quality of all women which I knew you were perfect when I saw your picture and profile! I made up my mind that I've got to have you! I have found my missing rib.' Wilma's internal voice started singing 'I am a Barbie girl.' He continued, 'I love you, our enjoyable conversations. I would love to have an intimate relationship with you.' Wilma remembered it had been a while since the 'cave of forbidden dreams' was visited and thought it might need landing lights to be found. He persistently declared, 'I will love you always without any reservations. I see you as my destiny and my world.' Wilma recalled the Boddington's adverts where Melanie Sykes says, 'By heck, it's still gorgeous.' She responded firmly, 'You are looking for a goddess! I am nothing of your belief, and I'm just a plain ordinary person!' He replied, 'Who says you are not my goddess, and I am craving for you.' Wilma couldn't understand why he saw her as a sexy lady with a Cadbury's Flake. She tried to clarify, 'I have never been anybody's goddess.' His next text said, 'I want you to think about this very well and tell me you love me too.' Wilma replied, 'Nut job,' and sent back, 'I think this is crazy!' He persisted, 'Baby, I want you to think about this very well and tell me you love me too.' She replied, 'Nut job,' and clarified, 'I just want a private relationship with you, just between us, you know what I mean in time. 'Wilma didn't want to know the image he had in his head, maybe fantasizing about her as Princess Leia in a bikini. She thought he could come and rescue her with his amazing light saber! She replied, 'I don't have a problem growing a friendship with you; we are chatting with each other.' She knew from his next text that he was disappointed that she'd rejected his love. He asked, 'What are you doing now?' She replied, 'I am just joining a writing class.' She always enjoyed these classes; they were genuinely fun with a person who ran them. She didn't hear anything until late evening when he said, 'Hope you're okay!' Wilma responded, 'Yes, of course, okay. I have had an enjoyable day with friends.' He replied, 'That's good. What are you up to now?' Wilma had bumped into Calamity Jane and learned about her plans over the next few weeks. She replied, 'I might have a drink with friends and catch up.' He said, 'Okay, then you enjoy yourself and text me when you get home.' She didn't bother telling him about her evening or the fun she had with her friends. The next morning, she greeted him with a 'morning' to which he replied, 'Enjoy the miracles of this beautiful morning! Let the beauty of the day fill your heart with joy.' Thanking him, she asked if he was enjoying a relaxing weekend. 'How are you doing today?' he asked. 'I'm doing well, thanks for asking,' she replied. He followed up with 'What are you up to now?' She responded, 'It's a beautiful day, and I'm going out for a walk. I hope you've had breakfast.' She mentioned to him that she had already had her breakfast; she had made sausage and egg muffins for herself, and Mr. G. Wilma carried on with her day, just like any other day. Later in the evening, he messaged her, 'I hope you're having a good day.' She decided to ask about his day, 'Yes, I am. How has your day been going? Are you travelling again?' She'd seen his Instagram pictures of the beautifully set concert filled with fake candles. He replied, 'Yes, I will be going to Switzerland tomorrow.' She checked online, confirming this information and wished him a safe journey and a pleasant stay. He teased, 'Yes, babe, you want to come with me, ha-ha.' She laughed it off and replied, 'I would love to; however, I am busy working at the moment.' Then, she shared a humorous anecdote about Toblerone and Switzerland, remembering Billy Connolly's take on it. The conversation continued about Toblerone, and Wilma jokingly mentioned ending up with 'an alp being stuck up my nose' while eating it. He found it amusing and asked if she'd tasted Toblerone which was a daft question really and she answered "Of course". The next morning, he sent another message about the beauty of the morning. Wilma, still half-asleep, replied, 'Morning, enjoy your day!' He asked, 'How are you doing today? I hope you had a pleasant sleep.' She responded, 'I did sleep well, thanks; I had a great evening catching up with my friends.' He found it lovely and asked about her plans for the day. She mentioned studying, focusing on the new online version of Writing Helper, and avoiding details about her Open University assignment. She joked about writing about scary movies. He chuckled and inquired about her current activity. Wilma sent a photo of Writing Helper and mentioned she was writing. In the evening, he wished her well and informed her about his upcoming shows in Switzerland. She wished him good luck for the show, and they both enjoyed a peaceful evening. The next morning, while sitting in her cat basket, she found a midnight message from him saying, 'Good night, babe, sweet dreams.'" "He sends, 'I wish you a comfortable morning and a peaceful day, all of which you deserve!' She replies, 'Good morning to you too. I hope you have an enjoyable day.' He responds, 'Yes, dear, and you. Hope you slept well!' Wilma, on autopilot, replies, 'I don't sleep too badly, but I am still feeling a bit sleepy.' He teases, 'Then you need to go back to sleep.' She laughs it off, saying, 'No, I will not be going back to sleep; will wait for the coffee to set in!' As the day progresses, he asks, 'What are you doing now?' Wilma carries on with her work without texting much. Later in the evening, he messages, 'Hello dear, how are you doing? I hope you're having a wonderful day.' She responds, 'It has been a productive day, thanks. So, what have you been up to yourself?' She had seen on Instagram that he recently put up a picture saying he was packed up and ready to go back to Germany. He confirms, 'I am heading back to Germany; I'm exhausted right now!' Wilma wonders if this is one of the teams playing around, knowing about the various frauds regarding his identity. He then asks, 'What have you been doing?' She explains, 'I went to the hospital to have my ankle x-rayed. I might have arthritis in it.' Concerned, he inquires, 'What happened to you?' She shares, 'It was from an accident I had years ago. I smashed my leg and ankle up and needed an operation to superglue it back together. The physio terrorist is checking everything out before torturing me with new exercises.' He expresses empathy, but she reassures him, 'I just have to live with it.' He continues to ask, 'Are you okay?' Wilma affirms, 'Yes, it's just a massive pain in my ankle!' He persists, 'Well, I'm still sorry. So, what are you up to now? I hope you've had dinner.' She assures him, 'Yes, of course I've had dinner. I am just sitting watching some TV, normal stuff. How was your power nap?' He responds affirmatively and playfully. Then, as the conversation winds down, he wishes her good night. The next morning, he sends a message emphasizing the beauty of the morning. Wilma replies later with a song recommendation and then continues the conversation. He informs her about his plans for the day, which she suspects might be a fraud. She shares her plans for a lecture and meeting up with friends for tapas. They exchange good wishes for the day, and she spends an enjoyable evening with Mr. G and their friends. The next morning, he sends another morning greeting, and she responds with a song link. He asks how she is doing, to which she replies positively and inquires about his well-being." "Mr G was on holiday, and they planned a day off together, enjoying a walk around the city and heading to the Chinese supermarket for supplies. After sharing some plans, he responds positively, mentioning it'd be nice to try her cooking. Curiously, he asks about her plans, to which Wilma responds that she visited a Thai supermarket and stocked up on various cooking ingredients, planning to experiment with new recipes. She jokes about her 'sad' hobbies. He shifts the conversation to Wilma's past, asking about it. She hesitates, then discloses her struggles with dyslexia and the years spent battling self-doubt due to negative remarks from others. She expresses her determination to change that narrative. He responds with an insensitive laugh, prompting her to assert her imperfections and reject any notion of being a perfect 'goddess.' She emphasizes that people can accept her flaws or leave. He continues probing, asking about the most interesting part of her. Wilma replies with humility, stating she's just human and values treating others as she wishes to be treated. She candidly explains the challenges of processing information differently due to dyslexia and how she's been undermined and belittled in the past. His response tries to highlight her strength, but Wilma dismisses it as a load of nonsense in her mind. She shares how people have told her to get a 'proper job' despite already having a decent-paying one. He questions her about her current job, but Wilma decides to keep that information to herself. The conversation ends with his inquiry about her job, to which she leaves unanswered." Wilma is suspicious and asks, "Why do you ask? You are a millionaire travelling around the world and doing the job that you love. I love what I do, and I do not bring my business into conversations unless someone wants my coaching. If they do, I have a consultation on how much I charge! I am sorry if I have overstepped the boundary." He probes again, "Do you support charity organizations?" The voice in her head says, "Here we go again, what a prick," and types, "Why are you asking this question?" Then adds, "Whatever charities you support is up to you and none of my business! Everyone has their boundaries; you are just exploring where we have boundaries!" Wilma goes to bed shortly after typing this to the star. The next morning, he sends, "A new day has come, it is time for you to rise and shine like a star. I'm awake thanks, hope you had a good night." "Yes, love, thank you. How was your night?" "It was a peaceful evening." "Well, that sounds good. So, what are your plans today?" It was Friday and Wilma always had the helpline in the morning. She told him, "Well, I'm just jumping on the helpline now and then I have a meeting with your fellow freelancer later today." "Okay, then. I hope you had breakfast." "Yes, I had breakfast earlier. You have an excellent day." "Thank you, love you." Wilma gets on with a busy day and then goes out for a few fruit ciders with Mr. G. Eventually returns home to her cat basket with a glass of wine when she receives, "Good night, love," to which she replies, "Sweet dreams." As expected, he sends, "Good morning bestie, and may all your days ahead be radiant sunshine." It was April Fools' Day; however, Wilma couldn't be bothered thinking of any practical jokes to play on her friends. "So, what are your plans today? I hope you slept well." "Yes, I slept well. No plans for today, but that can change." She then tells him, "I hope you have a nice relaxing day." He returns with, "Well, I will try, but I will be at the Luxembourg Philharmonic for my concert." Wilma checked online, and this information is correct. She sends back, "That's cool. You fairly get in about." Later, when she knows he's going to perform, she says, "Enjoy life, feel alive, face the crowds, be proud, perform showing your brightest love every minute of it. Amaze them. You have a formidable evening." Wilma is sitting typing up her book about the secret life of a dyslexic criminologist when he sends a good night love, "Talk to you tomorrow." She sends a gif of Britney Spears saying, "Sweet dreams." He is up super-duper early and sends, "Wilma, there is a beautiful morning calling out to you to enjoy its extraordinary beauty! You cannot miss this morning anyway." Wilma had made herself a cup of coffee and was going through her messages as usual and sent back, "You are up super early this morning, why? I thought you might be having a long lie this morning." He sent her, "I had a headache when I woke up, so I had a glass of water. How are you doing?" Wilma thought he could have taken some paracetamol to help with his headache.

She was empathetic and sent it back, "I hope your head is covered up. I am well, thank you. Just chilling out and doing some creative writing later. I am feeling better now." "That is good. Are you going to the grocery store today?" It was Sunday, and Wilma always liked to be creative on a Sunday. She replied, "That is good to hear, and I have no plans for going shopping today." He sent back, "That was a question." "I know that was a question. I have plenty of food in the house." "That's good. I just thought I'd ask you to get something for me." Wilma thinks, "Here we go," and asks, "Which card does he want? Google, Stream, Apple, iTunes?" She explores the question and asks, "What could you possibly need from the store?" "A gift card," Wilma decides to act naïve, "Would you need me to buy you a birthday card? How on earth would I post it to you while you're travelling a lot?" "No, I mean an Apple card." "I don't understand what an Apple card is." He sends a photo and says, "When you get to the grocery store, ask for an Apple card, and they will show it to you." "Oh really, I didn't know. I do not usually look for that in my local supermarket after all; it is only a small place. I will take a look next time I'm in your supermarket now!" Wilma was getting ready to go for a walk and just said, "No, I am at home drinking a cup of coffee." He seemed happy enough and sent back, "Okay, love, for me." Wilma has no intention of buying his card and says, "I will see what I can do. "I hope you've had breakfast already?" "Yes, I had a lovely breakfast. Hope you're planning to have a nice lunch or dinner with your friends?" "Definitely! I think I will have chicken pizza for my lunch, what about you?" "Well, that sounds fantastic. I am thinking of making something spicy but have not decided yet. Maybe I will make a Thai green papaya salad." "That will be nice because I'm coming to join you for lunch, ha-ha." Wilma bursts out laughing when she sees this message and sends it back, "Laughing aloud! I am sure you have found somewhere nice in Luxembourg unless you're travelling again. Presently, I'm in a rented apartment with my management." She looks up his schedule and knows that he has a day off and says, "Nice, I hope you have some time for a bit of sightseeing. Hopefully, you have nice weather for wandering around." He replies, "Definitely." "Are you wishing you were here with me?" he asks. Wilma laughs and remembers the conversation she was having with Calamity Jane the previous evening. Calamity's adventures in Switzerland involved drinking lots of wine with people skiing roundabout her. Wilma replies, "It would be a delightful place to explore. My friends were telling me about their adventures in Switzerland yesterday. I would like to see the Eiger; however, the closest I've been to the Eiger has been watching mountaineer Joe Simpson climbing it on TV." "Do you want us to go and visit the Eiger for a vacation, just the two of us?" Wilma laughed and texted, "How sweet of you! However, you're on a tight schedule for your tour, and I'm not sure when I will get time off. However, it is a brilliant idea, Mwah!" Wilma thinks there is a fair chance of that happening. He asks, "What are you up to now?" Wilma was sitting waiting for her laptop to load up. However, she says, "I am sitting listening to music and doing a bit of art and design. I like making Sundays my creative time." She sends over one of the doodles that she had done previously. He sends back, "Your doodles are beautiful, my dear." "Oh, thank you." "Then she receives, 'I hope you had dinner?'" "Yes, I made my first Thai green papaya salad which was lush! I then followed this with a Thai green curry, how was your chicken pizza?" "It was delicious, ha-ha you missed it." She sent, "What? The pizza. So, what are you doing now, my love?" "Just sitting watching TV. What do you normally do on a Sunday evening?" "I am relaxing and I'm going to be going out with friends for a drink." She concludes it is his weekend and time off; he is going out with friends. "That's nice. I went out for a drink with my friends yesterday. I'm behaving as I go back to work tomorrow, enjoy your evening." As an afterthought, she says, "Be incredibly careful when you come back home with the kebabs, you don't want to end up falling asleep with it plastered to your face and ending up with chilli sauce in your eyes." In the morning, she receives, "Rise and shine because the world wouldn't have been as beautiful if you were not a part of it. Good morning." Wilma has a kettle on and sends it back, "Morning, I thought you would have still been fast asleep after a night out with your friends." "Ha-ha, I was not drunk last night." Wilma decides to inquire, "No problem, did you find a pretty lady to chat up with?" "No, I don't have time for that, ha-ha," he responds. He asks, "How was your night?" Wilma thinks he must be lying as the hair bear bunch is always talking about babe watch and eyeing up beautiful women. She tells him, "It was a nice and relaxed evening; I watched Jennifer Eight, it was a good movie." Then follows with, "You didn't find a pretty lady? All the guys I know who are single are always on babe watch at our local! However, we always leave as a group and walk home." Laughing aloud, he says, "I have no time for that." Wilma thinks, "Nah, he has been chatting up pretty ladies." He then asks the usual, "I hope you had breakfast." Wilma had made her usual bowl of porridge and replied, "Yes, I have had my breakfast. Do you know it's the most important meal of the day? You are breaking your fast from the night before. Please hang around to find out more completely useless facts." At lunchtime, he says, "Ha-ha, I hope you're okay." Wilma was studying "Invisible Crimes: Harms and Victims" as part of her Open University course. Eventually, she sent back, "Yes, everything is fine. I am working on a presentation right now. "In the evening, she continues the conversation with, "What are you doing now?" Wilma was talking to her fellow freelancer; she had the TV on in the background. "I'm just chilling out watching a film. How has your day been?" "My day has been good as well, and you?" She thinks that is nice and texts back, "I have had a remarkably busy, productive day. I have achieved several things on my ta-da list!" Wilma does not keep a to-do list; instead, when she completes a task, she says, "Ta-da! Another one bites the dust." "Well, that sounds good, my love. I hope you had dinner." "Yes, I made some lovely veggie chilli which she had put over plain nacho chips covered in cheese." He then says, "Sounds good, what are you up to now?" "I am watching a scary movie. What are you up to?" "I am just doing some research on my laptop. "Wilma wonders what he is researching and would love to be a fly on the wall because she is nosey. However, knowing Wilma's luck, she would probably be swatted with a magazine and be squashed. She sends back, "Research is great. I spend a lot of time researching stuff," and she loved looking at things such as forensics and all the different Open Learn course badges as part of her job. "That sounds good, my love. Where are you now?"

Wilma was just sitting in the house and said, "I'm just enjoying a cup of peppermint tea while watching Case 39. It's spooky!" She went to bed shortly afterwards the following morning Wilma woke up and went downstairs to find a message saying, "Another day, another opportunity to live and laugh. Make the best out of it, my friend. Wishing you an exceptionally good morning." Wilma was having Internet problems that morning; she had switched off and waited for the Internet to reboot. She eventually sends, "Morning, sorry I just received your message. Bloody Internet gremlins this morning." Later, he said, "It's okay, hope you're fine. What are you doing?" At that point, Wilma was talking to her friend, whom she works with on the helpline. "I'm having a fascinating chat about how disabilities are supported in the criminal justice system." The conversation revolved around Fred West, not as a promotion of his actions but discussing a program made about supporting him through the criminal justice system as a vulnerable person, which Wilma found fascinating. In the evening, she said, "Hello baby, how are you doing?" "I'm doing well, thanks. I hope your day has gone well." "Yes, babe, I have enjoyed myself today. How about you?" Wilma had been discussing a podcast with her fellow freelancer, inviting several people to talk about dyslexic journeys, which she found exciting. "Yes, I have had a momentous day! I have a lot of work to do over the next coming weeks. I'm looking forward to seeing it all coming together." "Ha-ha, can I aid you in anything?" She thought that was nice, but he couldn't help, so she sent laughing emojis in response. It was late, and Wilma was going to bed shortly when she received, "What are you doing?" "I am watching the end of an episode of Baywatch and heading to bed. You have pleasant dreams tonight. All right, babe, good night, my love." In the morning, she received, "Good morning love, may your day ahead be as lovely, sweet, cute, beautiful, and amazing as you!" Wilma laughed and returned a simple "morning." She sat with a cup of coffee, yawning away, and asked, "How are you doing? How was your night?" "I had a good sleep, and presently, I am just trying to wake up. Once the coffee kicks in, I will be fine." "That's good. What are you doing now? What are your plans for today?" "I have a busy day with webinars for CPD certifications and renewal of licenses in assistive technologies." Then followed this with, "I hope you have a good day." "Thank you, dear. And you, take care. I will talk to you when I'm less busy, okay?" Wilma attended her webinars, absorbing a lot of information, and felt drained by the end. She went out for a walk afterwards, listening to Brother Johnson singing "Strawberry Letter 23," a favourite tune from the film "Jackie Brown," along with The Delfonics' "Didn't I (Blow Your Mind This Time)." It helped clear her head. The star was busy, so she didn't hear anything until the following morning. "Good morning, my love. I wish you an incredible day full of happiness." Wilma was on autopilot, heading to the kitchen to make a pot of porridge for herself and Mr. G. She returned with a mug of coffee, half yawning, and sent a message with a picture of Bugs Bunny, half-asleep, saying "am awake." "How are you doing today?" "I'll be fine when I eventually wake up." "Ha-ha, are you still in bed?" Wilma laughed and replied, "No, I'm sitting, waiting for my coffee to cool down. I am waiting for my porridge, which I am cooking for breakfast." "Well, that sounds delicious. I think I will join you for breakfast, ha-ha." Wilma asks, "Do you usually have porridge for breakfast?" "No, however, I will come and try yours," Wilma laughs and texts back, 'Crawler.' He asks, "What are your plans for today?" "I am working on a project with a fellow freelancer, which is a podcast. We hope to get it up and running shortly." "That is amazing. So, what are you doing now?" She tells him, "Well, I am trying to eat my breakfast." At lunchtime, he sends, "Hey babe, hope you're okay." It was Good Friday, and Wilma had the day off from the helpline, so she replied, "Everything is fine. You don't have to worry about me." He follows up with, "Just if you are getting out and buying some Easter eggs for Sunday." "That is good. Have you seen what I asked you to get me the other day?" Wilma decides to forget and sends back lots of question marks. She just says no, not bothering to explain it's a fraud at this point. With her laptop set up and studying at the Open University online, she tells him, "I'm at work." He asks, "Can you get it for me today?" Wilma sends a short, simple "No." Surprisingly, he doesn't argue and informs her, "I will be going to Switzerland tomorrow." She already knew this from the Internet and replied, "That will be nice for you. The Swiss love their chocolate; another completely useless fact I found on a Zoom call." She then sends a gif of Julie Andrews singing from "The Sound of Music." He asks, "What have you seen?" So, she sends a gif of Arnold Schwarzenegger starring in "The Sound of Music" and tells him to have a safe journey. He continued the conversation, asking, "How are you doing?" Wilma found out she had been subcontracted again to train people with assistive technology and was renewing important documentation over the Easter weekend. "That is good to know. What is making you so happy?" "I have been invited back as a speaker for this year's Texthelp virtual conference. I am doing my talk next week." "Wow, that is amazing. I am happy to hear that from you." Wilma thinks that is nice and replies, "Thank you." "Where are you now? What are you doing?" Wilma is sitting in her cat basket, watching "Rush Hour" on Amazon Prime. "I am just sitting, watching TV, and chilling out 😊." He then avoids the question about travelling to Switzerland and asks, "OK, have you eaten?" Wilma had enjoyed her dinner but decided to play a prank by saying, "No, I have not eaten. Why, what are you waiting for?" Wilma grins and sends back, "Gotcha," with a gif of Gordon Ramsay saying, "Fucking phenomenal." He responds with an unimpressed gif blowing a kiss. Wilma, feeling mischievous, sends Rimmer from Red Dwarf with Mr. Flibble saying, "We cannot possibly do that! Who would clear up the mess?" He gives up at this point, saying, "I am going to sleep. Good night and sweet dreams." Wilma sends him a kiss back. The next morning, she receives, "Good morning! I'm thinking of you and sending my good wishes as you start a new day." Wilma returns her usual "morning." Later in the mid-morning, he sends, "Hope you are having a good day." Wilma was receiving messages on LinkedIn from online teaching. She discusses catching up with the amazing teaching staff after the Easter break and responds, "I am having a momentous day 😊. I hope you have a wonderful journey over to Switzerland." In the afternoon, while out for her walk along the shore, she sends him a TikTok she had made of the walk along the shore. It was a beautiful view, and the music attached was Annie Lennox singing "A Thousand Beautiful Things." She had seen on Instagram that he had arrived safely. Late at night, he said, "Good night love," and she replied, "Sweet dreams." Wilma had also chatted with her friend in Switzerland, who said she would make him a cake for his concert. They both had a good laugh about the latest scammers they were chatting to. The next morning, as expected, she received, "Good morning, my love! May you have a productive and blessed day ahead." Wilma sent a morning message wishing the star a lovely time in Switzerland after seeing beautiful pictures on Instagram. She enjoyed her morning coffee while planning tapas for the hair bear bunch and watching football. At lunchtime, she shared a photo of the salads and black olive tapenade she made. She teased about a "pigeon delivery service" getting lost, earning a laugh from the star. Later, Wilma cooked special fried rice, receiving a call from Mr G, who invited her for drinks. As she cooked, she chuckled about the hair bear bunch's antics over a phone call. She jokingly described their adoration for a performer named Lola who played the piano and had an incredible set of legs, much to her amusement. When asked what she was doing, she mentioned feeding her friends homemade fried rice, which was a hit. Mr D complimented her cooking, a rare occurrence, after all, she was up against Gordon Ramsey! The star praised her cooking skills, and Wilma reciprocated the compliment, appreciating the friendly banter. He expressed warm sentiments about their friendship, which left Wilma a bit puzzled but glad to have a friend. They chatted about watching YouTube videos, and Wilma, slightly tipsy, shared comedic clips. She got absorbed in watching "Still Game" and didn't reply further that night. The next morning, they exchanged Easter greetings, and Wilma shared her plans for a fun day ahead. She later went out for a walk with the hair bear bunch and their children, making a stop for refreshments. Wilma felt sore after a brisk walk without breaks. As she relaxed with a glass of wine, she received a message expressing missed company and well wishes. She assured him of her well-being but queried the "missed" sentiment, only to receive no response. The next morning brought a cheerful greeting and a wish for a momentous day. Wilma playfully responded, acknowledging her soreness from the walk, and preparing for a busy week. Seated with her laptop, she loaded writing tools and organized documents for an upcoming assignment. Frustrated by her dictation software's errors, she joked about its mishaps, comparing it to dyslexia or dementia. Later, she teased him about getting lost using a posh GPS, aware of his travel plans, before receiving an apology for a momentary distraction. Wilma confirmed she'd eaten breakfast and was planning lunch. Curious about his plans, she discovered he was heading back to Germany, performing at the Cologne Philharmonic. Wilma cleverly connected his location with OrCam, an assistive technology company she worked with, and praised their innovations aiding visually impaired and learning-disabled individuals. She shared a picture of her OrCam Learn. He expressed interest and asked if she had one. Knowing he was back in Germany from Facebook updates, she explained the OrCam Learn, Read, and My Eye features, marvelling at its capabilities akin to science fiction. She encouraged him to witness the technology in action. He thanked her and inquired about her current activities. Wilma discovered a Jason Statham movie, "Operation Fortune," and found it darkly humorous and highly entertaining. However, she expressed her lack of time for movies due to the upcoming concert. Reminiscing about conversations with friends, she suggested watching the comedy "Spy" featuring Jason Statham and Melissa McCarthy, finding it hilarious. She encouraged him to relax and take care during his time off before returning to work. Mischievous from her recent silly conversation with friends, she humorously described their talk about travelling, visualizing a comical scenario with "fat guys in silver budgie smugglers." She playfully teased the hair bear bunch with banter and how they tended to embarrass her. He questioned why her friends behaved in such a way, to which Wilma, knowing it was all in genuine fun, explained their jesting nature, accustomed to being treated like one of the guys. She added a humorous touch, mentioning how they'd sometimes tell her things she'd rather not know. He encouraged her not to endure their behaviour, and she responded with witty comebacks, like finding a man's willy with a magnifying glass and tweezers. Impressed by her humour, he expressed his liking for her and asked about her plans. Wilma admitted her disorganization, often unable to plan beyond a week. She highlighted her collaboration with others facing similar challenges, adding humour by describing how her preparations for conferences involve last-minute packing and administrative assistance. Playfully, she described her forgetfulness, stressing how living with dyslexia and dyspraxia confuses others who may not understand these challenges. He then asked about the best decision she had ever made. Wilma candidly mentioned leaving her previous job after a nervous breakdown, opting to change her career during the pandemic. She now focuses on educating and supporting dyslexic individuals through assistive technology in education and the workplace. Wilma shared a team photo from the Dyslexia Conference in Malaga, recalling her invitation last year for the Dyslexic Compass launch. He inquired whether she was paid for her work, which irked her a bit. She responded assertively, emphasizing she prefers not to discuss money and aims for friendship. The next day, he greeted her with his usual cheerful messages, prompting Wilma to ponder his disposition on tough days. She responded politely, wishing him a good morning, and inquiring about his sleep. He wished her well and asked about her plans. Wilma, with a busy schedule ahead, explained her packed week, including talks and renewing subcontracts. He offered advice, and Wilma, feeling his reverse psychology, playfully countered by sharing her use of the Pomodoro technique. Later, after a nap, she responded to his message. Meanwhile, Mr. G returned home, and Wilma, feeling tired, retired for the night. The following day, he checked in again, and Wilma confessed to some organizational issues due to dyslexia, even missing a writing class. She noticed a mysterious follower on TikTok with a familiar name and number but chose not to engage. While attending a tutorial for her final TMA at the Open University, she missed his midday message. Wilma was amazed at nearing the end of her third year and sent over podcast questions. She anticipated the star being busy in Copenhagen. Later, she updated him on her day, watching "Zombieland: Double Tap" and enjoying dinner. He went quiet afterwards, and Wilma noticed his Facebook post about flying to Copenhagen. The next morning, he expressed a powerful desire for their friendship to last, which Wilma sceptically received, replying with a simple greeting. He mentioned a headache, and Wilma advised some remedies, suggesting he visit an ophthalmologist if it persists. As he inquired about her activities, she mentioned cooking breakfast and preparing for a pre-recorded talk for Texthelp's virtual conference on May 4th. Amazingly, she sent such a simple thank you. As it was drawing towards a break in the stars tour he brought his mission to Wilma's attention. "I just received a call from a charity organization I support in Africa." Wilma smiled, curious about his actions, and replied, "That's amazing! You being an ambassador supporting charities in Africa." As she expected, he disappeared, likely to reconnect later. Soon after, the star returned to Wilma, sharing, "Yeah, there's a child who's sick and needs a kidney transplant. The charity wants to send him to India for treatment." She found it intriguing and messaged, "Wow, that was quick to find a kidney! I hope it's the correct match, as the wrong one can cause massive problems." He responded, "That's why we're transferring him to India for proper treatment." With her background as a first aider, Wilma knew the importance of proper transportation and the safety of hospital care. She informed the star, "It's a massive undertaking. Transporting the child might pose risks during the flight." He replied, "There are two options: taking him to India or flying the doctor to Africa." Wilma considered it and said, "My medical knowledge suggests it's safer to take the doctor to Africa for the child. Transporting the kidney is also complicated, given the time constraints. At least the child is currently receiving care, dialysis, and the necessary drugs while awaiting the right kidney to be found and transported safely." He continued, trying to persuade Wilma, "I know, so I'll ask the charity to contact the doctor and arrange for them to fly to Africa. I'll need to raise a substantial amount of money; fundraising seems necessary." Wilma, sitting in her comfort zone, smiled, and responded, "I'm sure a public fundraising event through a registered charity would work best, avoiding any suspicions of scams. There are too many scams happening nowadays." He acknowledged the concern about scams but stated, "I'll have to raise the funds privately. I hope you'll assist us on this mission." Wilma found the situation amusing and shared it with a friend, who was alarmed by the potential fraud. She politely declined the star's request for help, suspicious of his intentions. The star became defensive, and Wilma expressed her admiration for his intelligence but maintained her cautious stance on charities. She suggested making the charity's work public instead of seeking private donations. He offered to publish her name if she wished, to which Wilma responded with consideration. As the conversation dwindled, Wilma didn't anticipate hearing from the star again but was surprised by a message greeting her. She responded, acknowledging his concert in Copenhagen, and expressing wishes for his lovely day. Their conversation shifted to her busy schedule and his inquiries about her work and solitude. Feeling a bit uncomfortable, Wilma evaded the question about being alone. The star later mentioned inviting the doctor to Africa, and Wilma wished him relaxation after his concert. The star continued asking about Wilma's dinner and whether she was alone, prompting her confusion and a quick laptop shutdown, citing a busy day ahead. The next morning, he sent his customary morning wishes, and Wilma reciprocated with a Scooby-Doo gif. Engrossed in a podcast recording and helpline duties, Wilma responded to the star's messages, discussing his upcoming trip to Germany and her dyslexic moments. Later, she wished him a formidable weekend with a YouTube video of Steps singing "Stomp." Excited about her podcast project, Wilma shared her enthusiasm with the star, detailing the informative discussion with Dr Dodgy Shoes about dyslexia and achieving a PhD. The star praised her dedication, calling her industrious, which triggered a hint of imposter syndrome within Wilma. Their conversation shifted to their respective jobs, with Wilma noting the differing perspectives on dyslexia between Germany and the UK. ." In the morning, he sent, "Good morning, beautiful. Please start your day with a smile and a grateful heart; it will lead to a day full of positivity and happiness." Wilma, who had been watching a documentary on Patrick Swayze, replied, "Ditto." In the afternoon, after returning from her walk around the shore, she received, "Hope you are having a good day." Wilma and her partner had launched the podcast with Dr. Dodgy Shoes and were receiving a good response. She had researched and sent questions to their next guest and was planning her assignment and study. She replied, "Super-duper. It's a bit hectic, but I will get there 😊." He asked, "Okay, where are you now?" She replied, "I am at work," as she was loading up her laptop. He then brought up the doctor from India who had arrived in Africa concerning the surgery, reminding her, "I am waiting for your feedback about what I told you the other day." Wilma thought to herself, "Oh yeah, I was ignoring that." She replied, "It is such a complex bit of surgery, replacing a kidney. This can be a life-threatening operation. I can only hope that it is successful. However, there is no guarantee, or how long someone will live. It could be a complete success or disaster." He confidently told her, "It will be a complete success." Wilma, concerned, thought, "You are treating a human being; this is not like changing a part of an engine in a car!" But she replied, "You can hope for this to be the case; there is no guarantee." He tried to push for more, "Okay then, let us see what the doctor has to say. I hope to hear from him before the concert." Wilma advised, "That's for the best. It is an extremely complicated process. The body might reject the kidney even if it is a match. Surgery is such a complex process, as I remember reading 'Coma' written by Michael Crichton." She also recalled her own life-threatening surgery after her accident and how frightening the process had been. Wilma, whose parents had medical backgrounds, was concerned about someone pushing something they had no knowledge of. She concluded, "I hope you have good news; however, be prepared if you receive shocking news." He persisted, "Okay, that is good. Hope for the future. Can you still help? In fact, will you help? "Wilma, being savvy, responded, "What sort of help do you need from me?" She suspected a ploy and retorted, "Anyway, you know you can help!" She then added, "No, I don't know how to help, that's why I'm asking you." As she looked up stats for her assignment, she stumbled upon scamming statistics indicating that 36 million people are targeted in the UK alone. Wilma recognized common scamming tactics aiming for sympathy, leveraging her nurturing role in society. With the star not performing for a couple of weeks, she pondered whether they'd leave her alone or if she'd end up blocking them soon. The challenge was set, and she awaited what would unfold next. Late in the evening, he sent Wilma a message: "Good night, dear. I will talk with you tomorrow. Sweet dreams."

The following morning, he greeted her with, "Love, I hope you wake up feeling amazing, because you are amazing. Have a great day." Wilma simply replied, "Morning." He was awake and eager to chat, asking, "How are you doing today? Hope you slept well." Wilma responded, "I am well, thank you," and an hour later, she mentioned, "I am organizing the next podcast 😊." When he inquired, "That is nice, where are you now?" Wilma thought it was none of his business and retorted, "You're full of daft questions today." As she expected, he messaged her, "I got a message from the doctor last night..." detailing a request for funds for a kidney purchase, aiming for 5000 euros more to complete the transaction. Wilma burst out laughing; she saw through the scheme. She replied, "After our chat yesterday, I did some research. Did you know that there are seventy-nine scams like this running currently? I feel you're trying to leverage my caring nature as a woman. I also found out that thirty-six million people are targeted by scammers in my country. Please tell me more." He responded defensively, "I am not sure what you are talking about. Are you trying to say I am a scammer?" Wilma stood her ground, "It's a matter of choice. I am pointing out research I've done on this subject. I'm interested in your thoughts." He tried to justify, "I am not asking you to help me with all the money. You can donate as much as you want to support this cause." Wilma decided, "Well, presently, I choose not to support your cause." He immediately asked, "Why?" Wilma countered, "You have provided me with no information about your charity. You expect me to blindly follow your advice despite pointing out reasons and research on the subject. I choose not to help you." He asked, "What information do you require?" Wilma, with a hint of sarcasm, responded, "Oh, now you want to tell me information! How strange. My answer remains no." He accepted, "Okay, thank you." Wilma ended the conversation, "Take care and enjoy your day." However, the star never sent any more messages. As suspected, the perfect relationship that the star had tried sell Wilma was non-existent.

www.ingramcontent.com/pod-product-compliance
Lightning Source LLC
Chambersburg PA
CBHW071257110526
44591CB00010B/703